THE INFORMATION MILLIONAIRE

Building Massive Wealth Through Information Marketing

STEPHEN AKINTAYO

Disclaimer

This book is not intended for use as a source of legal, business, accounting or financial advice. All readers are advised to seek he services of competent professionals in legal, business, accounting and finance fields.

Table of Content

1. WHAT IS INFORMATION MARKETING?..........................6

    The Best Information Packaging Formats..........................10

2. 6 REASONS YOU SHOULD BUILD INFORMATION
    MARKETING BUSINESS..13

3. SUCCESS STORIES IN INFORMATION
    MARKETING..18

    Successful Information Marketer in
    Nigeria...21

4. 7 INSIDERS STEPS TO INFORMATION

    MARKETING

    BUSINESS..26

5. GET
    STARTED!...39

    9 Tips for Creating Killer Product Videos......................40

    HOW TO START YOUR OWN PODCAST..............43

    Six Reason To Become A White Label
    Mobile...61

    App Reseller..61

6. INFORMATION..70

Foundation for a Free Information Infrastructure...83

    Access to Public Information...107

7. INFORMATION AND COMMUNICATION TECHNOLOGY...116

    Types of Information System..127

8. MOBILE INFORMATION MARTKETING...139

    The 5 best digital marketing success stories

9. ENTREPRENEURSHIP...151

    Financing..177

10. SUCCESS STORIES OF INFORMATION MILLIONARES.......................................182

11. MARKETING INFORMATION SYSTEM..261

12. LESSONS FROM INFORMATION MILLIONAIRES...................................274

    10 Lessons Every Entrepreneur Must Learn..325

CHAPTER ONE

WHAT IS INFORMATION MARKETING?

WHETHER B2B OR B2C, I BELIEVE PASSIONATELY THAT GOOD MARKETING ARE THE SAME. WE ARE ALL EMOTIONAL BEINGS LOOKING FOR RELEVANCE, CONTEXT AND CONNECTIONS.

Beth Comstock, CMO of General Electric

Do you have something important to share? Are you an expert in areas others would like to know about as well? Do you know that your knowledge is valuable?

Information marketing business is the business of providing useful information to information seekers to helping them solve their problems and charging for it.

The internet has become the fastest and easiest medium to get information of just about anything and millions of people are turning to it every day to get different information. If you have any useful information about anything people are looking for, you can market it to people and make money. This process is called *Information Marketing*.

No matter what type of business you're in, you could be making a healthy side income by sharing your information at a reasonable price.

Information marketing is about creating, promoting and selling information products. After creating an eBook, video or audio course; you can resell it again and again. DVDs, workshops and traditionally published books also fall under the information marketing business.

Taking your existing business or life experience and rolling it into an information marketing business is easier than you think. There are virtually no start-up costs – you just start putting your best tips, ideas and strategies into a form that works best for your target market. Once you have your product is ready, you promote it and see the sales come in.

Information marketing can be used as a standalone business, or it can complement your service-based business as well. If there is valuable insight that you could share with your existing service business clients, you can create an information product that you can sell again and again.

Businesses in every category can benefit from information marketing. To get started, dig into your own knowledge bank and discover topics that your target market would love to learn about. Narrow down your list to a few top ideas and then start creating your own information products.

With information marketing, you can leverage what you already know and make income from it again and again. You can move beyond one-to-one transaction in your business and start multiplying your income without multiplying your time.

In 2013, I created a blog called mypastquestion.com. There, I simply packaged exam past questions and answers and I sold to candidates who were preparing for exams.

There, I had past questions for POST-UTME, JAMB, WAEC, NECO, GCE, scholarships and job interviews. Could you imagine, there was no single day that I did not sell something on that website?

The amount for each item was cheap (most of the products were less than $5, but people who needed the information were many. I had a very good customer service and I made more sales.

That was just to show you that I'm good at this information marketing business. You too can start your own information marketing and make money from it.

Why Launch Information Products?

There are many reasons why information products rock! In fact, it's the best business you can start if you are a job seeker.

These are the major advantages of starting information marketing in Nigeria.

1. No or low budget for Product Creation: Unlike many other businesses, you can seemingly create an information product without spending a dime.

    It doesn't cost anything to compile a list of resources and sell to people who need them. A friend of mine compiled and sold "list of products for new-born babies." He even went ahead to make even more money from Konga Affiliate Program because he embedded affiliate links on where to buy those products.

He's selling this product for $6 (₦2,000) and he makes at least 3 sales a week. What this means is that you can sell virtually any type of information products especially when there are people who want to buy them. And as earlier stated, you don't need any money to create the product.

2. It can be delivered Anywhere Anytime: Unlike any other types of business or products, information products can be sold to anybody at any time.

   so, it's easy to be delivered to the buyers since most of them will only need a download link. Like some of my products, people can buy it even while I'm sleeping. Everything is automated.

   Once the user buys the product, a download link is automatically delivered to the buyer's email address and they will download the product. They don't need to call you and you will be making your sales come rain or shine.

3. Large Profit Margin: There is a very large profit margin with information products. Considering the fact that you have not invested anything in producing it, so you will virtually make over 1000% sales profit. In addition, information marketing business is fully scalable. This means that you can do it at any level – as large as possible or as small as you can control. Generally, there is a serious profit-margin in this business.

The Best Information Packaging Formats

There are many ways you can package information products and sell them to people who already need them. I am going to share with you 5 popular types that you can create and sell. These are:

1. PDF:

PDF is a short form of Portable Data File. It's usually opened by Adobe Acrobat Reader DC and other PDF applications. This is the most popular form of information product. Although, Amazon sells eBooks in the form of Kindles, there are many other top eBooks market like Click Bank, ejunky etc.

The reason PDF is popular is that it's easy to create while the file can be opened by almost all the devices. Buyers can also print out PDF files from their computers.

It's very easy to create PDF files from your computer whether you use Windows or Mac. There are many Microsoft Word add-ons to convert file to PDF. I personally use Nitro Pro 8 software to create my PDF files. With this software, you can encrypt your information products to avoid indiscriminate copying or editing.

2. Videos:

Another form of information products are videos. Videos are as powerful as PDFs. Video products are preferable if you are selling tutorials, site seeing, cooking tips, yoga guides as well as *how-to* guides. You can visit YouTube to see things for yourself. A typical video market is udemy.com. There you will find awesome video tutorials and trainers who are making millions of dollars by just selling videos.

It's not hard to create a video product. All you need is to procure video-capture devices. These are video cameras, lighting systems, audio capture devices and more. Once you setup your mini studio, you can start to create your videos. More on this later

3. Audio and Podcast:

Many professional online marketers interview experts in their fields and sell the recordings at a very high price.

These recording are in the form of podcast. Other forms of audio information products are audio book. Audio books are recorded paragraphs of books that buyers only listen to instead of reading it.

4. Apps:

Many information products are sold in the form of Android or iOS apps. Most of my friends turn their blogs to apps while they sell subscription service to the users

CHAPTER TWO

6 REASONS YOU SHOULD BUILD INFORMATION MARKETING BUSINESS

Here are six advantages of information marketing business;

> **"MARKETING IS REALLY JUST ABOUT SHARING YOUR PASSION."**
>
> Michael Hyatt

1.   It Replaces Manual Labour By "Multiplying Yourself" and Leveraging What You Know:

Whether you're working for someone else or you're a professional selling your services by the hour or by the job, you're being paid for what you produce. The moment you stop producing, you stop getting paid.

Trying to multiply yourself by hiring employees to increase the amount of product you can sell is also full of hassles. Employees leave and take clients with them. You have liability

issues even if the employee does a good job. There are hundreds of ways an employee can get a business owner into trouble. The work and the aggravation never end.

With an information marketing business, you create a product once, and you're done. It takes a lot of work to create the product, but you can sell it many times, often over a period of several years, without having to do any additional work. Creating an information marketing business is a terrific way to multiply yourself in a way that few other businesses allow.

With an information marketing business, everything you need to create a new product is already inside *you*. You don't need dozens of experts or new-fangled distribution methods. An information marketing business allows you to take the information, secrets, techniques, and the things you already know, and leverage them. That's the easy way to multiply yourself.

2. Buyers Of Your Information Products Will Buy More:
The people who buy your information product will buy other information products from you, whether they're products you create yourself or products you license from others. You can also partner with other information marketers to sell your products or pay them to create products for you. Once you find a customer

who wants information about a particular subject, that customer will continue to buy information from you on that subject.

Encouraging repeat business helps you further leverage yourself. You spend a certain amount upfront to identify potential customers and sell them your information product. That first product can then be used to sell them other information products. Once you've gotten a customer, you're going to be able to sell that customer many things as long as you continue to provide high-quality information at a good price.

3. A Small Amount of Interaction with Buyers is Possible:

One of the best things about the information marketing business is that very few customers insist on coming to your business location to buy your products. This means you can work at home and you don't have to worry about customers showing up at your door to buy your new book. You can create products and sell them online from your beach home or as you vacation around the world. As long as you've got a way to create a product, you don't have to be in any particular location for people to buy it. Not only is this exceptionally convenient, but it helps you get into this business with very little overhead expense.

4. It Takes Just a Small Investment to Get Started:

The information marketing business doesn't require a lot of equipment, fancy offices, furniture or multiple computers. It doesn't require special licenses (in most cases) or special education or degrees. You just need to leverage the information you already know. How? By identifying a market of people who are excited about the information you have, creating a product those people want, and offering it to them in a persuasive way. That's why you can get into this business with a low startup budget. Of course, you must be willing to put *some* money on the table to find potential customers and market your product to them. If you try to do this business without any investment at all, you're certain to fail.

5. There's A Large Profit Potential: Many info-marketers are making million-dollar incomes through their information marketing businesses. They researched potential customers, found out what those customers wanted the most, offered it to them in a compelling way,  and then continued to sell their products until they were making a lot of money. This is a business that's completely scalable; you can make it as small or as large as you want.

But don't think an information business doesn't require work. It does. You'll have to work hard, just the same as any other entrepreneur does. The good news is, if you put in the necessary work, you can eventually replace your manual labor by multiplying yourself and leveraging what you know to create new products. Your customers are going to buy more from you in the future. You can run your business with little interaction with your customers. You can be successful using a very small staff. It takes a small investment, and the payoff can be huge–if you stick with it and continue to develop your business.

6.   Few Staff Members Are Necessary:

The information marketing business is a terrific business because you don't need a lot of people to run it. Many info-marketers have no employees and instead pay an independent contractor to help maintain the customer database, ship products, and handle customers' questions. This is known as "outsourcing." You can literally operate a business that makes well over $1 million a year with very little staff and very little operating overhead.

CHAPTER THREE

SUCCESS STORIES IN INFORMATION MARKETING

They love working with people who want to improve their health and fitness levels. Very much like you, they're passionate about what they do. However, that's where their similarities stop. Peter's in his 40's, has a wife and three kids and a busy Chiropractic practice just outside of Houston, TX. Travis is in his 20's, lives in Omaha, NE, and owns the Forged Athlete gym and Fit Body Boot Camp.

If you have a passion for a niche, it will succeed. Neither gluten free eating nor super hard-core training are big wide-open niche markets like, say; fat loss. But both Peter and Travis are killing it online because they are living and sharing their passion with people.

But Peter and Travis have one more thing in common...they're both into information marketing. In addition to running successful off lines businesses, these guys are also super passionate about taking their message to the masses.

In fact, Dr. Peter Osborne is also known as the *Gluten Warrior* and he's made it his mission to educate the world on the harming effects of gluten and the havoc it plays on a person's ability to lose weight.

Through his info products he's helped thousands of people regain their health simply by educating them on gluten and how it can damage the body. That's something to feel good about!

Travis, on the other hand, loves hardcore training. If it involves a sandbag, kettlebell, ropes, chains, sleds, sledge hammers or anything rusty, heavy and misshapen – Travis will use it with his clients.

Just like Peter, Travis' offline business is rocking! is clients love him and the style of training he delivers. But that wasn't enough for Travis. He joined a Fitness Info Mastermind group with the focus of creating info programs that will help anyone who wants to be faster, stronger, and train more aggressively for REAL functional strength.

Travis makes more than $10,000 monthly. We're not talking about $10K with offline and online business. We're talking about $10K with ONLY his online info business...

When asked to share what helped him get to his first $10,000 month online... this is what Travis said:

"Had my mindset on 110% H.A.M. mode – This "110% H.A.M." mode is something I tell my clients and athletes to have in order to achieve their own goals, I follow this same mindset as well –this mindset means doing whatever it is you need to do to get the job done.

"My goal isn't about having a ton of money (while it is nice to have), it's about helping people that will accept my help and having freedom to be able to do the things I LOVE most in my life. That's what keeps me in 110% H.A.M. mode. (You'll have to ask Travis what H.A.M. stands for) Connect Connect Connect – I know that in order to be a success you have to have a STRONG team of people around you.

For me this means having a good group of people I can reach out to for help and in return HELP THEM as well. I'm always looking to connect with other coaches and people that are passionate about helping people as I am.

"I recently connected with Mike Whitfield with an idea I had in regards to Workout Finishers. Long story short, we created a product called, "Hard-core Workout Finishers" together that was HIGHLY valuable and we were able to get it out to a lot of people. This was done all through connecting and networking!

"I always want to make sure I'm supplying a TON value to those that are able to help me out in some way. It's the law of reciprocity – I try to give and over deliver no matter what and never expect anything in return. I do this with both my joint venture partners and clients.

"Getting things back in return is just the way nature works. One rule of thumb I follow at all times is to deliver ten times the value of whatever it is I'm doing.

"You're only as good as the thoughts and ideas you can think up yourself, but when you can get together with other like-minded people who also have amazing thoughts and ideas, the ideas you create from there are unimaginable! This can only be done through the power of combining thoughts and ideas through masterminding with other people."

Successful Information Marketer in Nigeria

SUNNY OBAZU-OJEAGBASE

Sunny is a Nigerian business success coach, author, pastor and business mogul. He is best known to be the founder of Complete Communications Limited, a company that houses *Complete Sports* newspaper.

Sunny has worked as a sports reporter for several media houses including *Herald Newspaper, Daily Times*,

Concord Group of Newspapers and *The Guardian*. In 1983, he started publishing a weekly sports newspaper called *Sports Souvenir* after he quit his job as a reporter for *The Guardian* and he went on to publish *Complete Football* with the former becoming the first Nigerian sports newspaper while the latter became the first Nigerian all-color monthly football magazine.

He is one of the pioneer of Information marketing revolution in Nigeria and built his publishing business empire said to worth close to 2 million Dollars (600 Million Niara) through information marketing business.

Some of Sunny Obazu-Ojeagbase published works include: *How to Make It in Nigeria – Building Your Wealth from Ground Floor Up* and *How to Bullet Proof Yourself from Poverty, Ideas – The Starting Point of All True Riches.*

AKIN ALABI

Akin is a Nigerian politician, entrepreneur, and philanthropist. He is the author of the popular business and marketing book, *Small Business Big Money.*

A kin started his business career in 2003 writing and selling books, manuals and other information products. He proceeded to launching his own seminar and training company specializing in teaching and consulting for other young people starting their own small businesses. He also started publishing a business opportunity newspaper titled INCOME (now rested) which became a bible for small business owners. To add to his publishing enterprise, Akin launched, *World Soccer News*, a weekly sports newspaper.

Akin has gone on to build many other businesses from scratch; one of them being NairaBET, Nigeria's first online sports betting portal, with outlets across Nigeria.

Nairabet.com has its headquarters in Lagos with its operations licensed by the Lagos State Lotteries Board. A very talented information marketer and sales pitch copywriter, Mr. Alabi built his sports betting company and other businesses (currently worth over 3 million Dollars) purely with the money he made from information marketing.

Akin Alabi is involved in the Nigerian entertainment industry and he currently manages award-winning pop duo of *Skuki* and upcoming artistes, *Sheliroy* and *Benijamz*. He owns state-of-the-art recording and rehearsal studios among others. He is one guy I admire his tactics and selling skills very much.

EFE IMIREN

She calls herself Information Marketing Queen and I think she truly is. This lady has a unique marketing ability through which she has conquered many information marketing niches in Nigeria. She has been able to calve a niche for herself in Information Marketing business in

Nigeria. She currently boasts of some multimillion Naira investments in and outside information business in Nigeria.

She is widely considered Nigeria's foremost, leading and very successful Female Expert on information marketing as a business. She enjoys an impactful career as a Speaker, Author, Consultant and Portfolio Entrepreneur.

Efe started honing her entrepreneurship skills while an undergraduate and eventually turned her passion and ideas into a profitable business named ServiceForts Ltd. The ServiceForts brand name has grown into four major operations including Technologies, Travels, Publishing and Business Academy.

Over the years Efe has discovered what works and what does not work in doing business both on and off the internet. Her discoveries lead to the creation of www.IdeaForts.com the headquarters of the business training outfit – ServiceForts Business Academy and www.Facebook.com/BusinessForts where she hangs out with most of our clients and students

DARLINTON OMEH

In February 2007, Darlington attended a seminar on Internet Marketing, and it was a significant moment in his life as he discovered that it was to do business on the internet. Six years later, he decided to move into professional blogging and content management by starting his first company, Palness Media. He also started blogging about business ideas, and founded a blog called *wealthresult.com.*

OLUWAFISAYO AKINLOLU

I used to be a subscriber to Akiolu's newsletter in those days and got really inspired by the way he put things. He too is an Information Marketing business person and was very popular in *Success Digest* before it became a free-for-all platform. His Hulk group of

companies was conceived and delivered through Information Marketing business.

CHAPTER FOUR

7 INSIDERS STEPS TO INFORMATION MARKETING BUSINESS

Information marketing is a simple business. But it's not an EASY business. I have laid out a seven step plan for your success selling information products.

Step 1: Select Your Niche

Whenever I speak about selecting a niche, I always use a graphic to illustrate how to do this.

You have to look for the intersection between PASSION and PROFIT. There are some "supposed" gurus out there who claim that you don't need to care about whether or not you LIKE the niche you select. I adamantly disagree!

Unless you are excited about what you're selling, the chances of sustaining the enthusiasm you need to make it is slim.

But, you also have to pick a niche where there is money to be made. If you don't, this will turn into a non-profit business. You don't want that.

Write down a few things both personally and professionally you have interests in. Then go to the Google External Keyword tool and type in what you think people would use to search for that product or service. From there you can see how many people are searching for that and related terms. This will give you a good idea about whether your niche idea is financially viable. This will give you a

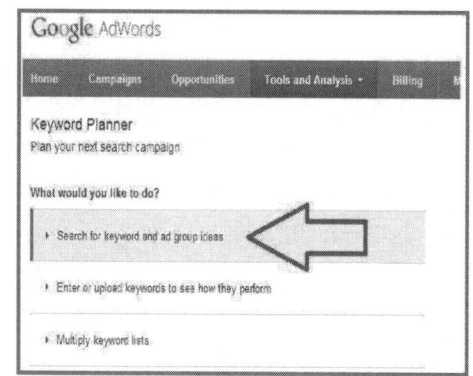

place to start TESTING your ideas. Make sure that there are at least 5,000 searches monthly for the niche you're thinking of targeting. Also, try and go after niches that are less than 100,000. If it's over 100k, you need to narrow the focus of your product. The niche is too broad.

Step 2: Write the Copy to Sell Your Product

Before you even create the product, you have to write the copy to sell your products. Why? It's like the cover of a book. It's always recommended that you write the book jacket copy before you even start writing your book. Once you know what you are offering people, THEN you can create the product to meet those promises.

Copywriting is a very valuable skill. You may be able to do it yourself (or you may not). The only way to find out is to give it a try.

Start by getting a hold of Bob Bly's book: *The Copywriter's Handbook*. His book on this topic is excellent. Even if you don't end up writing copy forever, you need to TRY and do it yourself the first few times. To do that, use this mini-template. Make sure you fill in all the elements. Feel free to use this site: *www.FredInfoBootcamp.com* as an example of a successful site. It closes people VERY well.

Here are the elements:

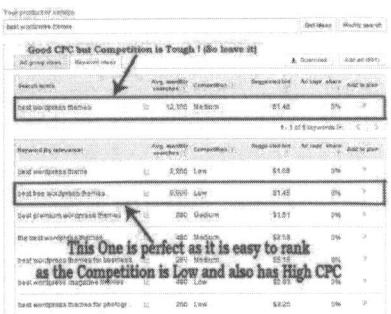

- Pre-Head

- Headline

- Post Head

- Salutation

- Opening Paragraph

- Bullet Points

- Testimonials Offer

- Price

- Bonuses

- Salutation

Remember that the worst your website will ever be is the first time you put it up. You'll want to be tweaking it constantly to improve your conversion rates.

Step 3: Create the
Product Itself

The most important element of product creation is to create a great outline.

So what does it take to create a great outline? Here are some suggestions.

First, write down every single element of whatever you are trying to teach. Don't worry about the order for now. Many people like to write each of these elements down on an index card.

Go fast. Don't worry if you repeat an item. Speed is the key. Once you have exhausted EVERY element you can think of, your next task is to put them into order. Put them in the order that you MUST do them to WORK. If not, people will get incredibly frustrated. Don't do that to them!

Since you KNOW what you are teaching, there is a tendency to both SKIP STEPS and to not be consciously aware of the order of the steps. Imagine that you're putting this information together for 3rd grader.

Do this and you're on your way.

Once you have all that done, you need to decide what form your product will be in. Will it be an audio, a video, or in eBook (written) form? You make THAT decision based on what will help your customers to BEST use and implement your ideas. Think of THEM when you make this decision. What form will help THEM learn this material quickest and best?

Step 4: Design the Website and Put it Online

Your first question to ask yourself is this: *Do you know how to do some of this technical "stuff" yourself or should you ask someone to help you?*

If you need some help, you can send a mail to gtextsoft@gtextgroup.com.ng. If you are fairly tech-savvy, then put up a WordPress site and reserve a domain name that includes some of the keywords you are targeting. You may even want to consider BUYING an existing domain name if you can't find a good one to use.

Stick with domains with the .com extension.

You'll also want to put up some "sales" sites and some "squeeze page" sites as well. Sales sites have only one purpose, to get people to BUY your product or service. Take a look below:

Squeeze pages have the goal of getting people to give you their names.

Examples of squeeze pages below:

To see a squeeze page, visit *http://gtexthomes.com/giveaway*

No matter how great your product and website, if no one finds it, you won't get any orders. There are four ways to drive traffic to your site. On and offline, paid and unpaid. This creates 4 categories of traffic driving methods. I'll only give you one example of each one of these four elements.

Unpaid – Offline: Publicity in a newspaper, magazine or on radio. If you do get coverage, people will find your site and it will cost you virtually nothing.

Unpaid – Online: Give away GREAT free material at my page: *stephenakintayo.com/1mdownload* is a good example. I give away a number of my books in eBook form. In the future, I'll be adding other books to this page. People will end up linking to this page to tell others about it. This will generate more traffic for me with NO additional out-of-pocket expense.

Paid – Offline: If the niche you operate in has a trade magazine, it may make sense to advertise your products or services there. It may cost you some money, but it can be well worth it.

Paid – Online: Pay-per-click advertising is the best example of this methodology. I'm no longer a big fan of most pay per click ads because the prices have gone WAY up. However, they are a good idea to use to see WHICH keywords will actually result in buyers. This way you can target those same keywords with your FREE S.E.O. efforts. I also boost my videos on Facebook to reach more people.

Step 6: Converting Visitors into Buyers/ Opt-ins
Once people get to your site, you have ONE SINGLE GOAL. Get them to BUY your product or service. If they don't buy, the goal is to get them to opt-in to your list, OR to download some of your free materials.

Your ultimate goal is to get folks to buy, but even a highly effective website only closes 5% of those who visit. This number depends on the price of the product or service and how good you are at converting them to buyers once they visit.

Here are 3 things you MUST do to increase your closing rates:

1.   Use Video. It works. Whether it's video email (www.CoolVideoTool.com) or using a video on your site to say hi and introduce yourself to your website visitors, video will increase your numbers.

2.   Guarantees are crucial. People will be reluctant to buy unless you give them good, solid guarantees. Take a look at your competition and make sure that what you offer is at LEAST as good as what they offer.

3.   Testimonials work. Again, video works better than audio or written testimonials here.

Step 7: Getting Customers to Buy More and More Often
Your final step is to get those who buy from you to buy more and to buy more often. The toughest sale to make is the first one. If you deliver a top notch product, people will be highly predisposed to buy from you again. That means that you have to start chunking out products.

If not, you'll miss opportunities to sell them something.

I've done thousands of hours of audio and video products. Unless you have other things to sell people after they buy your first, you are losing money. People will want to get more of what you have if what they get from you first is super good.

Don't disappoint them.

You'll also want to find other products that you can endorse.
Other people's products? Even competitors? Yes. Your buyers
will eventually find other people's material because of the site
called Google. Yours will not be the only product they find to
buy.

People are not monogamous when it comes to providers of
products and materials that they need or want. However, you can
and should get compensated for introducing them to those "other"
products. In the web world, we call this being an Affiliate for those
products. *This is covered in my book, Affiliate Marketing. Get it
here for Free:* stephenakintayo.com/1mdownload

If you find a product you really like and they do not have an affiliate
program, I would still recommend it to my customers. The key is to
never recommend something you haven't seen, tried, and liked. Also
make sure the person who is selling the product is above reproach. If
they turn out to be a fake, it will make you look bad

CHAPTER FIVE

HOW TO RESEARCH TOPICS FOR YOUR INFORMATION PRODUCTS

Like I said, ensure to do proper researches before you create any information product.

Your researches should answer these questions:

> "Make your marketing so useful people would pay you for it."
>
> – JAY BAER

- How large is your potential audience?

- Will people like the topic?

- How much will be the right price?

Answers to these questions will help you to create information products that will be profitable.

To research topics for your information product, follow the instructions below:

1. Prototype: Visit popular information products store. A typical example is Amazon and Clickbank. Now search for top sellers in any category of your choice. Top sellers means that there are more buyers. Afterwards, choose a product that you think you can create a prototype of it. Create it with a lot of improvements in it; make it a bit special than the one you saw.

2.   Inspiration: Many information product creators are simply inspired to get a topic that people will want to buy. They get inspiration from their environment, thoughts or feelings.

Once you discover a problem in the society, you can create information products in a bit to solve the problem and sell to those who already need them.

3.   Surveys: Another way to come up with a topic for your information product is by asking. You can ask your friends, relatives, followers about what they will like to buy. In most instances, professional information marketers use surveys to get responses from their respondents.

The result of this survey or questioning will definitely give you a clue about what information products people wants to buy.

Content Ideas that Sells like Hotcakes
Just like any other business, not all business ideas perform well. So, in information marketing business, you have to invest your time on creating information products that will sell like hotcakes.

In simple calculations, the more people who buys your products, the more money you will make.

I have compiled a list of content ideas that sells like hotcakes just for your inspiration. These are:

(1)   How-to tutorials

(2)   Cooking tips

(3)   Exercise tips

(4)   Yoga

(5)   Make money guide

(6)   Travel and Site seeing

(7)   Health tips

(8)   Internet Marketing

(9)   Design tips

(10)   Businesses

Most importantly, make sure you create information products on evergreen contents that can last for a very long time. Also, make sure that you have researched very well to be sure that people will like to buy them

CHAPTER SIX

GET STARTED!

Create PDF Using Nitro Reader

As I earlier said, I use Nitro Pro for my PDFs. Nitro Pro is one of the best multipurpose PDF tool software which can be used for professional as well as home uses. It is combined features of PDF reader, Editor, Creator, Converter and security. Nitro Pro is main competitor of the Adobe Acrobat, which selling is lower price and offers similar features inside it.

a. In Nitro Reader's Home tab, click Create from File b. Click
Browse to locate the file you wish to convert

c. Under the Make PDF files menu, select a profile based on how large the PDF file can afford to be. Size is related to quality, so smaller PDF files will also contain lower quality images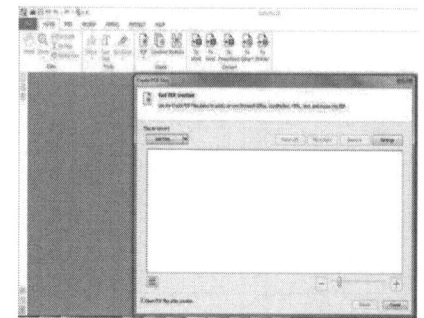

d. Under the Folder menu, choose where you wish to save the new PDF file

Tick Open PDF file after creation if you want your new PDF file to automatically open in Nitro Reader f. Click Create to finish

9 Tips for Creating Killer Product Videos

Whether you're selling a product or service, the ubiquitous product video can be the make-or-break moment for your potential customers. A truly great product video both informs and inspires viewers to give you their attention (and their wallets). Here are some rules for product videos and some examples of people who do it well:

1. Context is King

Don't just show off your slick product; show how it fits in the bigger picture of your customers' lives. What problem is your producting? How does it enrich your customers' lives? Is it inspiring a customer to do more? Is it increasing their overall happiness?

2. Show and Tell

A high-concept product trailer may be artistic and fancy, but if viewers don't know what you're selling at the end of it, they probably won't be inspired to become customers. Pretend you're back in first grade doing Show and Tell — show off your product, and tell your customers about it. It's that simple.

3. Tell Your Story – or Let Your Customers Tell it For You

When people look at a product video, they don't just want to know the technical specs of the product. They want to meet the people behind the product and the people who use it.

4. Beautify Your Home

Contrary to what your mother told you, it's not just what's on the inside that counts. The outside counts too, particularly in product videos. Your product video is essentially an advertisement for your product/service. As you may have heard, the Vimeo player makes your videos look great — customize it with your logo, and treat your viewers to zero pre-roll. Because the last thing a potential customer wants to watch is an ad before your ad.

5. Cater to Your Target Audience

Often when bands go on tour, they'll shout out the name of the city they're playing in. We recommend doing the same in your product video, figuratively or even literally. Whether it's a certain demographic or geographic audience you're targeting, you should customize your product video to be highly relevant to your potential customer.

6. Don't Use Scare Tactics

Nothing screams "cheap infomercial" like attempting to scare people into purchasing your product. By fear, we mean FOMO, what the kids say to refer to the fear of missing out. When businesses try to sell the risks of not buying their product, they're using fear as a cheap tactic to get people to buy. A great business like yours should be focusing on the benefits of your product/service in your product video, rather than on scare tactics.

7. Inject Your Video With Some Personality

Don't be afraid to use a product video to showcase your brand's identity. Showcasing your personality is a great way to differentiate your product from the millions of similar products out there.

8. Include a Call To Action (CTA)

Make it easy for potential customers to purchase your product/service once the video comes to an end.

How? Include a call to action, or a next step/destination. If a person makes it all the way to the end of your three-minute blender demonstration, they're probably pretty interested in buying that blender. If your product video is more of a proof-of-concept, try including an email capture or link to pre-order in your video.

9. Connect, Human To Human

It's all too easy to talk at your audience in a product video instead of them. Because your goal is to start a conversation with a potential customer, do your best to connect with the human on the other side of the screen.

HOW TO START YOUR OWN

PODCAST Step One: Audacity

Record yourself talking for a few seconds like before, then go to File, then export audio, and select MP3 Files in the 'Save as type' dropdown menu. Name your file something simple like "test1" and save it to your desktop.

Find the MP3 file on your desktop and before you rush into things, it's important to keep in mind that podcasts take a lot of effort to get going. They're not just recordings of people talking (not the good ones, anyway). Pat Flynn, host of the Smart Passive Income podcast, recommends you treat podcasting the same way you would any other big project: *"Podcasting is extremely fun and exciting, but there is one thing you must do before you start podcasting: Commit. You must internally commit to podcasting, as you must do with anything that is potentially beneficial but takes some time and effort to do."*

It's easy to assume that podcasts are easy to produce because they're audio only, but don't be fooled. They can take up a lot of time to put together, especially at first. Also, podcasts do best when they're released consistently. If you're interested in developing any kind of listener base, you have to be ready to release episodes on a regular basis. All in all, podcasting can be fun work, but it's still work and should be treated as such.

You also shouldn't expect to get rich from podcasting either. It's certainly possible to generate income from podcasting, but that usually requires advertisements and sponsorships—both of which you'll get after you've built up a listenership big enough to make it worthwhile to advertisers. If you're not interested in starting a podcast for the fun of it or to have your voice heard, you might not get much out of it unless you already have an audience.

What You Will Need for a Podcast

You can't start a podcast without equipment, and good equipment will go a long way. Here's what you'll need: Microphone(s): Any microphone will work for recording your podcast, but listeners can usually tell the difference between low and high quality microphones. As you shop around, you will also need to decide whether you want to use a USB or analog (XLR) microphone. USB mics convert analog sound into digital so you can plug a USB mic directly into any computer and start recording without much hassle, but you could potentially get lower audio quality compared to analog.

Considering you don't need any extra tools or devices to record with a USB mic, they can be a little cheaper in the long run. Analog microphones use XLR connectors, which means you need another device to get your audio onto your computer, but you can get higher audio quality and can use them with other sound equipment (if you had a PA system or wanted to play live music, for example).

Of course, if you have a gaming headset or other basic microphone around, you can easily use that too.

1. Portable XLR Recorder (optional): If you plan on using analog microphones for your podcast, you'll need something that captures your analog audio and converts it to digital. Portable XLR recorders can capture multiple microphone channels and allow you to do basic sound level adjusting and muting on the fly. Audio files automatically get organized and stored on a memory card that you can insert into a card reader or slot in your computer. These are amazing tools, but they can be expensive. You can find them for anywhere between $100 and $500, depending on how many channels and options you need.

3. Audio Interface (optional): If you want to record directly to your computer with your analog microphones, you'll need an audio interface. These devices allow you to plug in one or more analog microphones and will convert the analog audio to digital. Most audio interfaces will connect to your computer via USB or Firewire. Audio interfaces can cost as little as $30 and go as high as $300, depending on what you need. (You can see why a USB microphone is a cheaper option.)

4. A Computer: Any Windows computer or Mac should work fine to record, edit, and upload your podcast.

Thankfully, editing audio doesn't take a ton of computing power.

Additionally, depending on how you choose to record—directly to the computer or onto a dedicated recording device—your computer will also need the right ports. USB microphones, for example, will obviously need an open USB port. If you're using analog microphones with a portable XLR recorder or audio interface device, you'll need either a 3.5 mm audio-in jack, a USB port, or in some cases, a Firewire port. So before you spend any money on equipment, make sure you have a computer that can support it.

5. Audio Editing Software: For the actual recording and editing, you'll need a Digital Audio Workstation (or DAW), there are a lot of good options out there, but the licenses for some of them can cost a pretty penny, though. Licenses for professional level DAWs like Reason or Pro Tools can cost anywhere between $300 and $900. Apps like *Hindenburg* offer simpler audio editing software for under $100, Reaper is a fully loaded audio production app for $60, and Adobe's audio editing software

Audition CC is available with a $19.99 monthly subscription, but you probably shouldn't start dumping money into podcasting software if you're just starting out. Because of that, most people will recommend free open source programs like Audacity when you're just getting started, and that's what we'll use an example throughout this how-to guide.

6. Pop Filters (optional): The clearer your audio can sound, the better. Pop filters, while not required, are fairly cheap and can keep your plosives from making a nasty sound on your recording. If you don't want to buy any, though, you can make some of your own. You might be thinking that all this equipment is pretty expensive, and you're not wrong. However keep in mind that decent audio equipment will last forever if you take care of it. It may be expensive to get started, but after the initial purchase, you're set.

7. Step One: Narrow Your Topic and Find Your Niche

Just like blogs, there are a ton of podcasts out there. That means that you can probably find a podcast about everything under the sun already. Don't get discouraged! While just about every broad topic is already covered, you just have to find your spin on things to make an old idea something new.

For example, if you wanted to make a podcast about music, ask yourself if there's an audience out there for what you want to talk about. Maybe you narrow your idea down from music in general to bluegrass specifically. Now your coverage is specific: the music, people, and culture of bluegrass. Once you have your topic narrowed down, it helps to add a spin to it. Maybe you talk about bluegrass music and culture while sipping moonshine with your co-hosts. It's kind of true that everything has been done before, but it hasn't all been done the way you would do it. So find an angle that's personally interesting and you'll be better off.

Step Two: Download, Install, and Set Up Audacity

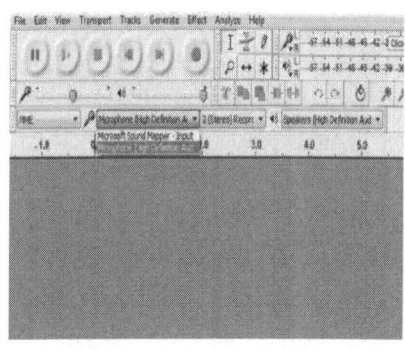

As mentioned earlier, Audacity is a great DAW for podcasting beginners. It's open source, free to use as long as you like, and is available for Windows, OS X, and Linux. Before you can jump into recording, however, there are a few tricks to getting it all set up properly:

1. Download Audacity 2.1.3 at *audacityteam.org* and install it.

2. Connect your microphone and open Audacity.

3. See if your microphone is being recognized by Audacity by checking the drop-down menu next to the small microphone icon. If you see your mic, go ahead and select it.

4. In the top-left corner, you should see the pause, play, stop, skip back, skip forward, and record buttons. Click the record button and talk into your mic to make sure it's working properly.

5. Stop recording and playback what you just recorded to make sure everything sounds okay.

6. You'll want to export your audio in the MP3 format later on. In order to do that, you'll need to download and install the Lame MP3 encoder for either Windows or Mac.

7. Once that's installed, close and reopen try playing it in your

MP3 player of choice, just to make sure everything is working properly.

If the audio in your MP3 test file sounds okay, you're ready to start recording your podcast in Audacity.

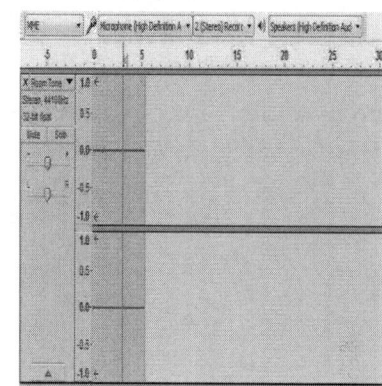

Step Three: Record and Edit Your Podcast in Audacity

Recording is pretty straightforward in Audacity, but there are a few things you should do before you jump into your first show:

1.   Connect your microphone and make a quick recording the same way as before to check your audio levels.

2.   You can adjust your recording volume with the slider right above the drop-down menu where you selected your recording device.

3.   When you've found a good level, go ahead and remove your recording test by clicking the small X at the top left of the track.

You don't need it anymore.

4.   Make sure your recording space is silent and record around 5 seconds of "silence." This is called room tone and you can use this to cut out things like swearing or even cover up some background noise that happens while you're recording. You can mute this track for now by clicking the mute toggle button on the left side of the track. You can also minimize it by clicking the arrow at the bottom-left of the track.

5.   Go to File, then Save Project As, and choose a name for your project.

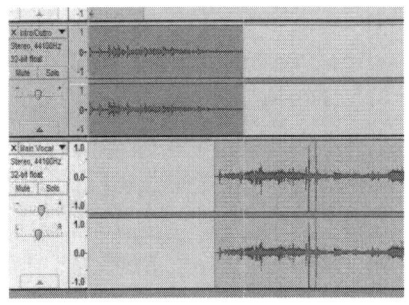

Keep in mind that this doesn't export any audio, just saves your progress.

Now you're ready to actually record the main part of your podcast. Just hit the record button and Audacity will start capturing your audio in a new track. When you're done recording, hit the stop button. It's as simple as that. Before you continue be sure to save your work. Now it's time to add music and make any necessary edits:

1.   Go to File, then Import, and then Audio. Locate the music you chose earlier (or your own if you made some), and click Open. The music will get dropped into Audacity as its own separate track.

2.   Now find the Selection Tool in the Audacity toolbar. It will look like a typing cursor.

3.   Drag the Selection Tool over the section of music you'd like to use for your intro and outro music.

4.   With that section of music currently selected, find the Trim Audio button on the Audacity toolbar and click it. You should be left with only the section of music you chose.

5.   While that section of music is still selected, find the Copy button on the toolbar and click it (you can also use CTRL+C or Command+C).

6.   On the same music track, click anywhere to the right of that music section. Then find the Paste button on the toolbar and click it (or CTRL+V or Command+V). You now have your intro and outro music, but it's still not quite ready.

7.   With the Selection Tool, select one of the music copies. Then go to Effect at the top and choose Fade Out. Do the same for the other music copy, but choose Fade In instead. You're intro and outro music is now ready to go.

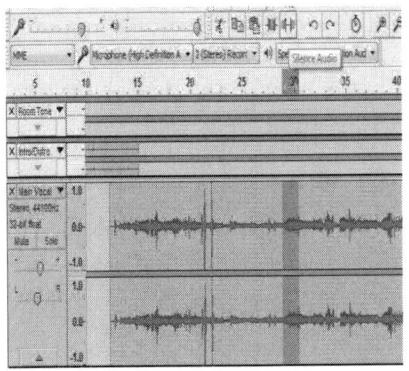 If you need to cut something out of your podcast—like swearing if you're trying to keep clean, or information that shouldn't be made public—it's easy to fix:

1.   Find the section of audio that needs to be cut out.

2.   Use the Selection Tool to select the entire section that needs to be removed.

3.   Find the Cut button on the toolbar and click. Boom, it's gone.

Alternatively, you could also use the Silence button.

4.   Now, remember the room tone you recorded earlier? You can copy a section of that and overlap it with the cut out portion so you have a less jarring silence.

With your music ready to go and your necessary edits made, you can now line everything up with the Time Shift Tool (two arrows connected by a thin line). Just slide each piece of audio in its respective track until you're happy with how all of the audio lines up. You might need to play around with it a little to find the sweet spot.

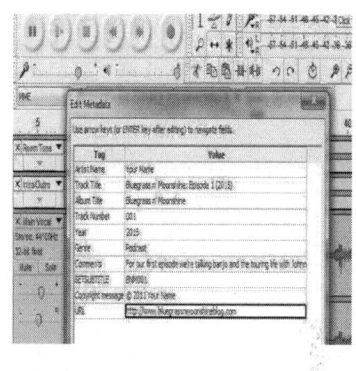

Step Four: Tag and
Export Your MP3 File in
Audacity

Exporting your podcast as an MP3 file should be easy now because you set up MP3 exporting before you started recording. There are still some important things to do when you export, though. To make sure your file is ready to be uploaded somewhere; you need to edit the file's metadata (also known as

"tagging"). Metadata is information that displays no matter what the filename is and includes things like title, track number, album, and the name of the artist.

Fortunately, Audacity lets you do that when you export your audio as an

MP3. Here's how to do that:

1.   Go to File, then Export Audio.

2.   Select MP3 Files in the 'Save as type' drop-down menu. Then name the file (your podcast name and the number of the episode, for example). Click Save.

3.   Now you'll see the Edit Metadata window. Enter all of the necessary information (will go over that shortly). You can also add and remove sections as you see fit here.

4.   Go down to the Template section and click Save. Save this template for future episodes so you don't have to fill out most of this information ever again.

5.   Click OK. Your MP3 should export and be

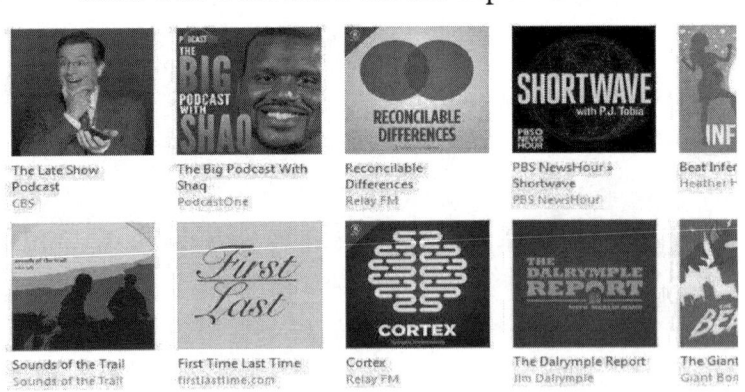

ready for uploading.

Step Five: Pick a Strong Name and Create a Cover Art Image

When it comes to people finding your podcast, the name you choose for it is important. If we return toa the bluegrass and moonshine example, it could be something straightforward, like"Bluegrass n' Moonshine," or something less obvious, but still gets the point across, like "Sippin' and Singin': The Bluegrass Podcast." The title gives you an idea of what the show is about, but more importantly, your show would likely pop up in someone's search for podcasts about bluegrass music.

You'll also need an image for your podcast. This is the first thing people will see when they come across your show, so it should look good. An image is also required in order to list your podcast in directories like iTunes, Stitcher, and BluBrry, as well as podcast managers like Pocket Casts and DoggCatcher.

Cover art can be a photo or piece of custom artwork, depending on how you want to represent your show. If the show is about you, you can even use a good photo of yourself. You can use a simple logo if you like, as long as it has something to do with what you talk about on the podcast. You want to make sure your image conveys what your show is really about as best it can. No matter what you choose to use for cover art, make sure the show's title is on the image. If you're not comfortable making the image yourself, don't be afraid to hire a designer to do it for you. Web sites like

Fiverr and 99designs lets you talk with and hire designers for cheap.

Podcast images need to be certain sizes as well, otherwise your artwork won't look as good when it's shrunken down. In fact, some directories won't even accept podcast feeds if your art isn't sized appropriately. Here's are the essentials you want to shoot for:

Image must be 1400 x 1400 pixels at minimum . Image must be Image in .jpg or .png format (.jpg preferred) . should look good—and readable— at 300 x 300 pixels. A good rule of thumb is to optimize your image for 150 x 150 pixels. If it looks good that small, you know you won't run into any problems. Daniel J. Lewis at The Audacity to Podcast also recommends that you treat certain types of images differently so they always look their best:

For photo/image-based artwork, acquire the largest version possible and design within its dimensions.

For color- or illustration-based artwork, design in a vector editor (like Adobe Illustrator) to make artwork that can scale to any size without losing quality.

You can do most of your image editing in Photoshop—or alternatives like GIMP and Pixelmator—with ease. When you have a good name and some decent art representing your show, you're just about ready to start recording.

Step Six: Find a Place to Host Your Podcast

When you've finished tagging and exporting your podcast, it's time to find a place to host the MP3 file. Getting your podcast hosted is essential so you can start distributing your show to podcast directories and apps via RSS feed. Here are some of the best options for beginners:

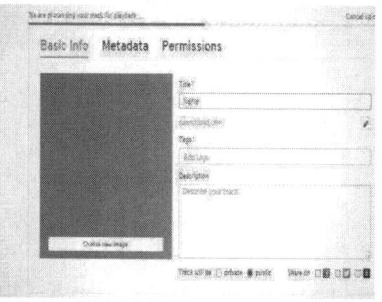

SoundCloud: SoundCloud offers free podcast hosting (in addition to two competitive paid options for when you get a little more serious), and lets you distribute your podcast via RSS. Your podcasts can also instantly publish to SoundCloud itself, which makes it really easy to share your podcast on social media, blogs, and other web sites.

Podbean: Podbean provides multiple tiers of hosting, including a free option (though the free hosting is fairly limited). The service has its own iOS and Android app for listening, as well as analytic tools, although, you will need to pay to get most of their best features.

Podomatic: Super user friendly and offers free hosting with enough bandwidth and storage for podcast beginners. There's also a pro option that allows for more bandwidth if you find that you like

Libsyn: Libsyn is one of the oldest dedicated podcast hosting sites and considered to be one of the best. Their lowest price plan is $5 a month with unlimited bandwidth, and there's no free option, but you get what you pay for.

Amazon S3: Amazon's hosting service offers a free plan, but limits your storage among other things. The paid service only charges you for the storage and bandwidth you actually use, meaning the cost can go up as your podcast grows in popularity.

Fireside: A new podcast hosting platform from the creator of the 5by5 podcast network, Fireside offers unlimited storage, downloads, episodes, analytics, and a site for your podcast (with custom domain support), for $19 per month. Each additional podcast is an extra $8 per month. You can easily import your older podcasts from any valid
odcast RSS feed in addition to other hosting sites including SoundCloud, Squarespace, and Libsyn. It also makes small details like chapter markers and metadata more accessible. If

you've got a few episodes under your belt and want to provide a better experience for both yourself and your audience, try it out.

If you're new to podcasting, or hosting media files online in general, try out the free services to see if you like the way they work. When you find one you like, it's worth paying for hosting if you're serious about continuing your podcast. Each host listed here will provide you with easy to follow instructions for how to upload your podcast audio file, but there are some basic steps to follow regardless of which service you choose:

1.   When you sign up for the service, use the name of your podcast (or the closest thing to it.

2.   Upload a cover art image that is at least 1400 x 1400 pixels.

3.   Fill out all sections of your profile, especially your show's description.

4.   Upload your MP3 file. Most hosting services let you listen to your podcast right within the site, so give it a listen to make sure everything sounds good.

5.   The file's metadata that you created before should fill in a lot of the necessary information. However, if something doesn't look right, now is the chance to make changes and fix it before you submit your RSS feed to any directories.

Once you're happy with how everything looks, you're ready to validate your feed and submit it to podcast directories.

Step Seven: Get Your Podcast on iTunes

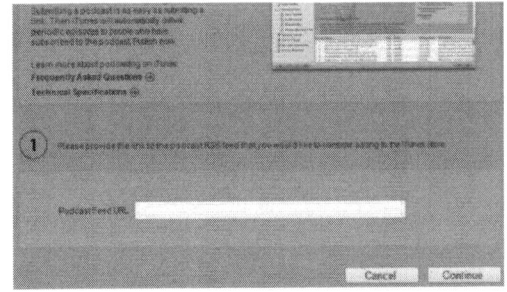

There are a lot of podcast directories out there that you can submit to, including Stitcher, Blubrry, and Miro. Most podcasters, however, will tell you that if there's only one directory you should try to get listed in, it's iTunes. It's the most popular and has the largest reach. Here's how to get listed in the iTunes podcast directory:

Check your title, author, description and cover art that's associated with your podcast audio file on your hosting service. iTunes uses those fields for search. For more information and tips, check out the official iTunes podcast specs here.

1.   Locate your podcast RSS feed URL and copy it.

3.   Make sure your podcast RSS feed is valid. Some hosts have a built-in validator and will say if your feed is valid. Otherwise

paste your feed URL into Cast Feed. Validator and see what podcasting

apps and directories will see. Make changes at the hosting site as necessary.

4.   Download and open iTunes.

5.   Find the More icon in the upper-left part of the window (the

"...". Select Podcasts.

6.   Locate the Podcast Quick Links section on the right side of the window. Click on the Submit a Podcast link.

7.   Copy your RSS feed URL in the field provided and click

"Next."

That should do it! If you don't see anything pop up in iTunes right away, don't stress. It can take from 24 hours to two weeks before your podcast is added (your podcast will be reviewed by a team of people). Fortunately, the process of getting listed in other podcast directories isn't much different. So once you've got iTunes figured out, the sky's the limit.

Finally, as exciting as it is to finally get your podcast out there for everyone to hear, consider waiting to submit your podcast until you've already got a few episodes in the can. Submitting only one episode can leave a lot to be desired for those that stumble upon your show. It's also less likely that you'll be featured or promoted as something new and noteworthy. So record three or four episodes before you start trying to grow your audience.

Six Reason To Become A White Label

Mobile App Reseller

Easy to use app building tools and white label mobile app reseller programs have opened the doors for small businesses to finally take

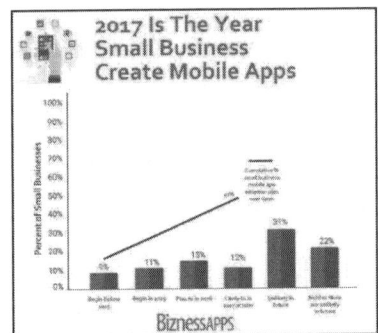

advantage of technology that was once only available to the Fortune 500. Whether you're an aspiring developer, with great ideas of apps, a marketer looking to add mobile apps to your offerings, or someone simply looking to seize the opportunity of this fast growing industry, becoming a white label mobile app reseller can open the door for you.

1.   The Demand For Mobile Apps And Small Businesses Is
      Very
High:

Mobile apps, are quickly becoming recognized as an indispensable tool for small businesses. In an age where customer experience reigns supreme, a brand's ability to offer an exceptional mobile experience is almost mandatory. The benefits of mobile apps for customers of small businesses range from increasing customer loyalty to increase customer engagement. You know, things that actually help a small business grow!

As more and more small business owners realize they can now afford these mobile applications, this demand is only going to increase. You'll be surprised how many businesses are shocked that you can supply them with a highly functional mobile app at a price they can afford. But more importantly, a mobile app that will increase their bottom line.

2.   Becoming a White Label Mobile App Reseller is
        Inexpensive:

Unlike other business opportunities out there, you don't need a ridiculous amount of money to start your own white label mobile app company. With a small investment in yourself or existing company, you can begin creating & selling mobile apps to small businesses for less than ~$1000 when all is said and done. The cost structure of mobile white label mobile app reseller programs are a small monthly fee but typically includes everything you need to be successful.

When evaluating any industry to break into, cost is always a concern, but more importantly you want to evaluate the potential return on your investment. With the mobile app market in full growth mode it is one of the best investments you can make due to the high demand and low competition. Alternatively, if you are already a local small business marketer, you can seamlessly integrate mobile apps into your current company and begin offering your clients a new mobile dimension to their businesses.

3.   Reseller Programs Make it Easy to Build & Sell Mobile
        Apps:

Practically anyone can become a white label mobile app reseller; you don't need the technical skills and experience to build an app from scratch. Do-it-yourself app building platforms are easy enough for most people to handle and begin building apps. Some mobile app reseller programs even include the ability for you to only focus on sales and not even worry about designing mobile apps as they offer a paid design service for you and your potential clients.

The key here is to pick the right partner when deciding whether or not reselling mobile apps is for you as you will want to work with a company that will be there to support you the whole way through. There should always be current and relevant publications, webinars and other educational materials that you can take advantage of and expand your knowledge of mobile development and how to sell mobile apps.

Not interested in designing mobile apps? Make sure whatever
company you work with offers a mobile app design service.

Don't have any existing clients? Make sure your mobile app partner has sales training available to help you secure your first customers.

Have an established brand with high profile clients? Ensure
you work with the leader in the space with the best technology and customer support.

Additionally, you have the freedom to rebrand, repackage mobile apps to make them appear custom, all under your own brand with white label mobile app reseller programs. So go ahead and customize them as you wish. You will likely learn your own lessons as you grow as a white label mobile app reseller.

4.   You're Able to Offer Mobile Apps at Prices Businesses Can
Afford

Offering white label mobile apps is undoubtedly a lucrative business.

The demand is there and you're offering a very expensive service at a much lower cost than what the market is used to seeing. The days of spending tens of thousands of dollars to create an app are over with white label mobile app reseller programs available. You can simply build an app, charge a set-up fee in the range of $1000-$3000 and also a recurring monthly fee from $50-$200/month depending on how much hand holding you do with your clients. This industry promises a hefty ROI and loads of potential clients, especially when you consider the high demand that exists and your low costs for being a white labeled mobile app reseller.

5.   The Mobile App Market is Expected to Double By 2020

Aside from the existing high demand, there is still a lot of growth left in the mobile app market. The mobile app industry is currently worth just over $50B, but it is expected to double by 2020 to over $100B.

That is a lot of growth in a short period of time. Mobile apps are here to stay and consumers are beginning to gravitate towards brands that have the best mobile experiences for them to benefit from.

This means that not only is there a growing market for mobile apps, but also a more diverse one. Today, mobile apps offer the opportunity to provide an app-based e-commerce platform for a retail store, takeaway ordering service for a restaurant, easy scheduling for a hair salon, ability to offer loyalty programs, and much more. The benefits you'll be able to provide to your small business clients with mobile apps can be as endless as the types of industries you can sell into.

6.   You Can Easily Measure Success as a White Label Mobile App Reseller

One of the hardest parts about starting a new business and running it successfully is knowing that you are making the right decisions and (perhaps more importantly) when you are making the wrong ones. Reselling mobile apps is no different; you want to know that your apps are serving their purposes, receiving downloads and actually being used once they are downloaded. In addition, you can easily measure your success by simply how satisfied your clients are or how much revenue you're generating from your mobile app company.

Luckily, the success of your apps (and thereby your company) is easy to measure. Aside from your client's input, your apps will also receive reviews on Google Play, the Apple App Store and other app marketplaces. These critiques provide vital information into what is working and what isn't, and allow you to improve your apps over time and ensure that you are staying ahead of emerging trends. Once you have your first few customers under your belt, you'll be able to build off of this momentum and really start forecasting a real new revenue stream for yourself or your existing business.

CONCLUSION

Creating your own company reselling mobile apps takes a lot of work but with the right partner it can be fairly easy. As you begin evaluating the mobile app market make sure that you're asking the right questions and doing your homework before jumping in head first as a white label mobile app reseller!

BONUS!

Make Money from Private Labeled
Right Information products

Apart from creating your information product, there are still many other products out there that you can market and still make money.

These products are called Private Label Rights. This means that you have the right to resell the products and keep all the profit for yourself.

Sometimes, you may not be allowed to edit the product or change things are on them. Others are public domains books.

You can use them as gift or bonus products, you can use them for opt-in to download products, you can also sell them for money depending on the copyright terms.

Popular Marketplaces to Sell your Information Products in Nigeria The next thing to think of is where to sell your information products and make money. In this section, I'll suggest the popular marketplaces that you can sell your information products right away. These are;

1. Amazon: Amazon is one of the popular information products market. There have millions of customers already who are ready to buy your products there.

You can convert your eBook to kindle and have access to over 500 million potential buyers. So, if you have an interesting information product, head over to Amazon and sell your product.

2. Create your Sales Page: You can create your sales page where you can sell your information products. It can be just one squeeze page and many pages website depending on what you are looking for.

It's actually easy to get it done with WordPress where you can easily integrate buy button and online payment system with the help of woocommerce plugin.

Other places are:

(3)   Konga.com

(4)   Gumroad.com

(5)   Clickbank.com
(6)   eJunky

(7)   Udemy.com

And many others...

Summary

We have come to the end of this book on how to start information marketing business. You can implement these ideas anywhere you are in the world and still make your money.

Implement these ideas and tell me how it goes.

Once again, if you're looking for QUICK MONEY, this is NOT the book for you and I'm NOT your guy. If that's what you want or expect, I suggest you play the lottery. Your chances of making the BIG BUCKS will be much greater than pursuing the BOGUS nonsense some of the SUPPOSED GURUS are dishing out.

CHAPTER SEVEN

INFORMATION

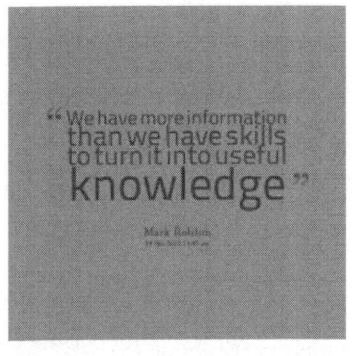

The ASCII codes for the word "Wikipedia" represented in binary, the numeral system most commonly used for encoding textual computer information

Information is that which informs. In other words, it is the answer to a question of some kind. It is thus related to data and knowledge, as data represents values attributed to parameters, and knowledge signifies understanding of real things or abstract concepts.[1] As it regards data, the information's existence is not necessarily coupled to an observer (it exists beyond an event horizon, for example), while in the case of knowledge, the information requires a cognitive observer.[2]

Information is conveyed either as the content of a message or through direct or indirect observation of anything. That which is perceived can be construed as a message in its own right, and in that sense, information is always conveyed as the content of a message.

Information can be encoded into various forms for transmission and interpretation (for example, information may be encoded into a sequence of signs, or transmitted via a sequence of signals). It can also be encrypted for safe storage and communication. Information reduces uncertainty. The uncertainty of an event is measured by its probability of occurrence and is inversely proportional to that. The more uncertain an event, the more information is required to resolve uncertainty of that event. The bit is a typical unit of information, but other units such as the nat may be used. For example, the information encoded in one "fair" coin flip is $\log_2 (2/1) = 1$ bit, and in two fair coin flips is $\log_2 (4/1) = 2$ bits.

The concept that *information is the message* has different meanings in different contexts.[3] Thus the concept of information becomes closely related to notions
of constraint, communication, control, data, form, education, knowledg e, meaning, understanding, mental
stimuli, pattern, perception, representation, and entropy.

Etymology

The English word apparently derives from the Latin stem (*information-*) of the nominative (*informatio*): this noun derives from the
verb *informare* (to inform) in the sense of "to give form to the mind", "to discipline", "instruct", "teach". *Inform* itself comes (via
French *informer*) from the Latin verb *informare*, which means to give form, or to form an idea of. Furthermore, Latin itself

already contained the word *informatio* meaning concept or idea, but the extent to which this may have influenced the development of the word *information* in English is not clear.

The ancient Greek word for *form* was μορφή (*morphe*; cf. morph) and also εἶδος (*eidos*) "kind, idea, shape, set", the latter word was famously used in a technical philosophical sense by Plato (and later Aristotle) to denote the ideal identity or essence of something (see Theory of Forms). "Eidos" can also be associated with thought, proposition, or even concept.

The ancient Greek word for *information* is πληροφορία, which transliterates (*plērophoria*) from πλήρης (*plērēs*) "fully"
and φέρω (*phorein*) frequentative of (*pherein*) *to carry through*. It literally means "bears fully" or "conveys fully". In modern Greek the word Πληροφορία is still in daily use and has the same meaning as the word *information* in English. In addition to its primary meaning, the word Πληροφορία as a symbol has deep roots in Aristotle's semiotic triangle. In this regard it can be interpreted to communicate information to the one decoding that specific type of sign. This is something that occurs frequently with the etymology of many words in ancient and modern Greek where there is a very
strong denotative relationship between the signifier, e.g. the word symbol that conveys a specific encoded interpretation, and the signified, e.g. a concept whose meaning the interpreter attempts to decode.

Information Theory Approach

From the stance of information theory, *information* is taken as an ordered sequence of symbols from an alphabet, say an input alphabet χ, and an output alphabet Υ. Information processing consists of an input-output function that maps any input sequence from χ into an output sequence from Υ. The mapping may be probabilistic or deterministic. It may have memory or be memoryless.[4]

As sensory input

Often information can be viewed as a type of input to an organism or system. Inputs are of two kinds; some inputs are important to the function of the organism (for example, food) or system (energy) by themselves. In his book *Sensory Ecology* [5]Dusenbery called these causal inputs. Other inputs (information) are important only because they are associated with causal inputs and can be used to predict the occurrence of a causal input at a later time (and perhaps another place). Some information is important because of association with other information but eventually there must be a connection to a causal input. In practice, information is usually carried by weak stimuli that must be detected by specialized sensory systems and amplified by energy inputs before they can be functional to the organism or system. For example, light is mainly (but not only, e.g. plants can grow in the direction of the lightsource) a causal input to plants but for animals it only provides information. The colored light reflected from a flower is too weak to do much photosynthetic work but the visual system of the bee detects it and the bee's nervous system uses the information to guide the bee to the flower, where the bee often finds nectar or pollen, which are causal inputs, serving a nutritional function.

As Representation and Complexity

The cognitive scientist and applied mathematician Ronaldo Vigo argues that information is a concept that requires at least two related entities to make quantitative sense. These are, any dimensionally defined category of objects S, and any of its subsets R. R, in essence, is a representation of S, or, in other words, conveys representational (and hence, conceptual) information about S. Vigo then defines the amount of information that R conveys about S as the rate of change in the complexity of S whenever the objects in R are removed from S. Under "Vigo information", pattern, invariance, complexity, representation, and information—five fundamental constructs of universal science—are unified under a novel mathematical framework.[6][7][8] Among other things, the framework aims to overcome the limitations of Shannon-Weaver information when attempting to characterize and measure subjective information.

As an influence that leads to transformation

Information is any type of pattern that influences the formation or transformation of other patterns.[9][10] In this sense, there is no need for a conscious mind to perceive, much less appreciate, the pattern. Consider, for example, DNA. The sequence of nucleotides is a pattern that influences the formation and development of an organism without any need for a conscious mind. One might argue though that for a human to consciously define a pattern, for example a nucleotide, naturally involves conscious information processing.

Systems theory at times seems to refer to information in this sense, assuming information does not necessarily involve any conscious mind, and patterns circulating (due to feedback) in the system can be called information. In other words, it can be said that information in this sense is something potentially perceived as representation, though not created or presented for that purpose. For example, Gregory Bateson defines

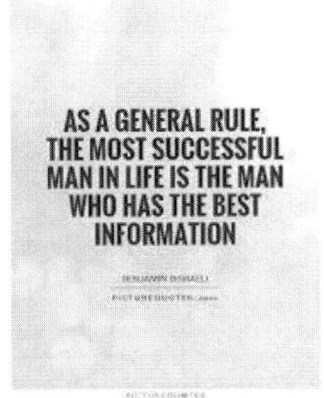

AS A GENERAL RULE, THE MOST SUCCESSFUL MAN IN LIFE IS THE MAN WHO HAS THE BEST INFORMATION

BENJAMIN DISRAELI
FIRST GREENHOUSE...

PICTUREQUOTES

"information" as a "difference that makes a difference".[11] If, however, the premise of "influence" implies that information has been perceived by a conscious mind and also interpreted by it, the specific context associated with this interpretation may cause the transformation of the information into knowledge. Complex definitions of both "information" and "knowledge" make such semantic and logical analysis difficult, but the condition of "transformation" is an important point in the study of information as it relates to knowledge, especially in the business discipline of knowledge management. In this practice, tools and processes are used to assist a knowledge worker in performing research and making decisions, including steps such as:

Review information to effectively derive value and meaning

Reference metadata if available

Establish relevant context, often from many possible contexts

Derive new knowledge from the information

Make decisions or recommendations from the resulting knowledge

Stewart (2001) argues that transformation of information into knowledge is critical, lying at the core of value creation and competitive advantage for the modern enterprise.

The Danish Dictionary of Information Terms [12] argues that information only provides an answer to a posed question. Whether the answer provides knowledge depends on the informed person. So a generalized definition of the concept should be: "Information" = An answer to a specific question". When Marshall McLuhan speaks of media and their effects on human cultures, he refers to the structure of artifacts that in turn shape our behaviors and mindsets. Also, pheromones are often said to be "information" in this sense.

As a property in physics

Information has a well-defined meaning in physics. In 2003 J. D. Bekenstein claimed that a growing trend in physics was to define the physical world as being made up of information itself (and thus information is defined in this way) (see Digital physics). Examples of this include the phenomenon of quantum entanglement, where particles can interact without reference to their separation or the speed of light. Material information itself cannot travel faster than light even if that information is transmitted indirectly. This could lead to all attempts at physically observing a particle with an "entangled" relationship to another being slowed down, even though the particles are not connected in any other way other than by the information they carry.

The mathematical universe hypothesis suggests a new paradigm, in which virtually everything, from particles and fields, through biological entities and consciousness, to the multiverse itself, could be described by mathematical patterns of information. By the same token, the cosmic void can be conceived of as the absence of material information in space (setting aside the virtual particles that pop in and out of existence due to quantum fluctuations, as well as the gravitational field and the dark energy). Nothingness can be understood then as that within which no matter, energy, space, time, or any other type of information could exist, which would be possible if symmetry and structure break within the manifold of the multiverse (i.e. the manifold would have tears or holes).

Another link is demonstrated by the Maxwell's demon thought experiment. In this experiment, a direct relationship between information and another physical property, entropy, is demonstrated. A consequence is that it is impossible to destroy information without increasing the entropy of a system; in practical terms this often means generating heat. Another more philosophical outcome is that information could be thought of as interchangeable with energy. Toyabe et al. experimentally showed in nature that information can be converted into work.[13] Thus, in the study of logic gates, the theoretical lower bound of thermal energy released by an *AND gate* is higher than for the *NOT gate* (because information is destroyed in an *AND gate* and simply converted in a *NOT gate*). Physical information is of particular importance in the theory of quantum computers.

In thermodynamics, information is any kind of event that affects the state of a dynamic system that can interpret the information.

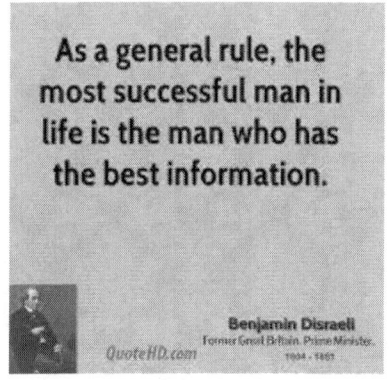

The application of information study

The information cycle (addressed as a whole or in its distinct components) is of great concern to Information Technology, Information Systems, as well as Information Science. These fields deal with those processes and techniques pertaining to information

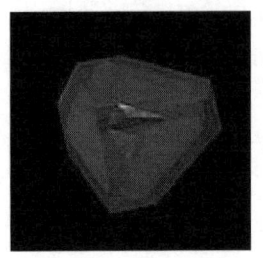 capture (through sensors) and generation (through computation, formulation or composition), processing (including encoding, encryption, compression, packaging), transmission (including all telecommunication methods), presentation (including visualization / display methods), storage (such as magnetic or optical, including holographic methods), etc. Information does not cease to exist, it may only get scrambled beyond any possibility of retrieval (within Information Theory, see lossy compression; in Physics, the black hole information paradox gets solved with the aid of the holographic principle).

Information Visualization (shortened as InfoVis) depends on the computation and digital representation of data, and assists users in pattern recognition and anomaly detection.

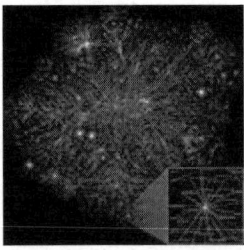

Partial map of the Internet, with nodes representing IP addresses

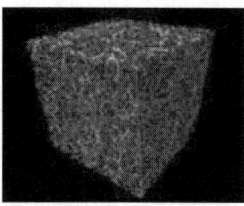

Galactic (including dark) matter distribution in a cubic section of the Universe

Information embedded in an abstract mathematical object with symmetry breaking nucleus

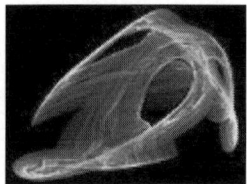

Visual representation of a strange attractor, with converted data of its fractal structure

Information Security (shortened as InfoSec) is the ongoing process of exercising due diligence to protect information, and information systems, from unauthorized access, use, disclosure, destruction, modification, disruption or distribution, through algorithms and procedures focused on monitoring and detection, as well as incident response and repair.

Information Analysis is the process of inspecting, transforming, and modelling information, by converting raw data into actionable knowledge, in support of the decision-making process. Information Quality (shortened as InfoQ) is the potential of a dataset to achieve a specific (scientific or practical) goal using a given empirical analysis method.

Information Communication represents the convergence of informatics, telecommunication and audio-visual media & content.

Technologically mediated information

It is estimated that the world's technological capacity to store information grew from 2.6 (optimally compressed) exabytes in 1986 – which is the informational equivalent to less than one 730-MB CD-ROM per person (539 MB per person) – to 295 (optimally compressed) exabytes in 2007.[14] This is the informational equivalent of almost 61 CD-ROM per person in 2007.[15]

The world's combined technological capacity to receive information through one-way broadcast networks was the informational equivalent of 174 newspapers per person per day in 2007.[14] The world's combined effective capacity to exchange information through two-way telecommunication networks was the informational equivalent of 6 newspapers per person per day in 2007.[15]

As of 2007, an estimated 90% of all new information is digital, mostly stored on hard drives.[16]

As records

Records are specialized forms of information. Essentially, records are information produced consciously or as by-products of business activities or transactions and retained because of their value. Primarily, their value is as evidence of the activities of the organization but they may also be retained for their informational value. Sound records management ensures that the integrity of records is preserved for as long as they are required.

The international standard on records management, ISO 15489, defines records as "information created, received, and maintained as evidence and information by an organization or person, in pursuance of legal obligations or in the transaction of business".[17] The International Committee on Archives (ICA) Committee on electronic records defined a record as, "a specific piece of recorded information generated, collected or received in the initiation, conduct or completion of an activity and that comprises sufficient content, context and structure to provide proof or evidence of that activity".

Records may be maintained to retain corporate memory of the organization or to meet legal, fiscal or accountability requirements imposed on the organization. Willis expressed the view that sound management of business records and information delivered "...six key requirements for good corporate governance...transparency; accountability; due process; compliance; meeting statutory and common law requirements; and security of personal and corporate information.

Semiotics

Michael Buckland has classified "information" in terms of its uses: "information as process", "information as knowledge", and "information as thing".[19]

Beynon-Davies [20][21] explains the multi-faceted concept of information in terms of signs and signal-sign systems. Signs themselves can be considered in terms of four inter-dependent levels, layers or branches of semiotics: pragmatics, semantics, syntax, and empirics. These four layers serve to connect the social world on the one hand with the physical or technical world on the other. Pragmatics is concerned with the purpose of communication. Pragmatics links the issue of signs with the context within which signs are used. The focus of pragmatics is on the intentions of living agents underlying communicative behavior. In other words, pragmatics link language to action.

Semantics is concerned with the meaning of a message conveyed in a communicative act. Semantics considers the content of communication. Semantics is the study of the meaning of signs - the association between signs and behavior. Semantics can be considered as the study of the link between symbols and their referents or concepts – particularly the way that signs relate to human behavior.

Syntax is concerned with the formalism used to represent a message. Syntax as an area studies the form of communication in terms of the logic and grammar of sign systems. Syntax is devoted to the study of the form rather than the content of signs and sign-systems.

Nielsen (2008) discusses the relationship between semiotics and information in relation to dictionaries. He introduces the concept of lexicographic information costs and refers to the effort a user of a dictionary must make to first find, and then

understand data so that they can generate information.

Communication normally exists within the context of some social situation. The social situation sets the context for the intentions conveyed (pragmatics) and the form of communication. In a communicative situation intentions are expressed through messages that comprise collections of inter-related signs taken from a language mutually understood by the agents involved in the communication. Mutual understanding implies that agents involved understand the chosen language in terms of its agreed syntax (syntactics) and semantics. The sender codes the message in the language and sends the message as signals along some communication channel (empirics). The chosen communication channel has inherent properties that determine outcomes such as the speed at which communication can take place, and over what distance.

Foundation for a Free Information Infrastructure

The Foundation for a Free Information Infrastructure (FFII) is a non-profit organization based in Munich, Germany, dedicated to establishing a free market in information technology, by the removal of barriers to competition. The FFII played a key organizational role and was very active in the campaign which resulted in the rejection of the EU software patent directive in July 2005.

CNET awarded the FFII the Outstanding contribution to software development award for this work, which was the result of years of research, policy, and action.[1] After the July 2005 victory, FFII has continued to defend a free and competitive software market by working towards adequate patent systems and open standards. Currently the FFII fights against software patents lobbies, not only in Europe but also in other parts of the world.

Views

FFII's view is that software patents present a burden, not a benefit to society. It backs this position up citing extensive studies.[2] FFII is a European NGO on this issue. Through its partnership with many other European organizations with the same goal, it has a reach across all nations of the EU.

FFII has been active on this front since 2000 when, according to the FFII, an attempt to change the European Patent Convention to legitimise software patents failed. In 2003, it strongly but indirectly lobbied the European Parliament against the proposed Directive on the patentability of computer-implemented inventions.

The EuroLinux anti-software-patent petition, supported and promoted by FFII, was signed by more than 1,500 SMEs, many thousand software developers, tens of thousands of software users system administrators as well as a number of scientists, academics and economists for a total of 400,000 signatories.

FFII organizes conferences about the topic, usually in Brussels, such as the conference which took place on April 14, 2004 together with a demonstration of more than 400 people against software patents the one on November 9–10, 2004. In Karlsruhe, FFII organised a demonstration of about 1,000 people against software patents. In 2005 FFII organised an *online demo* supported by 1,200 web sites.[3]

Structure

The FFII was funded originally by donations from SuSE and Infomatec. The Open Society Institute has contributed regularly, as have Red Hat, and Stichting NLnet. The historical list of donors from 1999 to 2005 can be found on the FFII web site.[4] Partners in Europe include EFFI, EuroLinux, FSF Europe, and SKOSI.

The FFII exists as a mother organization[5] with more or less formal chapters in many countries. The national FFII chapters (such as FFII France)[6] handle national membership, media and lobbying, while the mother organization operates at the EU level and in countries where there is no formal FFII organization.

As of 14 December 2013, the FFII board consists of Benjamin Henrion (President), Rene Mages (Vice president), Stephan Uhlmann (Treasurer), André Rebentisch (Secretary), Hartmut Pilch.

Campaigns

Besides software patents, FFII promotes various campaigns aimed at disencumbering computing and software development. These include supporting author's rights and Interoperability enforcements, such as working to improve copyright regulation by providing technical analysis, amendments and voting recommendations that may influence the European Parliament.

Freedom of information

Freedom of information is an extension of freedom of speech, a fundamental human right recognized

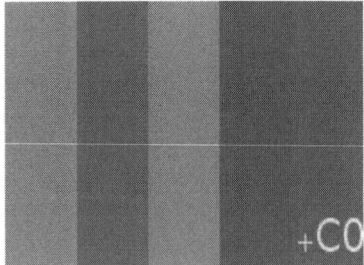

in international law, which is today understood more generally as freedom of expression in any medium, be it orally, in writing, print, through the Internet or through art forms. This means that the protection of freedom of speech as a right includes not only the content, but also the means of expression.[1] Freedom of information also refers to the right to privacy in the content of the Internet and information technology. As with the right to freedom of expression, the right to privacy is a recognized human right and freedom of information acts as an extension to this right.[2] Lastly, freedom of information can include opposition to patents, opposition to copyrights or opposition to intellectual property in general.[3] The international and United States Pirate Party have established political platforms based largely on freedom of information issues.[4]

In law

In June 2006 nearly 70 countries had freedom of information legislations applying to information held by government bodies and in certain circumstances to private bodies. In 19 of these countries the freedom of information legislation also applied to private bodies.[5] Access to information was

INFORMATION IS THE
CURRENCY OF
DEMOCRACY.

Thomas Jefferson
3rd U.S. President
QuoteHD.com (1743-1826)

increasingly recognised as a
prerequisite for
transparency and accountability of governments, as facilitating consumers' ability to make informed choices, and as safeguarding citizens against mismanagement and corruption. This has led an increasing number of countries to enact freedom of information legislation in the past 10 years.[6] In recent years, private bodies have started to perform functions which were previously carried out by public bodies. Privatisation and de-regulation saw banks, telecommunications companies, hospitals and universities being run by private entities, leading to demands for the extension of freedom of information legislation to cover private bodies.[7]

Government Bodies

As of 2006, 70 countries had comprehensive freedom of information legislation for public bodies, nearly half of which had been enacted in the past 10 years. Such legislation was pending in a further 50 countries.[6]

Private Bodies

As of 2006, the following 19 countries had freedom of information legislation that extended to government bodies and private bodies: Antigua and Barbuda, Angola, Armenia, Colombia, the Czech Republic, the Dominican Republic, Estonia, Finland, France, Iceland, Liechtenstein, Panama, Poland, Peru, South Africa, Turkey, Trinidad and Tobago, Slovakia, and the United Kingdom. The degree to which private bodies are covered under freedom of information legislation varies, in Angola, Armenia and Peru the legislation only applies to private companies that perform what are considered to be public functions. In the Czech Republic, the Dominican Republic, Finland, Trinidad and Tobago, Slovakia, Poland and Iceland private bodies that receive public funding are subject to freedom of information legislation. Freedom of information legislation in Estonia, France and UK covers private bodies in certain sectors.[8] In South Africa the access provisions of the Promotion of Access to Information Act have been used by individuals to establish why their loan application has been denied. The access provisions have also been used by minority shareholders in private companies and environmental groups, who were seeking information on the potential environmental damage caused by company projects.[9]

Consumer Protection

In 1983 the United Nations Commission on Transnational Corporations adopted the United Nations Guidelines for Consumer Protection stipulating eight consumer rights, including "consumer access to adequate information to enable making informed choices according to individual wishes and needs". Access to information became regarded as a basic consumer right, and preventive disclosure, i.e. the disclosure of information on threats to human lives, health and safety, began to be emphasized.[10]

Investors

Secretive decision making by company directors and corporate scandal led to freedom of information legislation to be published for the benefits of investors. Such legislation was first adopted in Britain in the early 20th century, and later in North America and other countries.[11] Disclosure regimes for the benefit of investor's regained attention at the beginning of the 21st century as a number of corporate scandals were linked to accounting fraud and company director secrecy.[12] Starting with Enron, the subsequent scandals involving Worldcom, Tyco, Adelphia and Global Crossing prompted the US Congress to impose new information disclosure obligations on companies with the Sarbanes-Oxley Act 2002.[13]

Internet and Information Technology

Freedom of information (or information freedom) also refers to the protection of the right to freedom of expression with regard to the Internet and information technology. Freedom of information may also concern censorship in an information technology context, i.e. the ability to access Web content, without censorship or restrictions.

The Information Society and freedom of expression

The World Summit on the Information Society (WSIS) Declaration of Principles adopted in 2003 reaffirms democracy and the universality, indivisibility and interdependence of all human rights and fundamental freedoms. The Declaration also makes specific reference to the importance of the right to freedom of expression for the "Information Society" in stating:

We reaffirm, as an essential foundation of the Information Society, and as outlined in Article 19 of the Universal Declaration of Human Rights, that everyone has the right to freedom of opinion and expression; that this right includes freedom to hold opinions without interference and to seek, receive and impart information and ideas through any media and regardless of frontiers. Communication is a fundamental social process, a basic human need and the foundation of all social organization. It is central to the Information Society. Everyone, everywhere should have the opportunity to participate and no one should be excluded from the benefits the Information Society offers.[14]

The 2004 WSIS Declaration of Principles also acknowledged that "it is necessary to prevent the use of information resources and technologies for criminal and terrorist purposes, while respecting human rights".[15] Wolfgang Benedek comments that the WSIS Declaration only contains a number of references to human rights and does not spell out any procedures or mechanism to assure that human rights are considered in practice.[16]

Hacktivismo

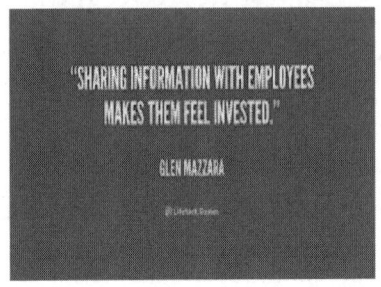

The digital rights group Hacktivismo, founded in 1999, argues that access to information is a basic human right. The group's beliefs are described fully in the "Hacktivismo Declaration" which calls for the Universal Declaration of Human Rights and the International Covenant on Civil and Political Rights (ICCPR) to be applied to the Internet. The Declaration recalls the duty of member states to the ICCPR to protect the right to freedom of expression with regard to the internet and in this context freedom of information.[17] The Hacktivismo Declaration recognises "the importance to fight against human rights abuses with respect to reasonable access to information on the Internet" and calls upon the hacker community to "study ways and means of circumventing state sponsored censorshipof the internet" and "implement technologies to challenge information rights violations".

The Hacktivismo Declaration does, however, recognise that the right to freedom of expression is subject to limitations, stating "we recognised the right of governments to forbid the publication of properly categorized state secrets, child pornography, and matters

related to personal privacy and privilege, among other accepted
restrictions." However, the Hacktivismo Declaration states "but we oppose the use of state power to control access to the works of critics, intellectuals, artists, or religious figures."[17]

Global Network Initiative

On October 29, 2008 the Global Network Initiative (GNI) was founded upon its "Principles on Freedom of Expression and Privacy". The Initiative was launched in the 60th Anniversary year of the Universal Declaration of Human Rights (UDHR) and is based on internationally recognized laws and standards for human rights on freedom of expression and privacy set out in the UDHR, the International Covenant on Civil and Political Rights (ICCPR) and the International Covenant on Economic, Social and Cultural Rights (ICESCR).[18] Participants in the Initiative include the Electronic Frontier Foundation, Human Rights Watch, Google, Microsoft, Yahoo, other major companies, human rights NGOs, investors, and academics.[19][20]

According to reports Cisco Systems was invited to the initial discussions but didn't take part in the initiative. Harrington Investments, which proposed that Cisco establish a human rights board, has dismissed the GNI as a voluntary code of conduct not having any impact. Chief executive John Harrington called the GNI "meaningless noise" and instead calls for bylaws to be introduced that force boards of directors to accept human rights responsibilities.[21]

Internet censorship

Main article: Internet censorship Jo Glanville, editor of the Index on Censorship, states that "the internet has been a revolution for censorship as much as for free speech".[21] The concept of freedom of information has emerged in response to state sponsored censorship, monitoring and surveillance of the internet. Internet censorship includes the control or suppression of the publishing or accessing of information on the Internet.

According to the Reporters without Borders (RSF) "internet enemy list" the following states engage in pervasive internet censorship: Cuba, Iran, Maldives, Myanmar/Burma, North Korea, Syria, Tunisia, Uzbekistan and Vietnam.[22] A widely publicised example is the Great Firewall of China (in reference both to its role as a network firewall and to the ancient Great Wall of China). The system blocks content by preventing IP addresses from being routed through and consists of standard firewall and proxy servers at the Internet gateways. The system also selectively engages in DNS poisoning when particular sites are requested. The government does not appear to be systematically examining Internet content, as this appears to be technically impractical.[23] Internet censorship in the People's Republic of China is conducted under a wide variety of laws and administrative regulations. In accordance with these laws, more than sixty Internet regulations have been made by the People's Republic of China (PRC) government, and censorship systems are vigorously implemented by provincial branches of state-owned ISPs, business companies, and organizations.[24][25]

In 2010, U.S. Secretary of State Hillary Clinton, speaking on behalf of the United States, declared 'we stand for a single internet where all of humanity has equal access to knowledge and ideas'. In her 'Remarks on Internet Freedom' she also draws attention to how 'even in authoritarian countries, information networks are helping people discover new facts and making governments more accountable', while reporting President Barack Obama's pronouncement 'the more freely information flows, the stronger societies become'.[26]

Access to public information in Europe

First edition of CFOI journal 'Secrets'

Access to public information and freedom of information (FOI) refer to the right
to access information held by public bodies also known as

"right

to know". Access to public

information is considered of fundamental importance for the effective functioning of democratic systems, as it enhances governments' and public officials' accountability, boosting people participation and allowing their informed participation into public life. The fundamental premise of the right to access public information is that the information held by governmental institutions is in principle public and may be concealed only on the basis of legitimate reasons which should be detailed in the law.[1] Access to public information builds on the principle that in a democratic system people should be in the condition of accessing a wide range of information in order to effectively participate in public life as well as on matters affecting them.

The right of access to public information is a component of the fundamental right of freedom of expression set forth by Article 19 of

the Universal Declaration of Human Rights (1948) which states that the fundamental right of freedom of expression encompasses the freedom "to seek, receive and impart information and ideas through any media and regardless of frontiers". Access to public information and freedom of information are recognised as human rights in the three main regional systems of human rights, namely within the Americas, Europe and Africa, as well as in major international instruments.[2]

The right to access information places two obligations on public bodies. First, the proactive duty to make public key information on the activities of authorities and governments; second, the reactive obligation to respond to people's requests for information, either by releasing public original documents or copies of the documents held.[3]

Over the past 10 years, the right to information and access to public information has been recognised in an increasing number of countries and several FOI lawshave been adopted all over the world, including in the developing countries. If in 1990 only 13 countries had a national freedom of information law, today there are 100 such laws across the world.[4][5]

In 2015 The UNESCO General Conference voted to designate Sept. 28 as "International Day for the Universal Access to Information" or, as it is more commonly known, Access to Information Day. The date had previously been celebrated as "Right to Know Day" since 2002. The UNESCO resolution recommends approval by the UN General Assembly.[6]

CHAPTER EIGHT
FREEDOM OF INFORMATION IN THE 21st CENTURY

The right to access information builds on the principle that the public has a right to know how power is exercised and public money is spent, given that public bodies are elected by people and sustained by taxpayers. The access to public information is a

precondition for governments' and public officials' accountability and it enables the adoption of informed decisions by citizens, hence representing a fundamental element for the proper functioning of democratic systems. International standards and evolving jurisprudence have confirmed that information held by public bodies belong to the public.[7] The Council of Europe Convention on Access to Official Documents (2009) states that "all official documents are in principle public and can be withheld subject only to the protection of other rights and legitimate interests".[8]

More than 100 countries around the world have now adopted national access to information laws to make the right to know effective. The first law on access to public information was adopted in Sweden in 1766, but after that one should wait almost one century to have the second law approved in Finland in 1951 and in the United States in 1966. During the 1970s and 1980s there has been a small but constant growth in FOI's laws, with a real expansion after 1989 due to the activism of civil society groups in Central and Eastern Europe during the post-Communist transitions to democracy. Indeed, the big push forward in the field of access to information leading to the broadening of the definition and of the scope of the right of access to information came together with a coordinated civil society reaction to contrast the control over the information exercised by Communist regimes in the Soviet bloc. It was this movement which gave a sound contribution to the development of access to information as a right in the sense of a human right. A 1992 decision of the Hungary's Constitutional Court established that access to information is a "fundamental right" essential for citizen oversight on the lawfulness and efficiency of the government.[9] Moreover, environmentalist groups and consumer associations also contributed to the affirmation of the right to know.[10]

All the eight former communists countries which joined the European Union in 2004 had a freedom of information law; also Romania and Bulgaria had their own law when joined the EU in 2007 and Croatia had already had an access to information law in force for ten years when it joined the EU in 2013.[11] Nowadays, in the OSCE region 48 of the 56 member states have specific access to information laws.[12]

The right to access information places two obligations on governments and public bodies. First, the duty to make public key information on the activities implemented by public bodies; second, the obligation to respond to people's requests of accessing documents, either by making available the original documents or by sharing copies of documents and information held.[13]

Access to information is a right which comprises two parts. The first is a proactive component, namely the positive obligation of public bodies to provide, make public and disseminate information about their activities, budgets and policies so that citizens can understand what public bodies are doing, can participate in public life and can monitor the behaviour of public authorities. The second component is a reactive one, entailing the right of all persons to requests information and documents to public bodies, along with the right to receive an answer.

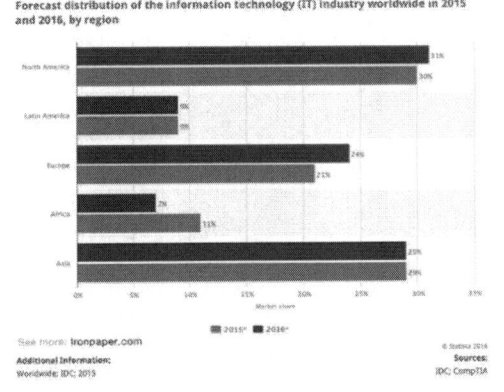

In principle, all the main information held by public bodies should be available, while exceptions to disclosure should be grounded on the protection of other values, such as privacy, national security or commercial interests. On the occasion of the first officially-recognised Access to Information Day celebrated on 28 September

2016, European civil society groups working to enhance the right of access to public information raised some concerns as, despite significant progress, there are still far-reaching shortcomings especially with regard to transparency of decision-making.[14] According to such organizations, among the main obstacles to government openness there is the inadequate record keeping of public bodies' information: minutes of public officials' meetings are not recorded, exchange with lobbyists are not available, public decisions are adopted without proper justification or documented evidence available to the public.[15][16] An additional problem concerns the over-application of exceptions with particular regard to the use of the privacy reasons, applied to not disclose the activities of public officials when performing public functions. Moreover, European civil society organizations are particularly concerned for the lack of transparency around the decision-making process at both national and EU level, as in the case of the refusal by the EU to disclose documents on the EU-Turkey refugee deal.[17]

Access to information as a human Right

A big push forward the advancement of the right to access information as a fundamental right was due to the activism of civil society movements which contrasted the regimes' control over information in the Communist countries in the Soviet bloc. A fundamental document in this sense is a 1992's decision of the Hungarian Constitutional Court which established that access to information is a "fundamental right" essential for citizen oversight on the lawfulness and efficiency of the government.[18]Progressively, several national and international courts decisions have been treating access to information as a basic human right, thus providing a strong legal case for citizens resorting to courts to defend any refusals by authorities to provide access to public information.[19] Such decisions are grounded on a series of international declarations, human rights covenants and conventions at international, regional and EU levels. In the first place, the right to access public information is recognized as a fundamental right and as a component of the right of freedom of expression in the Article 19 of the Universal Declaration of Human Rights; in the Article 19 of the International Covenant of Civil and Political Rights; and in the Article 13 of the American Convention on Human Rights. At regional level, all the three main regional systems of human rights, namely within the Americas, Europe and Africa, have recognized freedom of information as a universal human right.[20] In July 2011, the United Nations Human Rights Committee confirmed that the right to freedom of expression enshrined in Article 19 of the International Covenant on Civil and Political Rights includes the right of access public information.[21]

At the European Union level, Article 42 of the European Charter of Fundamental Rights establishes the right of access to EU institutions documents, as recognized also by Article 15 of the Treaty on the Functioning of the EU ("Treaty of Lisbon"). In 2009, the European Court of Human Rights on the basis of Article 10 of the European Convention on Human Rights, which is the article on freedom of expression, acknowledged the fundamental right of access to information held by public bodies. Specifically, the Court established that the right to information is protected in particular in case of "information monopoly", namely when the public bodies are the only ones owning the requested information, and when the information is needed by media or civil society organizations for public accountability purposes. The decision of the European Court embraced a 2006 decision by the Inter-American Court of Human Rights which endorsed Article 13 of the American Human Rights convention stating that individuals have the right to request information to public authorities and public authorities have the positive obligation to provide such information.[22]

Finally, many countries across the world recognize the right to information or access to documents in their Constitutions, either within the frame of the right to freedom of expression or separately and specifically as the right of access to information or documents. At least 50 countries all over the world, including 29 OSCE countries, have Constitutions including such provisions.[23]

Societal benefits of access to public information: accountability, participation, efficiency

Transparency enhanced through the right to access public information entails a series of core benefits for democratic societies, in particular accountability, participation and efficiency. First, access to public information enhances public accountability as it contributes to make governments and public officials more accountable for their actions and decisions. Second, the right to know boost people participation as it makes available information that can help citizens to make more effective decisions on matters that directly affect their lives and to participate with informed opinions in public debates and in the decision-making process. Third, access to public information contributes to the efficiency of decision-making as disclosure encourages public institutions to better manage and organize information and may help to improve communication between public bodies.[24] Also, access to information serve some other social goals. For instance, access to medical records can help individuals to improve personal decision-making and make better decisions about medical treatment, financial planning and the like. Finally, access to information can facilitate effective business practices as some of the information held by public bodies related to economic issues can be very useful for enterprises and can therefore contribute to increasing the effectiveness of the business sector.[25][26]

International standards and laws

At national level access to public information is regulated by freedom of information laws. In addition to national legislation, principles and standards for access

to public information are set forth into several international declarations and treaties that have authoritatively recognized the fundamental and legal nature of the right to freedom of information along with the need for effective legislations that should guarantee the respect of that right in practice.[27] Such international laws and standards include:

Civil society standards and declarations: these include the Ten Principles on the Right to Know by the Justice Initiative (2005); the Public's Right to Know - Principles on Freedom of Information Legislation by Article 19 (1999); the Atlanta Declaration and Plan of Action for the Advancement of the Right of Access to Information (2008); the Budapest Declaration on Right of Access to Information (2008); the Transparency Charter for International Financial Institutions: Claiming our Right to Know by the Global Transparency Initiative (2006); the Declaration on Parliamentary Openness (2012);

International treaties: these include the Council of Europe Convention on Access to Documents (2009) and the Aarhus Convention on Access to Information, Public Participation and Access to Justice in Environmental Matters (1999);

Inter-governmental Principles and Recommendations: these include the Principles on the Right of Access to Information by the Organisation of American States (2000); the Council of Europe Recommendation 2002(2) on access to official documents (2002); the Declaration of Principles on Freedom of Expression in Africa by the African Commission on Human and Peoples' Rights (2002); the UNESCO's Maputo Declaration on Fostering Freedom of Expression, Access to Information and Empowerment of People (2008); the UNESCO's Brisbane

Declaration on Freedom of Information; the Dakar Declaration on Media and Good Governance (2005);

Annual reports of the United Nations Special Rapporteur on Freedom of Opinion and Expression: the UN Special Rapporteur has addressed the issue of freedom of information in its annual reports since 1997. After that, the Commission on Human Rights endorsed the commentaries of the Special Rapporteur and asked him to elaborate further on the right to seek and receive information. As a consequence, the UN

Special Rapporteur expanded significantly his commentary on freedom of information in his 2000 annual Reports.[28]

Access to public information: guiding principles

The non-governmental organization ARTICLE 19 has published a set of principles called "The Public's Right To Know: Principles on Freedom of Information Legislation" which describes the best practices and standards on freedom of information legislation based on international and regional laws as well as on evolving national practices and legislations. Such principles, which are designed mainly for national laws, are also applicable to inter-governmental bodies such as the United Nations and the European Union.[29]

Principle 1: Maximum disclosure

The principle of maximum disclosure sets a presumption that all information held by public bodies should be covered by the scope of access to information laws. This presumption accepts only limited circumstances for exceptions. This principle incorporates the very basic rationale underpinning the concept of freedom of information. It entails that public authorities seeking to deny access to public information have the obligation to justifying their refusal. The principle of maximum disclosure provides for a broad definition of "public bodies" which are subject to the duty of releasing information. Such a broad interpretation includes all branches of government, e.g. local governments, elected bodies, nationalized industries and public corporations, judicial bodies and also private bodies carrying out public functions. Principle 1 requires the law to establish minimum standards regarding the maintenance and preservation of documents by public bodies.[30]

Principle 2: Obligation to publish

This principle implies the obligation for public bodies to respond to access to information requests and to publish and disseminate documents of public interest. Few reasonable limits based, for instance, on resources and capacity can be accepted. As a minimum, public authorities should make public the following types of information: operational information on the functioning of public bodies, including objectives, results and costs; information on any requests or complaints that people may take in relation of a given public body;

  information on how members of the public may provide their contribution to the policy-making process;
  the types and formats of information held by public bodies;

  Information on decisions and policies affecting the public, along with background information on those decisions and the evidence that led to their formulation.[31]

Principle 3: Promotion of open government

This principle calls governments to actively promote a culture of openness in order to enhance the respect of the right to know. This is important as experiences in different countries have shown that recalcitrant public authorities can undermine the application of even the most progressive legislations. National laws should therefore allocate adequate resources to the promotion of an open government culture and the goals of FOI laws, including by means of internal codes on access and openness, educational programs, media coverage and communications campaigns. Such activities should also be aimed at contrasting the culture of official secrecy within government for example through trainings for public officials.[32] An important step in this direction has been adopted in 2011 with the establishment of a new global alliance of democratic countries committed to the promotion of transparency, accountability and participation under the label Open Government Partnership [33]

Principle 4: Limited scope of exceptions

Exceptions to disclosure should be grounded on clearly and narrowly-defined exceptions. Public authorities should show that a refusal to provide the required information has passed a test through which to assess if the disclosure of a given information threaten to cause substantial harm to a legitimate aim and if the harm is greater than the public interest in having the information. Non-disclosure decisions should be taken on a case-by-case basis. National laws should provide an exhaustive list of the legitimate reasons that may justify non-disclosure. Such a list should be narrowly-defined and include only highly relevant interests to be protected, such as law enforcement, privacy, national security, commercial and other confidentiality, public or individual safety and the integrity of the decision-making process. However, even if can be demonstrated that disclosure would cause substantial harm to a legitimate interest, the information should be released when the benefits of disclosure prevail over the harm. In other words, the harm to the legitimate interest must be weighed against the public interest in having a given information publicly available.[34]

Principle 5: Processes to facilitate access

According to this principle requests for public information should be processed quickly and fairly and an independent review of any refusals should be made available to the applicant. Also, public

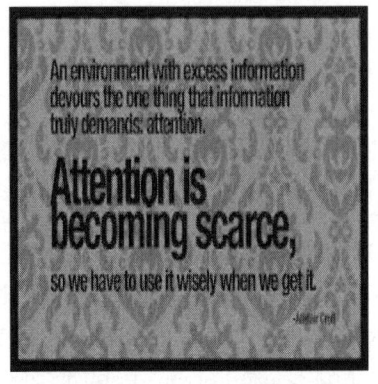

An environment with excess information devours the one thing that information truly demands: attention.

Attention is becoming scarce,

so we have to use it wisely when we get it.

-Aldfier Croll

bodies are called to set up open, accessible systems for implementing freedom of information laws and thus ensuring the public's right to receive the required information. Furthermore, the law should establish an individual right to appeal to an independent body for any refusal by a public body to release information. All members of the public should be in the condition of accessing to appeal procedures without incurring in undue costs and complicated procedures.[35]

Principle 6: Costs

This principle states that costs for accessing public information should not be so high as to deter applicants from making the request. Around the world there are different cost regimes, including, for instance, flat fees systems for each request and graduated fees depending on the actual cost of retrieving and reproducing the information and / or the documents requested.[36]

Principle 7: Open meetings

Freedom of information comprises the public's right to know how the government behaves on behalf of people and to participate to decision-making. Freedom of information law should thus incorporates the presumption that all relevant meetings of governing bodies, i.e. those involved in decision-making, should be open to the public. Meetings may be closed, but only when sound reasons for closure exist. Such reasons have to be clearly explained and closure have to comply with established procedures.[37]

Principle 8: Disclosure takes precedence

Other laws dealing with publicly-held information should be consistent with the principle of maximum disclosure and the other principles underpinning freedom of information. In particular, the regime of exceptions should be clearly defined in the freedom of information legislation; extensions of the exceptions regime should not be allowed by other laws.[38]

Principle 9: Protection for whistleblowers

Whistleblowers, i.e. individuals who make publicly available information on government's wrongdoings - including for instance corruption, dishonesty, maladministration, serious threat to health, safety or the environment, etc. - should be protected from any legal, administrative or other kind of sanctions. In this context the public interest refers to situations where the benefit of disclosure prevails over the harm, no matter how the disclosure has been conducted. This applies in particular when there are exceptionally serious reasons for releasing a certain information, such as a serious threat to public health or safety, or when there is a strong evidence that wrongdoing will be concealed or destroyed.[39]

Access to Public Information

Universal access

Being a fundamental and universal right, in principle access to information is a right to everyone: almost all national freedom of information laws recognize this by establishing that "anyone" may make a request to access public information. One noteworthy exception among the world's democracies is Canada where only citizens and residents are entitled to submit access to information requests.[40] Despite this, a major practical obstacle to the universal exercise of the right to access information is due to the obligation to submit the requests in the official language of the country which may hamper the exercise of the right to know for people that does not have a command of a country's official language.

In the EU, according to the treaties the right to access documents and the right to appeal to the European Ombudsman applies only to EU citizens, residents and companies registered inside the EU. While in general anyone whose right has been violated can appeal to the European Court of Justice, in the case of the right to access information the Court is obliged to accept cases made by EU citizens, residents and businesses.[41]

Kind of information and documents to be made available under access to information laws;

In principle, all information held by public bodies can be accessed upon a FOI's request, unless some exceptions can be applied (e.g. on the ground of protecting state interests; private interests or human rights, or to ensure effective governments). Some national laws refer to "access to information" while others to "access to documents": even if these definitions actually overlap, it can be useful for the applicant to be aware of the exact phrasing used by the law in order to formulate properly the access to information request, and thus, having more chance of success. Usually "documents" and "information" should be made available whatever it's medium, e.g. written on paper or in electronic format, or as a sound, visual or audiovisual.[42] The EU Regulation 1049/2001 specifies that documents subject to access to information are those concerning "policies, activities and decisions falling within the institutions' sphere of responsibility" and this applies to all documents held by the EU institutions "in all areas of activity of the European Union".[43]

Public bodies concerned by access to Information

In general in Europe the right of access to information applies to all administrative bodies, at any level of government, from central government to local authorities. Some rare exceptions to this can be found, as in the case of Ireland where police forces are exempted. In addition to administrative bodies, in national legislations which have been progressively approved the obligation to disclose information has been extended also to legislative and judicial bodies. Moreover, in many countries also some private bodies performing public functions or receiving public funds are obliged to respond to access to information requests. For instance, in Macedonia which adopted an access to information law in 2006, the right to access applies to local and national governments, legislative bodies and judicial authorities, and encompasses also private bodies with public functions.[44]

Inter-governmental Organisations

Many inter-governmental bodies hold information about policies and decisions affecting people's lives. While the EU has defined a set of rules regulating access to information held by EU institutions, the debate is still open about whether the right of access information applies to inter-governmental organisations which are outside the scope of national laws and have not signed international human rights conventions. Campaigning organisations have worked for the adoption of internal rules - called "disclosure policies" or "access to information policies" - so that inter-governmental organisations could apply rules similar to national access to information laws. The World Bank adopted its Access to Information Policy in July 2010.[45]

Standard exceptions to the right to information

Although in principles the right of access to information applies to all information held by public bodies, it is not an absolute right as there can be some exceptions not allowing the disclosure of certain kind of information. If released this information can violate some "legitimate interests", disturb public life or undermine other societal values. To justify the withhold of public information, authorities have the burden of the proof, thus have to demonstrate that disclosure would cause harm to a legitimate interest as specified by the law.

International laws and standards in the field of access to public information provide for three categories of standard exceptions. Specifically,

Exceptions to protect state interests or international relations, such as:

National security and defense of the state;

International relations;

Public safety or public order;

Economic, monetary and exchange rate policies of

the state; Exceptions aimed at ensuring effective government:

> Protection of internal public bodies' deliberations prior
> to decision-making (known as "space to think"
> exception);

> Protection of criminal enquiries;

Exceptions to protect private interests and human rights, such as:

> Privacy and other legitimate private interests;

> Commercial and other economic interests like, for
> instance, trade secrets;

> The environment;

Guaranteeing the effective administration of justice and
equality of parties before the courts.

However, even if the requested information or documents are
sensitive and exceptions apply, some part of it could be released
by public bodies on the ground of two factors. The first is the
right of partial access according to which authorities have the duty
of removing sensitive information and release the rest of the
document. The second "exception to exceptions" applies when
transparency overrides secrecy, thus even if the information is
sensitive the public interest in knowing it is stronger. In this
particular case public officials have to apply the so-called "public
interest test", meaning that they have to scrutinize and ponder

both the exceptions for not releasing information and the reasons of public interest in knowing the information required. Many national access to information laws foresees this kind of test.[46]

Right to appeal

Applicant have the right to appeal in case of "administrative silence" (i.e. the request is not answered), when public authorities reject the disclosure request or when their reply is not satisfying and does not meaningfully answer the question. Rules regulating the right to appeal depends on national legislations and vary from country to country. Generally, there are four main appeals mechanisms:

Internal or Administrative Appeal: internal review is addressed to the same authority that issued the denial or made a non-satisfying disclosure or to the administrative body which is immediately superior;
Administrative or Higher Court Appeal: appeal to administrative court is usually the step following internal review. This is regulated by administrative law and the competent authority entitled to examine the appeal are regional or national administrative courts. A further appeal to a higher court, including the European Court of Human Rights, is also possible.

Information Commission/er Appeal: in this case the appeal is scrutinized by a dedicated body whose specific role is to protect the right to access information. Such bodies can issue binding decisions as well as non-binding recommendations, depending on national laws. The decisions of the Information Commissioner can always go to appeal. In the OSCE region, Information Commissions exist in 16 countries.

Ombudsman Appeal: in some countries, the Ombudsman - which is the institution whose role is to protect the rights of citizens Vis à vis public authorities - has also the function to examine complains related to access to information. In many cases the Ombudsman's decision is only a recommendation, i.e. a non-binding measure, although usually his/her opinion is taken in due consideration by public authorities. At the EU level, the European Ombudsman is responsible for processing complaints concerning access to documents.

Access to public information in practice

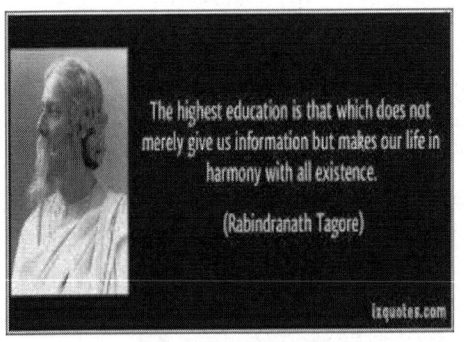

Request's contents

equests for accessing public information to the public authorities covered by the scope of national laws should be as clear and specific as possible about the information or documents required. A well-formulated request will facilitate the work of public officials and will more likely result in a positive answer or at least reducing the reasons for rejecting the request.[47] Usually the name and address of the person filing the request have to be provided. Giving also the e-mail address as well as a phone number might facilitate the exchange with public officials. In some countries requests made by resorting to pseudonyms or anonymously are permitted.

Procedure

In general, the procedure for requesting public information under national laws is simple and does not foresees many formalities. Usually requests can be filed in writing, either by post or hand-delivered to the concerned public authority. In most countries, submission is allowed also by e-mail. Moreover, some access to information laws permit oral requests, made, for instance, by phone or in person. However, in some cases, such as in Slovenia, oral request are not considered to be a formal basis for going to appeal. In some countries, such as in Armenia or Romania, rules and timeframes for written requests and oral requests are different.

Fees

Filing a request for accessing public information should always be free of charge, as confirmed by the Council of Europe Convention on Access to Official Documents which allows only costs for copying and delivering the documents, such as photocopying, postage costs, or costs of reproduction into other formats or materials in case of DVDs or CDs. As a rule, electronic delivery is free of charge. The majority of countries in the Council of Europe region comply with this rule, even if there are notable exceptions, such as Ireland and Germany where, however, the required fees can be significantly reduced on the ground of public interest.

Modalities of getting the information

In reply of a formal request of accessing public information, the examination of the required information can be allowed in different ways, including the inspection of original documents; photocopies sent by post or e-mails; copies in DVDs or CDs.

Timeframes for getting a reply

There is a great variability across Europe on the timeframes for public authorities to answer requests as well as for notifying the extension of the timeframe for justified reasons or for issuing a refusal. However, the average time is about 15 working days.[48] In Europe, the countries with the shortest timeframe for response are Norway and Sweden (1–3 days). On the contrary, the Albanian and Austrian access to information laws give the authorities a period of respectively 40 and 60 days to respond to people's requests. Most national laws allow the extension of the timeframe in case of requests which are particularly complex. In all cases such extension should be notified to the applicant, along with an explanation of the reasons that led to it. At the EU level, the Regulation 1049/2001 establishes 15 working days for issuing a response; an extension of up 15 additional working days may be applied in exceptional cases, for instance when the request relates to long documents or a large number of documents.

See also

CHAPTER NINE

INFORMATION AND COMMUNICATION TECHNOLOGY

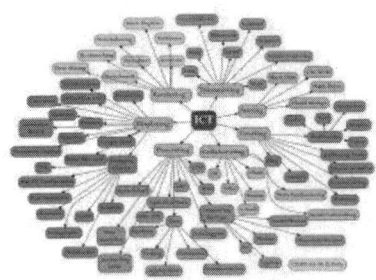

Information and communication technology (ICT) is an another/extensional term for information technology (IT) which stresses the role of unified communications[1] and the integration of telecommunications (telephone lines and wireless signals), computers as well as necessary enterprise software, middleware, storage, and audio-visual systems, which enable users to access, store, transmit, and manipulate information.[2]

The term *ICT* is also used to refer to the convergence of audio-visual and telephone networks with computer networks through a single cabling or link system. There are large economic incentives (huge cost savings due to elimination of the telephone network) to merge the telephone network with the computer network system using a single unified system of cabling, signal distribution and management.

However, definition, as "the concepts, methods and applications involved in ICT are constantly evolving on an almost daily basis."[3]

The broadness of ICT covers any product that will store, retrieve, manipulate, transmit or receive information electronically in a digital form, e.g. personal computers, digital television, email, robots. For clarity, Zuppo provided an ICT hierarchy where all levels of the hierarchy "contain some degree of commonality in that they are related to technologies that facilitate the transfer of information and various types of electronically mediated communications".[4] Skills Framework for the Information Age is one of many models for describing and managing competencies for ICT professionals for the 21st century.[5]

The phrase "information and communication technologies" has been used by academic researchers since the 1980s,[6] and the abbreviation *ICT* became popular after it was used in a report to the UK government by Dennis Stevenson in 1997,[7] and in the revised National Curriculum for England, Wales and Northern Ireland in 2000. But in 2012, the Royal Society recommended that *ICT* should no longer be used in British schools "as it has attracted too many negative connotations",[8] and with effect from 2014 the National Curriculum uses the word *computing,* which reflects the addition of computer programming into the curriculum.[9]

Variations of the phrase have spread worldwide, with the United Nations creating a "United Nations Information and Communication Technologies Task Force" and an internal "Office of Information and Communications Technology".[10]

Monetization

The money spent on IT worldwide has been most recently estimated as US $3.5 trillion and is currently growing at 5% per year, doubling every 15 years.[11] The 2014 IT budget of US federal government is nearly $82 billion.[12] IT costs, as a percentage of corporate revenue, have grown 50% since 2002, putting a strain on IT budgets. When looking at current companies' IT budgets, 75% are recurrent costs, used to "keep the lights on" in the IT department, and 25% are cost of new initiatives for technology development.[11]

The average IT budget has the following breakdown:[11]
  31% personnel costs (internal)

    29% software costs (external/purchasing category)

    26% hardware costs (external/purchasing category)

    14% costs of external service providers (external/services).

Technological capacity

The world's technological capacity to store information grew from 2.6 (optimally compressed) exabytes in 1986 to 15.8 in 1993, over 54.5 in 2000, and to 295 (optimally compressed) exabytes in 2007, and some 5 zettabytes in 2014.[13][14] This is the informational equivalent to 1.25 stacks of CD-ROM from the earth to the moon in 2007, and the equivalent of 4,500 stacks of printed books from the earth to the sun in 2014. The world's technological capacity to receive information through one-way broadcast networks was 432 exabytes of (optimally compressed) information in 1986, 715 (optimally compressed) exabytes in 1993, 1.2 (optimally compressed) zettabytes in 2000, and 1.9 zettabytes in 2007.[13] The world's effective capacity to exchange information through two-way telecommunication networks was 281 petabytes of (optimally compressed) information in 1986, 471 petabytes in 1993, 2.2 (optimally compressed) exabytes in 2000, 65 (optimally compressed) exabytes in 2007,[13] and some 100 exabytes in 2014.[15] The world's technological capacity to compute information with humanly guided general-purpose computers grew from 3.0×10^{8} MIPS in 1986, to 6.4×10^{12} MIPS in 2007.[13]

ICT Sector in the OECD

ICT Development Index

The ICT Development Index ranks and compares the level of ICT use and access across the various countries around the world.[17] In 2014 ITU (International Telecommunications Union) released the latest rankings of the IDI, with Denmark attaining the top spot, followed by South Korea. The top 30 countries in the rankings include most high-income countries where quality of life is higher than average, which includes countries from Europe and other regions such as "Australia, Bahrain, Canada, Japan, Macao (China), New Zealand, Singapore and the United States; almost all countries surveyed improved their IDI ranking this year."[18]

The WSIS process and ICT development goals

On 21 December 2001, the United Nations

General

Assembly approved Resolution 56/183, endorsing the holding of the World Summit on the Information Society(WSIS) to discuss the opportunities and challenges facing today's information society.[19] According to this resolution, the General Assembly related the Summit to the United Nations Millennium Declaration's goal of implementing ICT to achieve Millennium Development Goals. It also emphasized a multi-stakeholder approach to achieve these goals, using all stakeholders including civil society and the private sector, in addition to governments.

To help anchor and expand ICT to every habitable part of the world, "2015 is the deadline for achievements of the UN Millennium Development Goals (MDGs), which global leaders agreed upon in the year 2000."[20]>

In Education

Today's society shows the ever-growing computer-centric lifestyle, which includes the rapid influx of computers in the modern classroom.

Information and Communication Technology can contribute to

universal access to education, equity in education, the delivery of quality learning and teaching, teachers' professional development and more efficient education management, governance and administration. UNESCO takes a holistic and comprehensive approach to promoting ICT in education. Access, inclusion and quality are among the main challenges they can address. The Organization's Intersectral Platform for ICT in education focuses on these issues through the joint work of three of its sectors: Communication & Information, Education and Science.[21]

Despite the power of computers to enhance and reform teaching and learning practices, improper implementation is a widespread issue beyond the reach of increased funding and technological advances with little evidence that teachers and tutors are properly integrating ICT into everyday learning. Intrinsic barriers such as a belief in more traditional teaching practices and individual attitudes towards computers in education as well as the teachers own comfort with computers and their ability to use them all as result in varying effectiveness in the integration of ICT in the classroom. [22]

Today

In modern society ICT is ever-present, with over three billion people having access to the Internet.[23] With approximately 8 out of 10 Internet users owning a smartphone, information and data are increasing by leaps and bounds.[24] This rapid growth, especially in developing countries, has led ICT to become a keystone of everyday life, in which life without some facet of technology renders most of clerical, work and routine tasks dysfunctional. The most recent authoritative data, released in 2014, shows "that Internet use continues to grow steadily, at 6.6% globally in 2014 (3.3% in developed countries, 8.7% in the developing world); the number of Internet users in developing countries has doubled in five years (2009-2014), with two thirds of all people online now living in the developing world."[18]

However, hurdles are still at large. "Of the 4.3 billion people not yet using the Internet, 90% live in developing countries. In the world's 42 Least Connected Countries (LCCs), which are home to 2.5 billion people, access to ICTs remains largely out of reach, particularly for these countries' large rural populations."[25]ICT has yet to penetrate the remote areas of some countries, with many developing countries dearth of any type of Internet. This also includes the availability of telephone lines, particularly the availability of cellular coverage, and other forms of electronic transmission of data. The latest "Measuring the Information Society Report" cautiously stated that the increase in the aforementioned cellular data coverage is ostensible, as "many users have multiple subscriptions, with global growth figures sometimes translating into little real improvement in the level of connectivity of those at the very bottom of the pyramid; an estimated 450 million people worldwide live in places which are still out of reach of mobile cellular service."[23]

Favorably, the gap between the access to the Internet and mobile coverage has decreased substantially in the last fifteen years, in which "2015 [was] the deadline for achievements of the UN

Millennium Development Goals (MDGs), which global leaders agreed upon in the year 2000, and the new data show ICT progress and highlight remaining gaps."[20] ICT continues to take on new form, with nanotechnology set to usher in a new wave of ICT electronics and gadgets. ICT newest editions into the modern electronic world include smart watches, such as the Apple Watch, smart wristbands such as the Nike+ FuelBand, and smart TVs such as Google TV. With desktops soon becoming part of a bygone era, and laptops becoming the preferred method of computing, ICT continues to insinuate and alter itself in the ever-changing globe.

Information communication technologies play a role in facilitating accelerated pluralism in new social movements today. The internet according to Bruce Bimber is "accelerating the process of issue group formation and action"[26] and coined the term accelerated pluralism to explain this new phenomena. ICTs are tools for "enabling social movement leaders and empowering dictators"[27] in effect promoting societal change. ICTs can be used to garner grassroots support for a cause due to the internet allowing for political discourse and direct interventions with state policy [28] as well as change the way complaints from the populace are handled by governments.

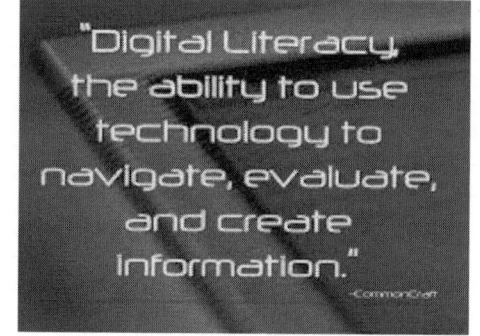

"Digital Literacy, the ability to use technology to navigate, evaluate, and create information."
-CommonCraft

Information system

An information system (IS) is an organized system for the collection, organization, storage and communication of information. More specifically, it is the study of complementary networks that people and organizations use to collect, filter, and process, create and distribute data.

"An information system (IS) is a group of components that interact to produce information. It focuses on the internal rather than the external."[1]

A computer information system is a system that a branch of Science composed of people and computers that processes or interprets information.[2][3][4][5] The term is also sometimes used in more restricted senses to refer to only the software used to run a computerized database or to refer to only a computer system.

Information Systems is an academic study of systems with a specific reference to information and the complementary networks of hardware and software that people and organizations use to collect, filter, process, create and also distribute data. An emphasis is placed on an information system having a definitive boundary, users, processors, storage, inputs, outputs and the aforementioned communication networks.[6] Any specific information system aims to support operations, management and decision-making.[7][8] An information system is the information and communication technology (ICT) that an organization uses, and also the way in which people interact with this technology in support of business processes.[9]

Some authors make a clear distinction between information systems, computer systems, and business processes. Information systems typically include an ICT component but are not purely concerned with ICT, focusing instead on the end use of information technology. Information systems are also different from business processes. Information systems help to control the performance of business processes.[10]

Alter[11][12] argues for advantages of viewing an information system as a special type of work system. A work system is a system in which humans or machines perform processes and activities using resources to produce specific products or services for customers. An information system is a work system whose activities are devoted to capturing, transmitting, storing, retrieving, manipulating and displaying information.[13]

As such, information systems inter-relate with data systems on the one hand and activity systems on the other. An information system is a form of communication system in which data represent and are processed as a form of social memory. An information system can also be considered a semi-formal language which supports human decision making and action.

Information systems are the primary focus of study for organizational informatics.[14]

Overview

Silver et al. (1995) provided two views on IS that includes software, hardware, data, people, and procedures.[15] Zheng provided another system view of information system which also adds processes and essential system elements like environment, boundary, purpose, and interactions. The Association for Computing Machinery defines "Information systems specialists [as] focus[ing] on integrating information technology solutions and business processes to meet the information needs of businesses and other enterprises."[16]

There are various types of information systems, for example: transaction processing systems, decision support systems, knowledge management systems, learning management systems, database management systems, and office information systems. Critical to most information systems are information technologies, which are typically designed to enable humans to perform tasks for which the human brain is not well suited, such as: handling large amounts of information, performing complex calculations, and controlling many simultaneous processes.

Information technologies are a very important and malleable resource available to executives.[17] Many companies have created a position of chief information officer (CIO) that sits on the executive board with the chief executive officer (CEO), chief financial officer (CFO), chief operating officer (COO), and chief technical officer (CTO). The CTO may also serve as CIO, and vice versa. The chief information security officer (CISO) focuses on information security management.

The six components that must come together in order to produce an information system are: (Information systems are organizational procedures and do not need a computer or software, this data is erroneous) (IE, an accounting system in the 1400s using ledger and ink utilizes an information system)

1. Hardware: The term hardware refers to machinery. This category includes the computer itself, which is often referred to as the central processing unit (CPU), and all of its support equipment. Among the support, equipment are input and output devices, storage devices and communications devices.

2. Software: The term software refers to computer programs and the manuals (if any) that support them. Computer programs are machine-readable instructions that direct the circuitry within the hardware parts of the system to function in ways that produce useful information from data. Programs are generally stored on some input/output medium, often a disk or tape.

3. Data: Data are facts that are used by programs to produce useful information. Like programs, data are generally stored in machine-readable form on disk or tape until the computer needs them.

4. Procedures: Procedures are the policies that govern the operation of a computer system. "Procedures are to people what software is to hardware" is a common analogy that is used to illustrate the role of procedures in a system.

5. People: Every system needs people if it is to be useful. Often the most overlooked element of the system are the people, probably the component that most influence the success or failure of information systems. This includes "not only the users, but those who operate and service the computers, those who maintain the data, and those who support the network of computers." <Kroenke, D. M. (2015). MIS Essentials. Pearson Education>

6. Feedback: it is another component of the IS, that defines that an IS may be provided with a feedback (Although this component isn't necessary to function).

Data is the bridge between hardware and people. This means that the data we collect is only data until we involve people. At that point, data is now information.

Types of Information System

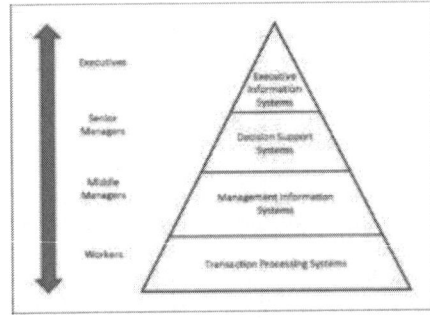

A four level

The "classic" view of Information systems found in the textbooks[18] in the 1980s was a pyramid of systems that reflected the hierarchy of the organization, usually transaction processing systems at the bottom of the pyramid, followed by management information systems, decision support systems, and ending with executive information systems at the top. Although the pyramid model remains useful since it was first formulated, a number of new technologies have been developed and new categories of information systems have emerged, some of which no longer fit easily into the original pyramid model.

Some examples of such systems are:

> data warehouses
>
> enterprise resource planning
>
> enterprise systems
>
> expert systems
>
> search engines
>
> geographic information system
>
> global information system
>
> Office automation.

A computer-based information system is essentially an IS using computer technology to carry out some or all of its planned tasks. The basic components of computer-based information systems are:

> *Hardware* these are the devices like the monitor, processor, printer and keyboard, all of which work

together to accept, process, show data and information.

Software are the programs that allow the hardware to process the data.

Databases are the gathering of associated files or tables containing related data.

Networks are a connecting system that allows diverse computers to distribute resources.

Procedures are the commands for combining the components above to process information and produce the preferred output.

The first four components (hardware, software, database, and network) make up what is known as the information technology platform. Information technology workers could then use these components to create information systems that watch over safety measures, risk and the management of data. These actions are known as information technology services.[19]

Certain information systems support parts of organizations, others support entire organizations, and still others, support groups of organizations. Recall that each department or functional area within an organization has its own collection of application programs or information systems. These functional area information systems (FAIS) are as the name suggest, each FAIS support a particular function within the organization, e.g.: accounting IS, finance IS, production /

operation management (POM) IS, marketing IS, and human resources IS. In finance and accounting, managers use IT systems to forecast revenues and business activity, to determine the best sources and uses of funds, and to perform audits to ensure that the organization is fundamentally sound and that all financial reports and documents are accurate. Other types of organizational information systems are FAIS, Transaction processing systems, enterprise resource planning, office automation system, management information system, decision support system, expert system, executive dashboard, supply chain management system, and electronic commerce system. Dashboards are a special form of IS that support all managers of the organization. They provide rapid access to timely information and direct access to structured information in the form of reports. Expert systems attempt to duplicate the work of human experts by applying reasoning capabilities, knowledge, and expertise within a specific domain.

Information system development Information technology departments in larger organizations tend to strongly influence the development, use, and application of information technology in the organizations. A series of methodologies and processes can be used to develop and use an information system. Many developers now use an engineering approach such as the system development life cycle (SDLC), which is a systematic procedure of developing an information system through stages that occur in sequence. Recent research aims at enabling

In today's knowledge-based economy, what you earn depends on what you learn. Jobs in the information technology sector, for example, pay 85 percent more than the private sector average.

(Bill Clinton)

lzquotes.com

measuring [21] the ongoing, collective development of such systems within an organization by the entirety of human actors themselves. An information system can be developed in house (within the organization) or outsourced. This can be accomplished by outsourcing certain components or the entire system.[22] A specific case is the geographical distribution of the development team (offshoring, global information system).

A computer-based information system, following a definition of Langefors,[23] is a technologically implemented medium for:

> recording, storing, and disseminating linguistic expressions,

> As well as for drawing conclusions from such expressions.

Geographic information systems, land information systems, and disaster information systems are examples of emerging information systems, but they can be broadly considered as spatial information systems. System development is done in stages which include:

> Problem recognition and specification

> Information gathering   [20] and

> Requirements specification for the new system

System design

System construction

System implementation

Review and maintenance.[24]

As an Academic Discipline

The field of study called *information systems* encompasses a variety of topics including systems analysis and design, computer networking, information security, database management and decision support systems. *Information management* deals with the practical and theoretical problems of collecting and analyzing information in a business function area including business productivity tools, applications programming and implementation, electronic commerce, digital media production, data mining, and decision support. *Communications and networking* deals with the telecommunication technologies. Information systems bridges business and computer science using the theoretical foundations of information and computation to study various business models and related algorithmic processes [25] on building the IT systems [26][27] within a computer science discipline.[

Computer information system(s)(CIS) is a field studying computers and algorithmic processes, including their principles, their software and hardware designs, their applications, and their impact on society,[41][42][43] whereas IS emphasizes functionality over design.[44]

Several IS scholars have debated the nature and foundations of Information Systems which have its roots in other reference disciplines such as Computer Science, Engineering, Mathematics, Management Science, Cybernetics, and others.[45][46][47][48] Information systems also can be defined as a collection of hardware, software, data, people and procedures that work together to produce quality information.

Differentiating IS from related disciplines

Information Systems relationship to Information Technology, Computer Science, Information Science, and Business.

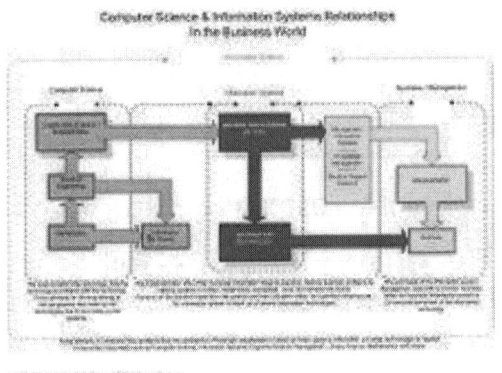

Similar to computer science, other disciplines can be seen as both related and foundation disciplines of IS. The domain of study of IS involves the study of theories and practices related to the social and technological phenomena, which determine the development, use, and effects of information systems in organization and society.[49] But, while there may be considerable overlap of the disciplines at the boundaries, the disciplines are still differentiated by the focus, purpose, and orientation of their activities.[50]

In a broad scope, the term *Information Systems* is a scientific field of study that addresses the range of strategic, managerial, and operational activities involved in the gathering, processing, storing, distributing, and use of information and its associated technologies in society and organizations.[50] The term information systems is also used to describe an organizational function that applies IS knowledge in industry, government agencies, and not-for-profit organizations.[50] *Information Systems* often refers to the interaction between algorithmic processes and technology. This interaction can occur within or across organizational boundaries. An information system is the technology an organization uses and also the way in which the organizations interact with the technology and the way in which the technology works with the organization's business processes. Information systems are distinct from information technology (IT) in that an information system has an information technology component that interacts with the processes' components.

One problem with that approach is that it prevents the IS field from
being interested in non-organizational use of ICT, such as in social networking, computer gaming, mobile personal usage, etc. A different
way of differentiating the IS field from its neighbors is to ask, "Which aspects of reality are most meaningful in the IS field and other fields?"[51] This approach, based on philosophy, helps to define not just the focus, purpose and orientation, but also the dignity, destiny and,

responsibility of the field among other fields. *International Journal of Information Management*, 30, 13-20.

Career pathways

Information Systems workers enter a number of different careers:

> Information System Strategy
>
> Management Information Systems
>
> Project Management
>
> Enterprise Architecture
>
> IS Development
>
> IS Organization
>
> IS Consulting
>
> IS Security
>
> IS Auditor

There is a wide variety of career paths in the information systems discipline. "Workers with specialized technical knowledge and strong communications skills will have the best prospects. Workers with management skills and an understanding of business practices and principles will have excellent opportunities, as companies are increasingly looking to technology to drive their revenue."[52]

Information technology is important to the operation of contemporary businesses, it offers many employment opportunities. The information systems field includes the people in organizations who design and build information systems, the people who use those systems, and the people responsible for managing those systems. The demand for traditional IT staff such as programmers, business analysts, systems analysts, and designer is significant. Many well-paid jobs exist in areas of Information technology. At the top of the list is the chief information officer (CIO).

The CIO is the executive who is in charge of the IS function. In most organizations, the CIO works with the chief executive officer (CEO), the chief financial officer (CFO), and other senior executives. Therefore, he or she actively participates in the organization's strategic planning process.

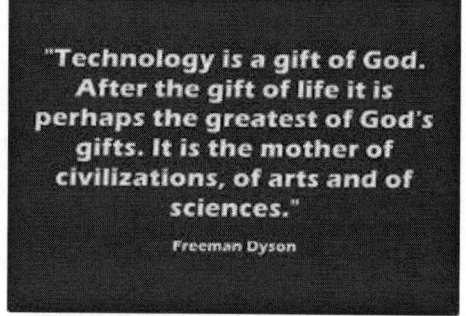

"Technology is a gift of God. After the gift of life it is perhaps the greatest of God's gifts. It is the mother of civilizations, of arts and of sciences."

Freeman Dyson

Research

Information systems research is generally interdisciplinary concerned with the study of the effects of information systems on the behaviour of individuals, groups, and organizations.[53][54] Hevner et al. (2004)[55] categorized research in IS into two scientific paradigms including *behavioural science* which is to develop and verify theories that explain or predict human or organizational behavior and *design science* which extends the boundaries of human and organizational capabilities by creating new and innovative artifacts.

Salvatore March and Gerald Smith[56] proposed a framework for researching different aspects of Information Technology including outputs of the research (research outputs) and activities to carry out this research (research activities). They identified research outputs as follows:

1. *Constructs* which are concepts that form the vocabulary of a domain. They constitute a conceptualization used to describe problems within the domain and to specify their solutions.

2. A *model* which is a set of propositions or statements expressing relationships among constructs.

3. A *method* which is a set of steps (an algorithm or guideline) used to perform a task. Methods are based on a set of underlying constructs and a representation (model) of the solution space.

4. An *instantiation* is the realization of an artifact in its environment.

Also research activities including:

1. *Build* an artifact to perform a specific task.
2. *Evaluate* the artifact to determine if any progress has been achieved.

3. Given an artifact whose performance has been evaluated, it is important to determine why and how the artifact worked or did not work within its environment. Therefore, *theorize* and *justify* theories about IT artifacts.

Although Information Systems as a discipline has been evolving for over 30 years now,[57] the core focus or identity of IS research is still subject to debate among scholars.[58][59][60] There are two main views around this debate: a narrow view focusing on the IT artifact as the core subject matter of IS research, and a broad view that focuses on the interplay between social and technical aspects of IT that is embedded into a dynamic evolving context.[61] A third view [62] calls on IS scholars to pay balanced attention to both the IT artifact and its context.

Since the study of information systems is an applied field, industry practitioners expect information systems research to generate findings that are immediately applicable in practice. This is not always the case however, as information systems researchers often explore behavioral issues in much more depth than practitioners would expect them to do. This may render information systems research results difficult to understand, and has led to criticism.[63]

In the last ten years, the business trend is represented by the considerable increasing of Information Systems Function (ISF) role, especially with regard the enterprise strategies and operations supporting. It became a key-factor to increase productivity and to support new value creation.[64] To study an information system itself, rather than its effects, information systems models are used, such as EATPUT.

The international body of Information Systems researchers, the Association for Information Systems (AIS), and its Senior Scholars Forum Subcommittee on Journals (23 April 2007), proposed a 'basket' of journals that the AIS deems as 'excellent', and nominated: *Management Information Systems Quarterly* (MISQ), *Information Systems Research* (ISR), *Journal of the Association for Information Systems* (JAIS), *Journal of Management Information Systems* (JMIS), *European Journal of Information Systems* (EJIS), and *Information Systems Journal* (ISJ).[65] A number of annual information systems conferences are run in various parts of the world, the majority of which are peer reviewed. The AIS directly runs the International Conference on Information Systems (ICIS) and the Americas Conference on Information Systems (AMCIS), while AIS affiliated conferences[66] include the Pacific Asia Conference on Information Systems (PACIS), European Conference on Information Systems (ECIS), the Mediterranean Conference on Information Systems (MCIS), the International Conference on Information Resources Management (Conf-IRM) and the Wuhan International Conference on E-Business (WHICEB). AIS chapter conferences[67] include Australasian Conference on Information Systems (ACIS), Information Systems Research

Conference in Scandinavia (IRIS), Information Systems International

Conference (ISICO), Conference of the Italian Chapter of AIS (itAIS), Annual Mid-Western AIS Conference (MWAIS) and Annual Conference of the Southern AIS (SAIS). EDSIG,[68] which is the special interest group on education of the AITP,[69] organizes the Conference on Information Systems and Computing Education[70] and the Conference on Information Systems Applied Research[71] which are both held annually in November.

CHAPTER TEN

MOBILE INFORMATION MARTKETING

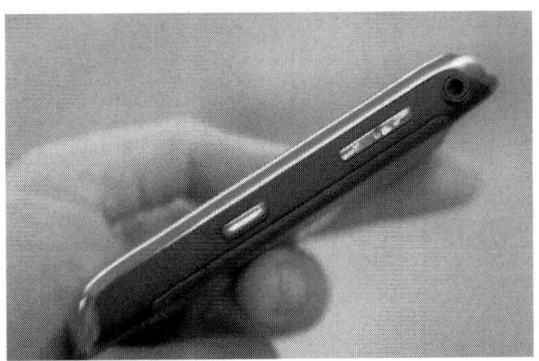

Mobile marketing

There are now more mobile devices in the world than there are people.

That stat is both startling and exciting. Mobile is opening up a whole new

landscape of communication that we can use to reach customers.

Have you thought about how your company can leverage mobile marketing to increase sales?

When the sky is the limit and the opportunities seem endless, it can be difficult to develop an initial strategy. Reading blog posts and reaching out to thought-leaders is a good way to gain knowledge, but how will you use that knowledge to craft a killer mobile strategy? Learning by example can help get you started.

Here are 7 mobile marketing success stories that will inspire your own mobile marketing efforts.

1) The North Face

The North Face, one of the world's leading providers of outdoor apparel, is using a mobile tactic called GEO-Fencing to lure more customers into their stores.

To sign up for the program, customers provide their mobile phone number and activate their mobile GPS feature. Then when they come within a certain distance of a store, they receive a text message from The North Face reminding them to stop in.

Based on the customer's location, The North Face can tailor the text message to the weather of the region, and they can target specific customers with certain promotions.

In urban areas, The North Face GEO-Fences extend up to a half a mile around the stores, and in suburban areas they are up to a mile.

Customers have responded well to this type of mobile marketing. 79% report they have increased their visits to the store once they started receiving reminders, and 65% made a purchase as a result of the reminder.

Action Steps:

– Location is everything. Consider segmenting your mobile customers to target specific audiences with certain promotions depending on their physical region.

– Offer an option for customers to sign up to receive reminders via text message.

2) Ikea Catalog App

In 2010, Ikea launched a free application integrated with their newest product catalog. The application had two main features. One feature helped users identify their own unique style by completing a series of tests. The other created an augmented reality that allowed customers to use their mobiles phones to see how furniture would look in their homes.

Users could download a picture of the product and then use their phone's camera feature to create a virtual 3-D image of how that piece of furniture would look in a certain area of the room.

For all the planners out there, it made purchasing furniture less of a headache. They could see how the colors matched and could even make sure the dimensions were appropriate before stepping into the store. No more eyeballing necessary.

For Ikea, the goal of the app was to inspire creativity and to stimulate customer interest in home furnishing. They also wanted to make the buying process easier and to encourage customers to engage with their catalog throughout the year, not just during the first few days they received it.

Action Steps:

– Use mobile to make the act of buying easier. Answer customers' questions before they even ask!
– Don't focus solely on generating sales. If you can interest and inspire customers first, the sales are likely to follow.
– Stimulate prolonged interest for your other marketing initiatives.

3) Intel

Compared to Ikea, Intel took a much simpler approach to mobile marketing. They didn't design a flashy new interface or produce their own augmented reality. Instead, they launched a B2B mobile paid search campaign to support its "Meet the Processors" brand campaign.

Intel used both exact and broad-match keyword search terms to drive people to their website in an attempt to educate customers on the features of their new processors, and they found that Bing mobile search was 40% more efficient than a normal online search.

To supplement their PPC campaign, they also ran advertisements on a number of popular mobile websites like CNN and CBS and saw lower bounce rates compared to normal Internet advertising. This can be attributed to the fact that customers tend to search for information on their phones with greater purpose.

Action Steps:

– Conduct mobile keyword research to see how your customers are searching on their cell phones.

– Don't focus solely on Google. Consider using Bing and Yahoo to attract mobile customers.

4) Chipotle

Some are saying this could be one of the best mobile marketing campaigns in history.

Chipotle, a fast-food Mexican grill that is attempting to revolutionize the fast-food experience, is known for its Food with Integrity initiative, a commitment to finding the very best ingredients that are raised with respect to the environment.

To promote this unique initiative, they produced and posted an animated film on YouTube and developed a new mobile game. In under two weeks, the film received over 6.5 million views on YouTube, and the game, Chipotle Scarecrow, was ranked among the top 15 free iOS applications in the iOS app store.

Experts attribute this success to the fact that the game's production value was very high. It wasn't just thrown together. It has well-developed characters, an emotionally driven plot, and it stays away from pushy advertisements. To users, it's actually a game, not just a marketing ploy.

Action Steps:

– Mobile games can be great advertising tools as long as you invest in a quality game that provides entertainment.
– Show customers you are interested in providing value, not just trying to make sales.
– Integrate multiple mobile platforms to broaden the awareness of your mobile campaigns.

5) Starbucks

When the mobile revolution took stride, Starbucks used the opportunity to make paying for coffee easier and quicker for customers. In January of 2011, nearly 6,8000 company-operated Starbucks in the United States started accepting mobile payments from the Starbucks Card Mobile payment program.

Consumers can download the application to their phones and load money onto the Mobile Card. Then when they make a purchase, the barista scans the barcode on the screen and the total is deducted from the account.

Just three months from when it was first introduced, the application gained over 3 million users.

There are a number of reasons why this app was so successful. Besides making buying coffee easier than ever, having the app encourages customers to revisit the store, and it promotes customer loyalty. Customers also get to engage regularly with the Starbucks brand in a new, innovative way.

Action Steps:

– Give customers a new mobile capability that they're excited to use.
– Use mobile to make your customers' lives easier on-the-go.
– Develop a type of mobile program to increase customer loyalty and to encourage users to interact with your brand more often.

6) McDonald's

McDonald's is leveraging Instagram, one of the most popular photo and video sharing apps in the world, to interact with customers in a new way. Back in March of 2013, the company ran a promotion encouraging customers to take pictures of their favorite meals using the application.

They then created a mobile ad asking users to "Share Your Biggest Instagram Moments." If users expanded the ad, they could share pictures of their food and even view a gallery of other photos.

McDonald's isn't a stranger to mobile marketing. When they were running their famous Monopoly promotion, they used mobile advertising to educate customers about the promotion. They also took to mobile to get the word out about their new product, Fish McBites.

This particular campaign was meant to broaden McDonald's Instagram presence, and it was successful because it brought fresh attention to older products. It also bolstered a ton of user-generated content, which tends to be more influential on customers.

Action Steps:

– Use the mobile channel to create a new conversation about an old topic.
– Go where your customers are already hanging out. Start developing a presence on mobile apps like Instagram and even Vine.

7) Target

Target is using both social media and paid advertising to broaden awareness of their new mobile application, which gives mobile users access to exclusive deals and discounts.

The Cartwheel app is more than just a mobile coupon. Many of the deals can be used over and over until the expiration date. They aren't one-and-done discounts. The deals are also personalized to help consumers save more on things they buy often, and the app rewards customers for staying active and inviting friends to join. Customers can also share their favorite deals with their friends on Facebook, helping the Target brand reach even more newsfeeds.

While most mobile promotions are like white noise to customers, Target should be applauded for creating an effective, interactive discount application.

Action Steps:

– Give customers special perks for interacting with you on a mobile device.
– Encourage mobile users to engage with you to receive discounts. Social media contests have been proven to boost engagement.

Final Thoughts

As we move into the age of mobile marketing, it can be both exciting and overwhelming to think about all the possibilities. It doesn't matter what industry you're in or who your customers are—mobile marketing can work for you.

These 7 brands are each using mobile differently to connect with customers and increase sales, and I hope they will serves as examples for when you sit down to start developing your own mobile strategy.

The 5 best digital marketing success stories of 2017

The retailers holding the five top spots, according to Internet Retailer's just-released Digital Marketing Report Series, range in size from the very large to the very small.

Digital ad spending among online retailers reached $12.91 billion last year—far outpacing the spend from any other industry, according to research firm eMarketer. Paid search spending among retailers ranked in the Internet Retailer Top 1000 alone reached $278.9 million per month in 2015—up 21.2% from 2014.

Of course those figures don't account for other spending on digital marketing, including fees to marketing and consulting firms, and the significant amounts of staff time and focus online retailers spend on crafting marketing content for email campaigns or social media posts, or optimizing their sites to make them more appealing to search engine crawlers.

The time and money online retailers are spending on digital marketing are benefiting some more than others, according to the recently released 2016 Digital Marketing Report Series. The report, available as a four-part downloadable PDF, scores retailers on effectiveness in the main channels of online marketing—social media, email, and paid and natural search.

Internet Retailer factored in 36 metrics to arrive at its scores, including such data points as the percentage of site traffic a retailer attracts from the various channels, monthly paid search spend, monthly volume of emails sent to consumers, and the size and relative engagement of the merchant's following on social networks.

Here are the merchants that ranked No. 1 in each channel, and a brief summary of how they earned that rank.

ADVERTISEMENT

Best Email Marketer in E-Commerce: Beyond the Rack (Score: 93 out of 100)

Discount flash-sale retailer Beyond the Rack gets 16.2% of its website traffic from customers clicking on its email campaigns, according to web traffic measurement firm SimilarWeb. This is nearly five times the average among Top 500 retailers (which get 2.6% of their traffic from email), and is a clear sign that the

ADVERTISING IS A BUSINESS OF WORDS, BUT ADVERTISING AGENCIES ARE INFESTED WITH MEN AND WOMEN WHO CANNOT WRITE. THEY CANNOT WRITE ADVERTISEMENTS, AND THEY CANNOT WRITE PLANS. THEY ARE HELPLESS AS DEAF MUTES ON THE STAGE OF THE METROPOLITAN OPERA

–David Ogilvy

Content of its emails are resonating with consumers enough to make them click.

Beyond the Rack sends on average of 65 e-mail campaigns to new signups per month—that's more than two per day and the eighth highest among the Top 500, according to a study conducted for Internet Retailer by email marketing firm Listrak. Clearly, the e-retailer is communicating often to customers, and that suggests the merchant places a high premium on email to drive sales.

Beyond the Rack has three of the four key email marketing features Internet Retailer and Listrak tracked for this report.
First, the merchant's emails are optimized for mobile devices. Second, it has a shopping cart abandonment program in place, meaning if customers are on the site, add an item to their cart then leave, the retailer will send them an email encouraging them to complete their purchase. Third, the retailer has a pop-up box on its home page that asks new website visitors for their email address.

Best Natural Search Marketer in E-Commerce: Amazon (Score: 80 out of 100)

Amazon dominates organic search, and the leading web retailer by sales earns its highest points in this score from the sheer number of visits per month it garners from natural search results—a number that basically blows away the competition. More than 55 million Amazon.com visits per month stem from organic search results, according to SimilarWeb, more than 662 times as many as the median among Top 500 retailers (84,000) and seven times as many as the second-highest number, Walmart.com's 7.7 million visits per month from natural search results.

In an Internet Retailer analysis of Alexa Inc. data on top keyword searches and the retailers garnering the highest rankings on those searches, Amazon scored in the top five—and often No. 1—in 14 of the 15 merchandise categories tracked.

Best Paid Search Marketer in E-Commerce: The New York Times Co.
(Score: 78 out of 100)

The New York Times Co., which sells gifts, photos and art on its online store, spent around $1.3 million monthly on paid search last year, according to estimates provided to Internet Retailer by search marketing firm AdGooroo. That's nowhere close to the roughly $38 million Amazon.com Inc. spent, but it is 48 times as high as the median spend among Top 1000 retailers ($27,141) when including those that don't invest in paid search. The merchant, therefore, earned a high score on this metric.

The merchant gets 19.9% of its site traffic from paid search ads, which translates to roughly 24.8 million monthly visits that stem from consumers clicking onto its site from a paid search ad— again, far ahead of the average. The scoring system tracks visits from paid search ads to retailers' home pages, and for the New

York Times Store, that happens to be NYTimes.com. That means some of those clicks may be from consumers clicking on ads with the intent of reading news, and not buying products.

Best Social Media Marketer in E-Commerce: Amazon.com Inc. (Score: 88 out of 100)

The primary reason for Amazon's lead in social media comes its sheer size and ability to direct large volumes of shoppers onto its site from social networks, even with only modest efforts. While the merchant gets only 1.5% of its website traffic from social networks, according to Similar Web, that equates to roughly 14 million visits to Amazon.com from consumers clicking from organic or paid content on Facebook, Twitter or one of the other large social networks.

Those 14 million visits, Internet Retailer estimates, lead to roughly $1.32 billion in direct online sales from social networks last year—far and away the largest among retailers tracked in this report.

Amazon also earns high scores for its large following on Facebook—it had more than 26 million Likes as of mid-2015, the seventh highest behind such big-name brands and entertainment companies as Starbucks Corp., Discovery Channel, Wal-Mart, WWE Inc., National Basketball Association, and Victoria's Secret.

Amazon's followers are also more engaged than other retailers, and that helped its score as well. For example, on average, each post on Facebook earns more than 4,791 comments, 7,303 shares, and 213,000 Likes, according to social media measurement firm Unmetric—far ahead of other retailers tracked. Each post on Twitter is retweeted on average 274 times.

America's Best Marketer in E-Commerce:
Wayfair LLC (Score: 69 out of 100)

Wayfair earned the coveted top spot in Internet Retailer's overall ranking because it scored highly in each of the four channels tracked— email (Wayfair ranked No. 7), social media (No. 131), paid search (65) and natural search (No. 47). Internet Retailer's overall score weighted the channels as follows given our opinion on the relative impact of each: email 30%, paid search 25%, natural search 25%, and social media 20%.

CHAPTER ELEVEN

ENTREPRENEURSHIP

Entrepreneurship is the process of designing, launching and running a new business which is often initially a small business and the people who create these businesses are called entrepreneurs. *verify*[2]

Entrepreneurship has been described as the "capacity and willingness to develop, organize and manage a business venture along with any of its risks in order to make a profit".[3] While definitions of entrepreneurship typically focus on the launching and running of businesses due to the high risks involved in launching a start-up, a significant proportion of businesses have to close due to "lack of funding, bad business decisions, an economic crisis, lack of market demand – or a combination of all of these.[4]

Elements

Entrepreneurs act as managers and oversee the launch and growth of an enterprise. Entrepreneurship is the process by which either an individual or a team identifies a business opportunity and acquires and deploys the necessary resources required for its exploitation. The exploitation of entrepreneurial opportunities may include:[5]

Developing a business plan

Hiring the human resources

Acquiring financial and material resources
Providing leadership

Being responsible for both the venture's success or failure

Risk aversion

The economist Joseph Schumpeter (1883–1950) saw the role of the entrepreneur in the economy as "creative destruction" – launching innovations that simultaneously destroy old industries while ushering in new industries and approaches. For Schumpeter, the changes and "dynamic disequilibrium brought on by the innovating entrepreneur [were] the norm of a healthy economy".[6]

While entrepreneurship is often associated with new, small, for-profit start-ups, entrepreneurial behavior can be seen in small-, medium- and large-sized firms, new and established firms and in for-profit and not-for-profit organizations, including voluntary-sector groups, charitable organizations and government.[7]

Entrepreneurship may operate within an entrepreneurship ecosystem which often includes:

Government programs and services that promote entrepreneurship and support entrepreneurs and start-ups

Non-governmental organizations such as small-business associations and organizations that offer advice and mentoring to entrepreneurs (e.g. through entrepreneurship centers or websites)

Small-business advocacy organizations that lobby governments for increased support for entrepreneurship programs and more small business-friendly laws and regulations

Entrepreneurship resources and facilities (e.g. business incubators and seed accelerators)

Entrepreneurship education and training programs offered by schools, colleges and universities

Financing (e.g. bank loans, venture capital financing, angel investing and government and private foundation grants) [8][

In the 2000s, the definition of "entrepreneurship" expanded to explain how and why some individuals (or teams) identify opportunities, evaluate them as viable and then decide to exploit them, whereas others do not [9] and in turn how entrepreneurs use these opportunities to develop new products or services, launch new firms or even new industries and create wealth. [10] The entrepreneurial process is fundamentally uncertain because opportunities cannot be discovered or identified prior to their actualization into profits. [11] What appears as a real opportunity ex-ante might actually be a non-opportunity or one that cannot be actualized by entrepreneurs lacking the necessary business skills, financial or social capital?

Entrepreneurs tend to be good at perceiving new business opportunities and they often exhibit positive biases in their perception (i.e. a bias towards finding new possibilities and seeing unmet market needs) and a tendency towards risk-taking that makes them more likely to exploit the opportunity.[12][13] An entrepreneur may be in control of a commercial undertaking, directing the factors of production –
the human, financial and material resources – that are required to exploit a business opportunity.

History

Historical usage

Emil Jellinek-Mercedes (1853–1918), here at the steering wheel of his Phoenix Double-Phaeton, was a European entrepreneur who helped design the first modern car

"Entrepreneur"
(/ˌɒntrəprəˈnɜːr/ (

🔊 listen)) is a loanword from French. The word first appeared in the French dictionary

entitled *Dictionnaire Universel de Commerce* compiled by Jacques des Bruslons and published in 1723.[14] Especially in Britain, the term "adventurer" was often used to denote the same meaning.[15] The study of entrepreneurship reaches back to the work in the late 17th and early 18th centuries of Irish-French economist Richard Cantillon, which was foundational to classical economics. Cantillon defined the term first in his *Essai sur la Nature du Commerce en Général*, or *Essay on the Nature of Trade in General*, a book William Stanley Jevons considered the "cradle of political economy".[16][17] Cantillon defined the term as a person who pays a certain price for a product and resells it at an uncertain price, "making decisions about obtaining and using the resources while consequently admitting the risk of enterprise". Cantillon considered the entrepreneur to be a risk taker who deliberately allocates resources to exploit opportunities in order to maximize the financial return.[18][19] Cantillon emphasized the willingness of the entrepreneur to assume the risk and to deal with uncertainty, thus he drew attention to the function of the entrepreneur and distinguished between the function of the entrepreneur and the owner who provided the money.[18][20]

Dating back to the time of the medieval guilds in Germany, a craftsperson required special permission to operate as an entrepreneur, the small proof of competence (*Kleiner Befähigungsnachweis*), which restricted training of apprentices to craftspeople who held a Meister certificate. This institution was introduced in 1908 after a period of so-called freedom of trade (*Gewerbefreiheit*, introduced in 1871) in the German Reich. However, proof of competence was not required to start a business. In 1935 and in 1953, greater proof of competence was reintroduced (*Großer Befähigungsnachweis Kuhlenbeck*), which required craftspeople to obtain a Meister apprentice-training certificate before being permitted to set up a new business.[21]

20th Century

In the 20th century, entrepreneurship was studied by Joseph Schumpeter in the 1930s and other Austrian economists such as Carl Menger, Ludwig von Mises and Friedrich von Hayek. While the loan from French of the word "entrepreneur" dates to the 1850, the term "entrepreneurship" was coined around the 1920s. According to Schumpeter, an entrepreneur is willing and able to convert a new idea or invention into a successful innovation.[22] Entrepreneurship employs what Schumpeter called "the gale of creative destruction" to replace in whole or in part inferior offerings across markets and industries, simultaneously creating new products and new business models, thus creative destruction is largely responsible for long-term economic growth. The idea that entrepreneurship leads to economic growth is an interpretation of the residual in endogenous growth theory and as such continues to be debated in academic economics. An alternate description by Israel Kirzner suggests that the majority of innovations may be incremental improvements such as the replacement of paper with plastic in the construction of a drinking straw that require no special qualities.

For Schumpeter, entrepreneurship resulted in new industries and in new combinations of currently existing inputs. Schumpeter's initial example of this was the combination of a steam engine and then current wagon making technologies to produce the horseless carriage. In this case, the innovation (i.e. the car) was transformational, but did not require the development of dramatic new technology. It did not immediately replace the horse-drawn carriage, but in time incremental improvements reduced the cost and improved the technology, leading to the modern auto industry. Despite Schumpeter's early 20th-century contributions, the traditional microeconomic theory did not formally consider the entrepreneur in its theoretical frameworks (instead of assuming that resources would find each other through a price system). In this treatment, the entrepreneur was an implied but unspecified actor, consistent with the concept of the entrepreneur being the agent of x-efficiency.

For Schumpeter, the entrepreneur did not bear risk: the capitalist did. Schumpeter believed that the equilibrium was imperfect. Schumpeter (1934) demonstrated that the changing environment continuously provides new information about the optimum allocation of resources to enhance profitability. Some individuals acquire the new information before others and recombine the resources to gain an entrepreneurial profit. Schumpeter was of the opinion that entrepreneurs shift
the production possibility curve to a higher level using innovations.[23]

Initially, economists made the first attempt to study the entrepreneurship concept in depth.[24] Alfred Marshall viewed the entrepreneur as a multi-tasking capitalist and observed that in the equilibrium of a completely competitive market there was no spot for "entrepreneurs" as an economic activity creator.[25]

Millennial entrepreneurs

The term "millennial entrepreneur" refers to a business owner who is affiliated with the generation that was brought up using digital technology and mass media—the products of Baby Boomers, those people born during the 1980s and early 1990s. Also known as Generation Y, these business owners are well equipped with knowledge of technology and have a strong grasp of its applications toward businesses. There have been many breakthrough businesses that have come from millennial entrepreneurs such as Mark Zuckerberg, who created Facebook.[26][27] Despite the expectation of millennial success, there have been recent studies that have proven this to not be the case. The comparison between millennials who are self-employed and those who are not self-employed shows that the latter is higher. The reason for this is because they have grown up in a different generation and attitude than their elders. Some of the barriers to entry for entrepreneurs are the economy, debt from schooling and the challenges of regulatory compliance.[28]

2000s

In 2012, Ambassador-at-Large for Global Women's Issues Melanne Verveer greets participants in an African Women's Entrepreneurship Program at the State Department in Washington, D.C.

In the 2000s, entrepreneurship has been extended from its origins in for-profit businesses to include social entrepreneurship, in which business goals are sought alongside social, environmental or humanitarian goals and even the concept of the political entrepreneur. Entrepreneurship within an existing firm or large organization has been referred to as intrapreneurship and may include corporate ventures where large entities "spin-off" subsidiary organizations.[29]

Entrepreneurs are leaders willing to take risk and exercise initiative, taking advantage of market opportunities by planning, organizing and deploying resources,[30] often by innovating to create new or improving existing products or services.[31] In the 2000s, the term "entrepreneurship" has been extended to include a specific mindset (see also entrepreneurial mindset) resulting in entrepreneurial initiatives, e.g. in the form of social entrepreneurship, political entrepreneurship or knowledge entrepreneurship.

According to Paul Reynolds, founder of the Global Entrepreneurship Monitor, "by the time they reach their retirement years, half of all

working men in the United States probably have a period of self-employment of one or more years; one in four may have engaged in self-employment for six or more years. Participating in a new business creation is a common activity among U.S. workers over the course of their careers".[32] In recent years, entrepreneurship has been claimed as a major driver of economic growth in both the United States and Western Europe.

Entrepreneurial activities differ substantially depending on the type of organization and creativity involved. Entrepreneurship ranges in scale from solo, part-time projects to large-scale undertakings that involve a team and which may create many jobs.

Many "high value" entrepreneurial ventures seek venture capital or angel funding (seed money) in order to raise capital for building and expanding the business.[33] Many organizations exist to support would-be entrepreneurs, including specialized government agencies, business incubators (which may be for-profit, non-profit, or operated by a college or university), science parks and non-governmental organizations, which include a range of organizations including not-for-profits, charities, foundations and business advocacy groups (e.g. Chambers of commerce). Beginning in 2008, an annual "Global Entrepreneurship Week" event aimed at "exposing people to the benefits of entrepreneurship" and getting them to "participate in

entrepreneurial-related activities" was launched.

Relationship between small business and entrepreneurship

The term "entrepreneur" is often conflated with the term "small business" or used interchangeably with this term. While most entrepreneurial ventures start out as a small business, not all small businesses are entrepreneurial in the strict sense of the term. Many small businesses are sole proprietor operations consisting solely of the owner—or they have a small number of employees—and many of these small businesses offer an existing product, process or service and they do not aim at growth. In contrast, entrepreneurial ventures offer an innovative product, process or service and the entrepreneur typically aims to scale up the company by adding employees, seeking international sales and so on, a [who?] process which is financed by venture capital and angel investments. Successful entrepreneurs have the ability to lead a business in a positive direction by proper planning, to adapt to changing environments and understand their own strengths and weakness.[34]

Ethnic entrepreneurship

The term "ethnic entrepreneurship" refers to self-employed, business owners who belong to racial or ethnic minority groups in the United States and Europe. A long tradition of academic research explores the experiences and strategies of ethnic entrepreneurs as they strive to integrate economically into mainstream U.S. or European society. Classic cases include Jewish merchants and tradespeople in large U.S. cities in the 19th and early 20th centuries as well as Chinese and Japanese small business owners (restaurants, farmers, shop clerks) on the West Coast.[35]

In the 2010s, ethnic entrepreneurship has been studied in the case of Cuban business owners in Miami, Indian motel owners of the U.S. and Chinese business owners in Chinatowns across the United States. While entrepreneurship offers these groups many opportunities for economic advancement, self-employment and business ownership in the United States remain unevenly distributed along racial/ethnic lines.[36] Despite numerous success stories of Asian entrepreneurs, a recent statistical analysis of U.S. census data shows that whites are more likely than Asians, African-Americans and Latinos to be self-employed in high prestige, lucrative industries.[36]

Institutional entrepreneur

The American-born British economist Edith Penrose has highlighted the collective nature of entrepreneurship. She mentions that in modern organizations, human resources need to be combined in order to better capture and create business opportunities.[37] The sociologist Paul DiMaggio (1988:14) has expanded this view to say that "new institutions arise when organized actors with sufficient resources [institutional entrepreneurs] see in them an opportunity to realize interests that they value highly".[38] The notion has been widely applied.[39][40][41][42]

Cultural entrepreneurship

According to Christopher Rea and Nicolai Volland, cultural entrepreneurship is "practices of individual and collective agency characterized by mobility between cultural professions and modes of cultural production". In their book *The Business of Culture* (2015), Rea and Volland identify three types of cultural entrepreneur: "cultural personalities", defined as "individuals who buil[d] their own personal brand of creativity as a cultural authority and leverage it to create and sustain various cultural enterprises"; "tycoons", defined as "entrepreneurs who buil[d] substantial clout in the cultural sphere by forging synergies between their industrial, cultural, political, and philanthropic interests"; and

"collective enterprises", organizations which may engage in cultural production for profit or not-for-profit purposes.[43]

Feminist entrepreneur

A feminist entrepreneur is an individual who applies feminist values and approaches through entrepreneurship, with the goal of improving the quality of life and wellbeing of girls and women.[44] Many are doing so by creating "for women, by women' enterprises". Feminist entrepreneurs are motivated to enter commercial markets by desire to create wealth and social change, based on the ethics of cooperation, equality and mutual respect.[45][46]

Entrepreneurial behaviors

British entrepreneur Karren Bradyhas an estimated net worth of $123 million[47]

The entrepreneur is commonly seen as an innovator—a designer of new ideas and business processes.[48] Management skills and strong team building abilities are often perceived as essential leadership attributes for successful entrepreneurs.[49] Political economist Robert Reich considers leadership, management ability and team-building to be essential qualities of an entrepreneur.[50][51]

Uncertainty perception and risk-taking

 Dell Women's Entrepreneur Network event in New York City

Theorists Frank Knight[52] and Peter Drucker defined entrepreneurship in terms of risk- taking. The entrepreneur is willing to put his or her career and financial security on the line and take risks in the name of an idea, spending time as well as capital on an uncertain venture. However, entrepreneurs often do not believe that they have taken an enormous amount of risks because they do not perceive the level of uncertainty to be as high as other people do. Knight classified three types of uncertainty:

Risk, which is measurable statistically (such as the probability of drawing a red color ball from a jar containing 5 red balls and 5 white balls)

Ambiguity, which is hard to measure statistically (such as the probability of drawing a red ball from a jar containing 5 red balls but an unknown number of white balls)

True uncertainty or Knightian uncertainty, which is impossible to estimate or predict statistically (such as the probability of drawing a red ball from a jar whose contents are entirely unknown)

Malala Yousafzai, a Pakistani activist, social entrepreneur and the youngest-ever Nobel Peace Prizewinner, was named in the *Forbes* 30list

Entrepreneurship is often associated with true uncertainty, particularly when it involves the creation of a novel good or service, for a market that did not previously exist, rather than when a venture creates an incremental improvement to an existing product or service. A 2014 study at ETH Zürich found that compared with typical managers, entrepreneurs showed higher decision-making efficiency and a stronger activation in regions of front polar cortex (FPC) previously associated with explorative choice.[53]

"Coachability" and advice taking

The ability of entrepreneurs to work closely with and take advice from early investors and other partners (i.e. their coachability) has long been considered a critical factor in entrepreneurial success.[54] At the same time, economists have argued that entrepreneurs should not simply act on all advice given to them, even when that advice comes from well-informed sources, because entrepreneurs possess far deeper and richer local knowledge about their own firm than any outsider. Indeed, measures of coachability are not actually predictive of entrepreneurial success (e.g. measured as success in subsequent funding rounds, acquisitions, pivots and firm survival). This research also shows that older and larger founding teams, presumably those with more subject expertise, are less coachable than younger and smaller founding teams.

Strategies

Strategies that entrepreneurs may use include:

Innovation of new products, services or processes[55]

Continuous process improvement (CPI)[55]

Exploration

Use of technology[55]

Use of business intelligence

Use of economical strategies

Development of future products and services[55]

Optimized talent management[55]

Designing individual/opportunity nexus

According to Shane and Venkataraman, entrepreneurship comprises both "enterprising individuals" and "entrepreneurial opportunities", so researchers should study the nature of the individuals who identify opportunities when others do not, the opportunities themselves and the nexus between individuals and opportunities.[56] On the other hand, Reynolds et al.[57] Argue that individuals are motivated to engage in entrepreneurial endeavors driven mainly by necessity or opportunity, that is individuals pursue entrepreneurship primarily owing to survival needs, or because they identify business opportunities that satisfy their need for achievement. For example, higher economic inequality tends to increase entrepreneurship rates at the individual level, suggesting that most entrepreneurial behavior is based on necessity rather than opportunity.[58]

Opportunity perception and biases

The ability of entrepreneurs to innovate relates to innate traits, including extroversion and a proclivity for risk-taking.[59] According to Joseph Schumpeter, the capabilities of innovating, introducing new technologies, increasing efficiency and productivity, or generating new products or services, are characteristic qualities of entrepreneurs.[60] One study has found that certain genes affecting personality may influence the income of self-employed people.[61] Some people may be able to use an innate ability" or quasi-statistical sense to gauge public opinion [62] and market demand for new products or services. Entrepreneurs tend to have the ability to see unmet market needs and underserved markets. While some entrepreneurs assume they can sense and figure out what others are thinking, the mass media plays a crucial role in shaping views and demand.[63] Ramoglou argues that entrepreneurs are not that distinctive and that it is essentially poor conceptualizations of "non-entrepreneurs" that maintain laudatory portraits of "entrepreneurs" as exceptional innovators or leaders [64][65]Entrepreneurs are often overconfident, exhibit illusion of control, when they are opening/expanding business or new products/services.[12]

Styles

Differences in entrepreneurial organizations often partially reflect their founders' heterogeneous identities. Fauchart and Gruber have classified entrepreneurs into three main types: Darwinians, communitarians and missionaries. These types of entrepreneurs diverge in fundamental ways in their self-views, social motivations and patterns of new firm creation. [66]

Communication

Entrepreneurs need to practice effective communication both within their firm and with external partners and investors in order to launch and growth a venture and enable it to survive. An entrepreneur needs a communication system that links the staff of her firm and connects the firm to outside firms and clients. Entrepreneurs should be charismatic leaders, so they can communicate a vision effectively to their team and help to create a strong team. Communicating a vision to followers may be well the most important act of the transformational leader. [67] Compelling visions provide employees with a sense of purpose and encourage commitment. According to Baum et al. [68] and Kouzes and Posner, [69] the vision must be communicated through written statements and through in-person communication. Entrepreneurial leaders must speak and listen to articulate their vision to others. [70]

Communication is pivotal in the role of entrepreneurship because it enables leaders to convince potential investors, partners and employees about the feasibility of a venture.[71] Entrepreneurs need to communicate effectively to shareholders.[72] Nonverbal elements in speech such as the tone of voice, the look in the sender's eyes, body language, hand gestures and state of emotions are also important communication tools. The Communication Accommodation Theory posits that throughout communication people will attempt to accommodate or adjust their method of speaking to others.[73] Face Negotiation Theory describes how people from different cultures manage conflict negotiation in order to maintain "face".[74] Hugh Rank's "intensify and downplay" communications model can be used by entrepreneurs who are developing a new product or service. Rank argues that entrepreneurs need to be able to intensify the advantages of their new product or service and downplay the disadvantages in order to persuade others to support their venture.[75] Links to sea piracy

Research from 2014 found links between entrepreneurship and historical sea piracy. In this context, the claim is made for a non-moral approach to looking at the history of piracy as a source of inspiration for entrepreneurship education [76] as well as for research in entrepreneurship [77] and business model generation.[78]

Psychological makeup

Apple co-founder and longtime leader Steve Jobs (pictured in 2010) led the introduction of many innovations in the computer, smartphone and digital music industry

Stanford University economist Edward Lazear found in a 2005 study that variety in education and work experience was the most important trait that distinguished entrepreneurs from non-entrepreneurs[79] A 2013 study by Uschi Backes-Gellner of the University of Zurich and Petra Moog of the University of Siegen in Germany found that a diverse social network was also important in distinguishing students that would go on to become entrepreneurs.[80][81]

Studies show that the psychological propensities for male and female entrepreneurs are more similar than different. Empirical studies suggest that female entrepreneurs possess strong negotiating skills and consensus-forming abilities.[82]Asa Hansson, who looked at empirical evidence from Sweden, found that the probability of becoming self-employed decreases with age for women, but increases with age for men.[83] She also found that marriage increased the probability of a person becoming an entrepreneur.[83]

Jesper Sørensen wrote that significant influences on the decision to become an entrepreneur are workplace peers and social composition.
Sørensen discovered a correlation between working with former
entrepreneurs and how often these individuals become entrepreneurs

themselves, compared to those who did not work with entrepreneurs.[84] Social composition can influence entrepreneurialism in peers by demonstrating the possibility for success, stimulating a "He can do it, why can't I?" attitude. As Sørensen stated: "When you meet others who have gone out on their own, it doesn't seem that crazy".[85]

Entrepreneurs may also be driven to entrepreneurship by past experiences. If they have faced multiple work stoppages or have

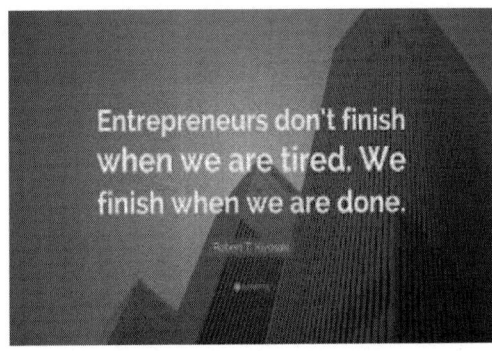

been unemployed in the past, the probability of them becoming an entrepreneur increases [83] Per Cattell's personality framework, both personality traits and attitudes are thoroughly investigated by psychologists. However, in case of entrepreneurship research these notions are employed by academics too, but vaguely. According to Cattell, personality is a system that is related to the environment and further adds that the system seeks explanation to the complex transactions conducted by both—traits and attitudes. This is because both of them bring about change and growth in a person. Personality is that which informs what an individual will do when faced with a given situation. A person's response is triggered by his/her personality and the situation that is faced.[86]

Innovative entrepreneurs may be more likely to experience what psychologist Mihaly Csikszentmihalyi calls "flow". "Flow" occurs when an individual forgets about the outside world due to being thoroughly engaged in a process or activity. Csikszentmihalyi suggested that breakthrough innovations tend to occur at the hands of individuals in that state.[87] Other research has concluded that a strong internal motivation is a vital ingredient for breakthrough innovation.[88] Flow can be compared to Maria Montessori's concept of normalization, a state that includes a child's capacity for joyful and lengthy periods of intense concentration.[89]Csikszentmihalyi acknowledged that Montessori's prepared environment offers children opportunities to achieve flow.[90] Thus quality and type of early education may influence entrepreneurial capability.

Research on high-risk settings such as oil platforms, investment banking, medical surgery, aircraft piloting and nuclear power plants has related distrust to failure avoidance.[91] When non-routine strategies are needed, distrusting persons perform better while when routine strategies are needed trusting persons perform better. This research was extended to entrepreneurial firms by Gudmundsson and Lechner.[92] They argued that in entrepreneurial firms the threat of failure is ever present resembling non-routine situations in high-risk settings. They found that the firms of distrusting entrepreneurs were more likely to survive than the firms of optimistic or overconfident entrepreneurs. The reasons were that distrusting entrepreneurs would emphasize failure avoidance through sensible task selection and more analysis. Kets de Vries has pointed out that distrusting entrepreneurs are more alert about their external environment.[93] He concluded that distrusting entrepreneurs are less likely to discount negative events and are more likely to engage control mechanisms. Similarly, Gudmundsson and Lechner found that distrust leads to higher precaution and therefore increases chances of entrepreneurial firm survival.

Researchers Schoon and Duckworth completed a study in 2012 that could potentially help identify who may become an entrepreneur at an early age. They determined that the best measures to identify a young entrepreneur are family and social status, parental role modeling, and entrepreneurial competencies at age 10, academic attainment at age 10, generalized self-efficacy, social skills, entrepreneurial intention and experience of unemployment.[94]

Leadership in entrepreneurship

Leadership in entrepreneurship can be defined as "process of social influence in which one person can enlist the aid and support of others in the accomplishment of a common task"[99] in "one who undertakes innovations, finance and business acumen in an effort to transform innovations into economic goods".[97] This refers to not only the act of entrepreneurship as managing or starting a business, but how one manages to do so by these social processes, or leadership skills. Entrepreneurship in itself can be defined as "the process by which individuals, teams, or organizations identify and pursue entrepreneurial opportunities without being immediately constrained by the resources they currently control".[100] An entrepreneur typically has a mindset that seeks out potential opportunities during uncertain times.[100] This leads us to see that an entrepreneur must have leadership skills or qualities in order to see potential opportunities and act upon them. At the core, an entrepreneur is a decision maker. Such decisions often affect an organization as a whole, which is representative of their leadership amongst the organization.

According to Fisher (1970), there are four phases of decision-making: orientation, conflict, emergence and reinforcement.[101] As a communicative approach, the orientation stage is where the members involved are becoming acquainted both with themselves as well as the problem at hand. The conflict stage is where the problem is analyzed with several possibilities presented to resolve the problem. Upon discussing these possibilities, the emergence phase becomes known when a decision is made about which solution is to be used. The reinforcement stage is the supportive of the decision.[102] These phases are not without objection from many theorists in the field. Morley and Stephenson (1977) claim that such a staged model of decision-making is not so rigid between phases and varies depending upon the types of decisions made.[103]

With the growing global market and increasing technologies throughout all industries, the core of entrepreneurship and the decision-making has become an ongoing process rather than isolated incidents This becomes knowledge management which is "identifying and harnessing intellectual assets" for organizations to "build on past experiences and create new mechanisms for exchanging and creating knowledge".[104] This belief draws upon a leader's past experiences that may prove useful. It is a common mantra for one to learn from their past mistakes, so leaders should take advantage of their failures for their benefit. This is how one may take their experiences as a leader for the use in the core of entrepreneurship-decision making.

Global leadership and entrepreneurship

It is important to note that the majority of scholarly research done on these topics have been from North America.[105] Words like "leadership" and "entrepreneurship" do not always translate well into other cultures and languages. For example, in North America a leader
is often thought to be charismatic, but German culture frowns on such

charisma due to the charisma of Adolph Hitler. Other cultures, like

some Europeans, view the term "leader" negatively, like the French.[106] The participative leadership style that is encouraged in the United States is considered disrespectful in many other parts of the world due to the differences in power distance.[107] Many Asian and Middle Eastern countries do not have "open door" policies and would

never informally approach their managers/bosses. For countries like that, an authoritarian approach to management and leadership works best as is custom.

Despite cultural differences, the successes and failures of entrepreneurs can be traced to how leaders adapt to local conditions.[108] With the increasingly global environment a successful leader must be able to make these adaptations and have some insight into other cultures. In response to the environment, corporate visions are becoming transnational in nature due to the changes an organization must make in order to operate or provide services/goods for other cultures.[109]

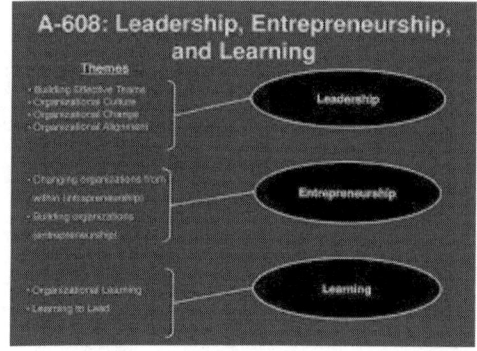

Educational effects

ichelacci and Schivardi[110] are a pair of researchers who believe that identifying and comparing the relationships between an entrepreneur's earnings and education level would determine the rate and level of success. Their study focused on two education levels, college degree and post-graduate degree. While Michelacci and Schivardi do not specifically determine characteristics or traits for successful entrepreneurs, they do believe that there is a direct relationship between education and success, noting that having a college degree does contribute to advancement in the workforce.

Michelacci and Schivardi state there has been a rise in the number of self-employed people with a baccalaureate degree. However, their findings also show that those who are self-employed and possess a graduate degree has remained consistent throughout time at about 33 percent. They briefly mention those famous entrepreneurs like Steve Jobs and Mark Zuckerberg who were college dropouts, but they call these cases all but exceptional as it is a pattern that many entrepreneurs view formal education as costly, mainly because of the time that needs to be spent on it. Michelacci and Schivardi believe that in order for an individual to reach the full success they need to have education beyond high school. Their research shows that the higher the education level the greater the success. The reason is that college gives people additional skills that can be used within their business and to operate on a higher level than someone who only "runs" it.

Project entrepreneurship

Project entrepreneurs are individuals who are engaged in the repeated assembly or creation of temporary organizations.[111] These are organizations that have limited lifespans which are devoted to producing a singular objective or goal and get disbanded rapidly when

the project ends. Industries where project-based enterprises are widespread include: sound recording, film production, software development, television production, new media and construction.[112] What makes project-entrepreneurs distinctive from a theoretical standpoint is that they have to "rewire" these temporary ventures and modify them to suit the needs of new project opportunities that emerge. A project entrepreneur who used a certain approach and team for one project may have to modify the business model or team for a subsequent project.

Project entrepreneurs are exposed repeatedly to problems and tasks typical of the entrepreneurial process.[113] Indeed, project-entrepreneurs face two critical challenges that invariably characterize the creation of a new venture: locating the right opportunity to launch the project venture and assembling the most appropriate team to exploit that opportunity. Resolving the first challenge requires project-entrepreneurs to access an extensive range of information needed to seize new investment opportunities. Resolving the second challenge requires assembling a collaborative team that has to fit well with the particular challenges of the project and has to function almost immediately to reduce the risk that performance might be adversely affected.

Another type of project entrepreneurship involves entrepreneurs working with business students to get analytical work done on their ideas.

Financing

Bootstrapping

At least early on, entrepreneurs often "bootstrap-finance"[114] their start-up rather than seeking external investors from the start. One of the reasons that some entrepreneurs prefer to "bootstrap" is that obtaining equity financing requires the entrepreneur to provide ownership shares to the investors. If the start-up becomes successful later on, these early equity financing deals could provide a windfall for the investors and a huge loss for the entrepreneur. If investors have a significant stake in the company, they may as well be able to exert influence on company strategy, chief executive officer (CEO) choice and other important decisions. This is often problematic since the investor and the founder might have different incentives regarding the long-term goal of the company. An investor will generally aim for a profitable exit and therefore promotes a high-valuation sale of the company or IPO in order to sell their shares. Whereas the entrepreneur might have philanthropic intentions as their main driving force. Soft values like this might not go well with the short-term pressure on yearly and quarterly profits that publicly traded companies often experience from their owners.

One consensus definition of bootstrapping sees it as "a collection of methods used to minimize the amount of outside debt and equity financing needed from banks and investors".[115] The majority of businesses require less than $10,000 to launch,[116] which means that personal savings are most often used to start. In addition, bootstrapping entrepreneurs often incur personal credit-card debt, but they also can utilize a wide variety of methods. While bootstrapping involves increased personal financial risk for entrepreneurs, the absence of any other stakeholder gives the entrepreneur more freedom to develop the company. Many successful companies, including Dell Computer and Facebook, started by bootstrapping.[117]

Bootstrapping methods include:[118]

Owner financing, including savings, personal loans and credit card debt

Working capital management that minimizes accounts receivable

Joint utilization, such as reducing overhead by co-working or using independent contractors

Increasing accounts payable by delaying payment, or leasing rather than buying equipment

Lean manufacturing strategies such as minimizing inventory and lean startup to reduce product development costs

Subsidy finance

Additional financing

Many businesses need more capital than can be provided by the owners themselves. In this case, a range of options is available including a wide variety of private and public equity, debt and grants.[119] Private equity options include:

Startup accelerators

Angel investors

Venture capital investors

Equity crowdfunding

Hedge funds

Debt options open to entrepreneurs include:

Loans from banks, financial technology companies and economic development organizations

Line of credit also from banks and financial technology companies

Microcredit also known as microloans

Merchant cash advance

Revenue-based financing

Grant options open to entrepreneurs include:

Equity-free accelerators[120]

Business plan/business pitch competitions for college entrepreneurs[121] and others

Small Business Innovation Research grants from the U.S. government

Effect of taxes

Entrepreneurs are faced with liquidity constraints and often lack the necessary credit needed to borrow large amounts of money to finance their venture.[122] Because of this, many studies have been done on the effects of taxes on entrepreneurs. The studies fall into two camps: the first camp finds that taxes help and the second argues that taxes hurt entrepreneurship.

Cesaire Assah Meh found that corporate taxes create an incentive to become an entrepreneur to avoid double taxation.[122] Donald Bruce and John Deskins found literature suggesting that a higher corporate tax rate may reduce a state's share of entrepreneurs.[123]

They also found that states with an inheritance or estate tax tend to have lower entrepreneurship rates when using a tax-based measure.[123] However, another study found that states with a more progressive personal income tax have a higher percentage of sole proprietors in their workforce.[124] Ultimately, many studies find that the effect of taxes on the probability of becoming an entrepreneur is small. Donald Bruce and Mohammed Mohsin found that it would take a 50 percentage point drop in the top tax rate to produce a one percent change in entrepreneurial activity.[125]

Predictors of success

Factors that may predict entrepreneurial success include the following:[126]

Methods

Establishing strategies for the firm, including growth and survival strategies

Maintaining the human resources (recruiting and retaining talented employees and executives)

Ensuring the availability of required materials (e.g. raw resources used in manufacturing, computer chips, etc.)

Ensuring that the firm has one or more unique competitive advantages

Ensuring good organizational design, sound governance and organizational coordination

Congruency with the culture of the society[127]

Market

Business-to-business (B2B) or business-to-consumer (B2C) models can be used

High growth market

Target customers or markets that are untapped or missed by others

Industry

Growing industry

High technology impact on the industry

High capital intensity

Small average incumbent firm size

Team

Large, gender-diverse and racially diverse team with a range of talents, rather than an individual entrepreneur

Graduate degrees

Management experience prior to start-up

Work experience in the start-up industry

Employed full-time prior to new venture as opposed to unemployed

Prior entrepreneurial experience

Full-time involvement in the new venture

Motivated by a range of goals, not just profit

Number and diversity of team members' social ties and breadth of their business networks

Company

Written business plan

Focus on a unified, connected product line or service line

Competition based on a dimension other than price (e.g. quality or service)

Early, frequent intense and well-targeted marketing

Tight financial controls

Sufficient start-up and growth capital

Corporation model, not sole proprietorship

Status

Wealth can enable an entrepreneur to cover start-up costs and deal with cash flow challenges

Dominant race, ethnicity or gender in a socially stratified culture[128]

CHAPTER TWELVE

SUCCESS STORIES OF INFORMATION MILLIONARES
Marissa Mayer

Marissa Ann Mayer (/ˈmaɪər/; born May 30, 1975) is an American information technology executive, formerly serving as the president and CEO of Yahoo!, a position she had held starting July 2012. In January 2017, it was announced that she will step down from the company's board upon the sale of Yahoo!'s operating

business to Verizon Communications.[8] She announced that resignation on June 13, 2017.[9] She is a graduate of Stanford and was a long-time executive, usability leader, and key spokesperson for Google.[10][11][12] Yahoo CEO Marissa Mayer may have launched her career in tech as one of Google's first employees, but her meteoric rise hasn't come without problems..[8]

Early life and education

Mayer was born in Wausau, Wisconsin, the daughter of Margaret Mayer, art teacher of Finnish descent,[13] and Michael Mayer, an environmental engineer who worked for water companies.[14][15][16] Her grandfather, Clem Mayer, had polio when he was 7 and served as mayor of Jackson, Wisconsin, for 32 years.[17][18][19] She has a younger brother.[14] She would later describe herself as having been "painfully shy" as a child and teenager.[20] She "never had fewer than one after-school activity per day," participating in ballet, ice-skating, piano, swimming, debate, and Brownies.[14] During middle school and high school, she took piano and ballet lessons, the latter of which taught her "criticism and discipline, poise, and confidence."[20] At an early age, she showed an interest in math and science.[21]

When she was attending Wausau West High School, Mayer was on the curling team and the precision dance team.[20] She excelled in chemistry, calculus, biology, and physics.[22] She took part in extracurricular activities, becoming president of her high school's Spanish club, treasurer of the Key Club, captain of the debate team, and captain of the pom-pom squad.[20] Her high school debate team won the Wisconsin state championship and the pom-pom squad was the state runner-up.[17] During high school, she worked as a grocery clerk.[23] After graduating from high school in 1993, [24] Mayer was selected by Tommy Thompson, then the Governor of Wisconsin, as one of the state's two delegates to attend the National Youth Science Camp in West Virginia.[25]

Intending to become a pediatric neurosurgeon,[26] Mayer took pre-med classes at Stanford University.[20] She later switched her major from pediatric neuroscience to symbolic systems,[27] a major which combined philosophy, cognitive psychology, linguistics, and computer science.[14] At Stanford, she danced in the university ballet's *Nutcracker*, was a member of parliamentary debate, volunteered at children's hospitals, and helped bring computer science education to Bermuda's schools.[28] During her junior year, she taught a class in symbolic systems, with Eric S. Roberts as her supervisor. The class was so well received by students that Roberts asked Mayer to teach another class over the summer.[20] Mayer went on to graduate with honors from Stanford with a BS in symbolic systems in 1997[27][28] and an MS in computer science in 1999.[29] For both degrees, her specialization was in artificial intelligence. For her undergraduate thesis, she built travel-recommendation software that advised users in natural-sounding human language.[26] In 2009, the Illinois Institute of Technology granted Mayer an honoris causa doctorate degree in recognition of her work in the field of search.[30][31]

Mayer interned at SRI International in Menlo Park, California, and Ubilab, UBS's research lab based in Zurich, Switzerland.[26] She holds several patents in artificial intelligence and interface design.[32][33]

Career

Google

Marissa Mayer speaking at the Google "Search On" event in 2010.

After graduating from Stanford, Mayer received 14 job offers,[27] including a teaching job at Carnegie Mellon University[28]and a consulting job at McKinsey & Company.[20] She joined Google in 1999 as employee number 20.[34][35] She started out writing code and overseeing small teams of engineers, developing and designing Google's search offerings.[11] She became known for her attention to detail which helped land her a promotion to product manager,[36] and later became director of consumer web products.[17][37] She oversaw the layout of

Google's well-known, unadorned search homepage.[37][38][39] She was also on the three-person team responsible for Google AdWords, which is an advertising platform that allows businesses to show their product to relevant potential customers based on their search terms. AdWords helped deliver 96% of the company's revenue in the first quarter of 2011.

Marissa Mayer at an interview while working for Google.

In 2002, Mayer started the Associate Product Manager (APM) program, a Google mentorship program aimed to recruit new talents and cultivate and train them for leadership roles within the company. Each year, Mayer selected a number of junior employees for the two-year program, which would see them take on a number of extracurricular assignments and intensive evening classes.[20][40] Notable graduates of the program include Bret Taylor and Justin Rosenstein.[40] In 2005 she became Vice President of Search Products and User Experience.[41] Mayer held key roles in Google Search, Google Images, Google News, Google Maps, Google Books, Google Product Search, Google Toolbar, iGoogle, and Gmail.[42]

Mayer was the vice president of Google Search Products and User Experience until the end of 2010, when she was asked by then-CEO Eric Schmidt to head the Local, Maps, and Location Services.[43] In 2011, she secured Google's acquisition of survey site Zagat for $125 million. While Mayer was working at Google, she taught introductory computer programming at Stanford and mentored students at the East Palo Alto Charter School.[17][26] She was awarded the Centennial Teaching Award and the Forsythe Award from Stanford.[44]

Yahoo

Michael Arrington and Marissa Mayer at TechCrunch Disrupt

On July 16, 2012, Mayer was

appointed president and CEO of Yahoo!, effective the following day. She is also a member of the company's board of directors.[45][46] To simplify the bureaucratic process and "make the culture the best version of itself", Mayer launched a new online program called PB&J. It collects employee complaints, as well as their votes on problems in the office; if a problem generates at least 50 votes, online management automatically investigates the matter.[47] In February 2013, Mayer oversaw a major personnel policy change at Yahoo! that required all remote-working employees to convert to in-office roles.[48] Having worked from home toward the end of her pregnancy, Mayer returned to work after giving birth to a boy, and built a mother's room next to her office suite—Mayer was consequently criticized for the telecommuting ban.[49] In April 2013, Mayer changed Yahoo!'s maternity leave policy, lengthening its time allowance and providing a cash bonus to parents.[50] CNN noted this was in line with other Silicon Valley companies, such as Facebook and Google.[51][52] Mayer has been criticized for many of her management decisions in pieces by *The New York Times* and *The New Yorker*.[53][54]

On May 20, 2013, Mayer led Yahoo! to acquire Tumblr in a $1.1 billion acquisition.[55][56] In February 2016, Yahoo! acknowledged that the value of Tumblr had fallen by $230 million since it was acquired. In July 2013, Yahoo! reported a fall in revenues, but a rise in profits compared with the same period in the previous year. Reaction on Wall Street was muted, with shares falling 1.7%.[57] In September 2013, it was reported that the stock price of Yahoo! had doubled over the 14 months since Mayer's appointment.[58] However, much of this growth may be attributed to Yahoo!'s stake in the Chinese e-commerce company Alibaba Group, which was acquired before Mayer's tenure.[59]

Mayer delivering a conference keynote.

In November 2013, Mayer instituted a performance review system based on a bell curve ranking of employees, suggesting that managers rank their employees on a bell curve, with those at the lowend being fired.[60][61] Employees complained that some managers were viewing the process as mandatory.[61] In February 2016, a former Yahoo! employee filed a lawsuit against the company claiming that Yahoo's firing practices have violated both California and federal labor laws.[62]

In 2014, Mayer was ranked sixth on *Fortune*'s 40 under 40 list,[63] and was ranked the 16th most-powerful businesswoman in the world that year according to the same publication.[64] In March 2016 *Fortune* would name Mayer as one of the world's most disappointing leaders.[65][53][54] Yahoo! stocks continued to fall by more than 30% throughout 2015, while 12 key executives left the company.[66]

In December 2015, the New York-based hedge fund SpringOwl, a shareholder in Yahoo Inc., released a statement arguing that Mayer be replaced as CEO.[67] Starboard Value, an activist investing firm that owns a stake in Yahoo, likewise wrote a scathing letter regarding Mayer's performance at Yahoo.[68] By January 2016, it was further estimated that Yahoo!'s core business has been worth less than zero dollars for the past few quarters.[69] In February 2016, Mayer confirmed that Yahoo! was considering the possibility of selling its core business.[70] In March 2017, it was reported that Mayer could receive a $23 million termination package upon the sale of Yahoo! to Verizon.[71]

Mayer announced her resignation on June 13, 2017.[72] In spite of large losses in advertising revenue at Yahoo! and a 50% reduction in staff during her 5 years as CEO, Mayer was paid a total of $239 million over that time, mainly in stock and stock options.[73] On the day of her resignation, Mayer publicly highlighted many of the company's achievements during her tenure, including: creating $43B in market capitalization, tripling Yahoo stock, growing mobile users to over 650 million, building a $1.5B mobile ad business,

 and transforming Yahoo's culture.[72]

On 8 November 2017, along with several other present and former **corporate CEOs; Mayer testified**

before the United States Senate Committee on Commerce, Science, and Transportation regarding major security breaches at Yahoo during 2013 and 2014. [74][75]

Mayer with the House
Democratic leader Nancy Pelosi, May 3, 2014

Allegations of WARN Act violations and gender-based discrimination

Scott Ard, a prominent editorial director, fired from Yahoo! in 2015, filed a lawsuit alleging that "Mayer encouraged and fostered the use of (an employee performance-rating system) to accommodate management's subjective biases and personal opinions, to the detriment of Yahoo!'s male employees." He claimed that, prior to his firing, he had received "fully satisfactory" performance reviews since starting at the company in 2011 as head of editorial programming for Yahoo!'s home page; however, he was relieved of his role, which was given to a woman who had been recently hired. [76][77]

An earlier lawsuit was filed by Gregory Anderson, who was fired in 2014, alleging the company's performance management system was arbitrary and unfair and disguised layoffs as terminations for the purpose of evading state and federal WARN Acts, making it the first WARN Act and gender discrimination lawsuit Yahoo! and Mayer faced in 2016.[78][79][80]

Boards

As well as sitting on the boards of directors of Walmart and Jawbone, Mayer also sits on several non-profit boards, such as Cooper–Hewitt, National Design Museum, New York City Ballet, San Francisco Ballet, and San Francisco Museum of Modern Art.[81][82][83][84]

Business investments

Mayer actively invests in technology companies, including crowd-sourced design retailer Minted,[85][86] live video platform Airtime.com,[86] wireless power startup uBeam,[86] online DIY community/e-commerce company Brit + Co.,[86][87] mobile payments processor Square,[86] home décor site One Kings Lane,[86][88] genetic testing company Natera,[86] and nootropics and biohacking company Nootrobox.[89]

Accolades

Mayer was named to *Fortune* magazine's annual list of America's *50 Most Powerful Women in Business* in 2008, 2009, 2010, 2011, 2012, 2013, and 2014 with ranks at 50, 44, 42, 38, 14, 8 and 16 respectively.[90] In 2008, at age 33, she was the youngest woman ever listed.

Mayer was named one of *Glamour Magazine*'s Women of the Year in 2009.[91] She was listed in *Forbes* Magazine's List of The World's 100 Most Powerful Women in 2012, 2013 and 2014, with ranks of 20, 32 and 18 respectively.

In September 2013, Mayer became the first CEO of a Fortune 500 company to be featured in a *Vogue* magazine spread.[14]

In 2013, she was also named in the *Time* 100, becoming the first woman listed as number one on *Fortune* magazine's annual list of the top 40 business stars under 40 years old.[92]

Mayer made *Fortune* magazine history in 2013, as the only person to feature in all three of its annual lists during the same year: Businessperson of the Year (No. 10), Most Powerful Women (at No. 8), and 40 Under 40 (No. 1) at the same time.[93] In March 2016, *Fortune* then named Mayer as one of the world's most disappointing leaders.[65]

On 24 December 2015, Mayer was listed by UK-based company Richtopia at number 14 in the list of 500 Most Influential CEOs.[94] Mayer appeared on the List of women CEOs of Fortune 500 companies in 2017, having ranked 498 of the top 500 Fortune 500 company CEOs.

Personal life

Marissa Mayer and Zachary
Bogue at Pre-White House
Correspondents' dinner reception
in 2014

Mayer married lawyer and investor Zachary
Bogue on December 12, 2009.[36][95][96]
On the day Yahoo! announced her hiring,
Mayer revealed that she was
pregnant;[97][98][99] she gave birth to a
baby boy on September 30,
2012.[100] Although she asked for suggestions via social media,[101] the
name Macallister was eventually chosen for her baby's name from an
existing list.[102]On December 10, 2015, Mayer announced that she had

given birth to identical twin girls,[103][104]
Marielle and Sylvana. [105]

Mayer is Lutheran,[106] but said,
referencing Vince Lombardi's "Your God,
your family and the Green Bay Packers"
quote, her priorities are "God, family and
Yahoo!, except I'm not that religious, so
it's really family and Yahoo!."[107] Since

2008, Mayer has lived on the 38th-floor penthouse suite at the Four Seasons Hotel in San Francisco.[20][42]

Ginni Rometty

Virginia Marie "Ginni" Rometty (born July 29, 1957)[4][5] is an American business executive. She is the current chairman, president,
and CEO of IBM, and the first woman to head the company.[6][7] Prior to becoming president and CEO in January 2012, she held the positions of senior vice president and group executive for sales, marketing, and strategy at IBM. She joined IBM as a systems engineer in 1981.

Rometty's tenure as CEO has been marked by prestigious awards including by *Bloomberg* who named her among the 50 Most Influential People in the World,[8][9][10] and *Fortune* naming her among the "50 Most Powerful Women in Business" for ten consecutive years.[11][12] Her tenure as CEO has been met by criticism related to executive compensation, outsourcing,[13][14] and IBM's 22 consecutive quarters of revenue decline.[15]

Early life and education

Rometty was born on July 29, 1957, in Chicago. She is oldest of four children. Her father left when she was fifteen years old and her mother worked multiple jobs to support her and her siblings. Rometty graduated from the Robert R. McCormick School of Engineering and Applied Science at Northwestern University in 1979 with high honors, receiving a bachelor's degree in computer science and electrical engineering.[16] Rometty was a member of the Kappa Kappa Gamma sorority, eventually serving as its president.[17]

Career

After graduation in 1979, Rometty went to work for General Motors Institute. In 1981, she joined IBM as a systems engineer in its Detroit office.[18] She joined IBM's Consulting Group in 1991. In 2002, she "championed the purchase of the big business consulting firm, PricewaterhouseCoopers Consulting, for $3.5 billion."[19] Rometty became senior vice president and group executive for sales, marketing, and strategy in 2009[18] and is "credited with spearheading IBM's growth strategy by getting the company into the cloud computing and analytics businesses. She was also at the helm of readying Watson, the *Jeopardy!* playing computer, for commercial use."[20]

On October 25, 2011, IBM announced that she was to be the company's next president and CEO, with Sam Palmisano stepping down but retaining his position as chairman.[18] Rometty's appointment marks the first time a woman has been CEO of IBM.[6] Regarding her promotion, Palmisano stated, "Ginni got it because she deserved it ... It's got zero to do with progressive social policies."[19]

On September 26, 2012, IBM announced that Rometty was taking on the added role of chairman of IBM, as Samuel Palmisano prepared to retire at the end of 2012. Rometty commenced her duty as chairman, president, and CEO of IBM on October 1, 2012.[7] One of her goals is to focus company efforts on the cloud and cognitive computing systems, such as Watson.[21]

Boards and honors

Rometty serves on the Council on Foreign Relations; the Board of Trustees of her *alma mater* Northwestern University; the Board of Overseers and Board of Managers of Memorial Sloan-Kettering Cancer n center;[22] and is a council member at the Latin America Conservation Council, a subsidiary of The Nature Conservancy.[23] She also served on the Board of Directors of AIG from 2006 until 2009.[24]

In 2014, Rometty was featured in the PBS documentary *The Boomer List*.[25] Also that year, she became the third female member of the Augusta National Golf Club.[26] She has received honorary doctoral degrees from Rensselaer Polytechnic Institute (2014) and Northwestern University (2015).[27][28]

In *Fortune*'s September 15, 2015 issue, Rometty ranked third on their Most Powerful Women List.[21] Named the eleventh most powerful woman on the 2016 *Forbes* list: The World's 100 Most Powerful Women.[29]

Criticism

Over Rometty's tenure as CEO she has been met by increasing criticism, most notably a confrontation with Mark Cuban, who said, "IBM is no longer a tech company" and "They have no vision", with IBM losing revenue for 22 consecutive quarters.[15] IBM employees have also criticized her for taking pay bonuses despite massive layoffs (replacing employees with cheaper talent offshore or with H1B Visa holders), as well as for poor performance.[14][30] Rometty has been named among the worst CEOs by several publications including The Motley Fool, 24/7 Wallstreet, *Forbes*, and *The Wall Street Journal*.[31][32][33][34]

Personal life

Rometty married Mark Anthony Rometty, a principal investor in the Bam Oil Company, who she met at General Motors while working there for two years after college. They have been married for 37 years and the couple has no children.[35]

Jack Canfield

Jack Canfield (born August 19, 1944[1][2]) is an American author, motivational speaker,[3] seminar leader, corporate trainer, and entrepreneur.[4]:453 He is the co-author of the *Chicken Soup for the Soul* series, which has more than  250 titles and 500 million copies in print in over 40 languages.[3][5] In 2005 Canfield co-authored with Janet Switzer *The Success Principles: How to Get From Where You Are to Where You Want to Be.*[4]

Early life and Education

Canfield was born in Fort Worth, Texas on August 19, 1944. He spent his teen years in Wheeling, West Virginia and graduated from the Linsly Military Institute in 1962.[1] Canfield received an A.B. in Chinese History from Harvard University in 1966.[1] He received his M.Ed. in 1973 from the University of Massachusetts Amherst.[1] Canfield received an honorary Ph.D. from the University of Santa Monica in 1981.[5]

Career

Canfield began his career in 1967 when he taught a year of high school in Chicago, Illinois. He worked at the Clinton Job Corps Center in Iowa and the W. Clement and Jessie V. Stone Foundation in Chicago.[5] In 1976 Canfield co-authored 100 Ways to Enhance Self-Concept in the Classroom: A Handbook for Teachers and Parents.[6] He ran a residential Gestalt center called the New England Center for Personal and Organizational Development [7] and was named one of the Ten Outstanding Young Men of America (TOYA) by the U.S. Jaycees in 1978.[5]

Canfield is the founder and CEO of The Canfield Training Group in Santa Barbara, California and founder of The Foundation for Self-Esteem in Culver City, California.[1][8] Canfield hosts a radio program and writes a globally syndicated newspaper column.[1] He holds a Guinness World Record for having seven books on the New York Times best-seller list at the same time.[8] In 2006 Canfield was featured in a self-development film called *The Secret.*[8] His best known books include: *The Power of Focus*, *The Aladdin Factor*, and *Dare to Win.*[1] In 2005 Canfield co-authored *The Success Principles: How to*

Get from Where You Are to Where You Want to Be.[9] He is a
founding member of the Transformational Leadership Council.[10][11]

Chicken Soup for the Soul

Main article: Chicken Soup for the Soul

Canfield coauthored *Chicken Soup for the Soul* with Mark Victor Hansen in 1993. According to *USA Today*, *Chicken Soup for the Soul* was the third best-selling book in the United States during the mid-1990s.[12] Canfield later co-authored dozens of additional books in the *Chicken Soup for the Soul* series.[13]

The Success Principles

In his book *The Success Principles: How to Get From Where You Are to Where You Want to Be.*[9] Jack Canfield has collected what he asserts to be 64 essential lessons for attaining goals and creating a successful life. The book is divided into six sections: The Fundamentals of Success, Transform Yourself for Success, Build Your Success Team, Create Successful Relationships, Success and Money, and Success Starts Now. These principles include the fundamentals, such as "Take 100%

Responsibility for Your Life", "Decide What You Want", and "Believe It's Possible", as well as those aimed at creating better relationships, such as "Keep Your Agreements", and "Speak with impeccability," and "Tell the Truth Faster." Canfield also presents ideas that he claims can create success with money, build a successful team, and how to overcome procrastination and get started.

In the traditions of Napoleon Hill, W. Clement Stone, Earl Nightingale and Maxwell Maltz Canfield emphasizes the importance of focusing on a vision and using visualization, i.e. the act of creating compelling and vivid pictures in one's mind, in order to achieve one's goals.[4]:81–89 Canfield cites neuropsychologists who study expectancy theory to support his view on the significance of visualization:

Scientists used to believe that humans responded to information flowing into the brain from the outside world. But today, they're learning that instead we respond to what the brain, based on previous experience, expects to happen next. In fact, the mind is such a powerful instrument; it can deliver literally everything you want. But you have to believe that what you want is possible... Through a lifetime's worth of events, our brain actually learns what to expect next—whether it eventually happens that way or not. And because our brain expects something will happen a certain way, we often achieve exactly what we anticipate.[4]:35–36

In January 2015 a 10th anniversary, revised and updated, edition of Jack Canfield's *Success Principles* came out. The new edition is meant to reflect changing times and address challenges and opportunities that define our digital age. The revised edition includes a new section, "Success in the Digital Age," that explains how to brand oneself with an online persona, use social media in a way that enhances one's reputation, and how to organize crowdfunding to finance projects.[14]:499–539

\Teaching & public influence

In July 2009, DoPeace[15] and MaestroConference co-hosted a Social Conferencing Event titled Being a Practical Visionary. Canfield was one of the expert speakers on personal growth.

Personal life[edit]

Canfield married in 1971 and had four children before he divorced in 1976. A few years later he remarried and had a fifth child. He divorced in 1999 and married for a third time in 2001.[1]

Mary Barra

Mary Teresa Barra (née Makela; born December 24, 1961) is the Chairman and CEO of General Motors Company. She has held the CEO position since January 15, 2014, and she is the first female CEO of a major global automaker.[3][4] On December 10, 2013, GM named her to succeed Dan Akerson as Chief Executive Officer, and prior to that, Barra served as the Executive Vice President of Global Product Development, Purchasing and Supply Chain at General Motors.[3][4]

Early life

Barra was born in Royal Oak, Michigan. Her father, Ray Mäkelä, worked as a die maker at Pontiac for 39 years.[5]Barra's parents are of Finnish descent.[6][7] Barra attended Waterford schools in Waterford, Michigan. She is a graduate of Waterford Mott High School.

Education

Barra graduated from the General Motors Institute (now Kettering University), where she obtained a Bachelor of Science degree in electrical engineering. She then attended Stanford Graduate School of Business on a GM fellowship, receiving her Masters in Business Administration degree in 1990.[8]

Career

General Motors

Barra started working for General Motors at the age of 18[9] as a co-op student in 1980 and subsequently held a variety of engineering and administrative positions, including being the manager of the Detroit/Hamtramck Assembly plant.[8]

In February 2008, she became Vice President of Global Manufacturing Engineering. In July 2009 she advanced to the position of Vice President of Global Human Resources, which she held until February 2011, when she was named Executive Vice President of Global Product Development.[8][10] The latter position included responsibilities for design; she has worked to reduce the number of automobile platforms in GM.[3] In August 2013, her Vice President responsibility was extended to include Global Purchasing and Supply Chain.[11]

During her first year as CEO, General Motors was forced to issue 84 safety recalls involving over 30 million cars.[12] Barra was called before the Senate to testify about the recalls and deaths attributed to the faulty ignition switch.[13] Barra and General Motors also came under suspicion of paying for awards to burnish the CEO and corporation's image during that time.[14]

Over the course of her tenure as CEO, Barra has pushed GM as a company transitioning into the tech space pushing forward in the automated driverless car space with major acquisitions including Strobe, a startup focused on driverless technology.[15] Also in 2017 she pushed GM to develop the Chevy Bolt EV, beating rival Tesla in developing the first electric car with a range of 200 miles.[16]

Disney

In August 2017, she was elected to the board of Disney.[17] She is the 12th person elected to this board. Robert Iger, the CEO of Disney, has this to say about Barra:

Beyond being an incredibly respected leader of a major U.S. company, Mary is recognized as an agent of change with a relentless focus on quality, safety and, most importantly, consumers. Her ability to adapt to a changing technological and consumer-focused landscape makes her uniquely suited for the Disney board.

Barra and GM are helping Disney with a new project called Test Track, located in the Epcot Center of Disney World in Orlando.[18]

Other Boards and Councils

Barra is a member of the General Dynamics Board of Directors. She serves on the Board of Directors of the Detroit Economic Club and as a member of The Business Council. She is also a member of the

Stanford University Board of Trustees, the Stanford Graduate School of Business Advisory Council and the Board of Trustees for the Detroit Country Day School.[19]

Awards and honors

Barra was listed as one of the world's most powerful women by *Forbes*, for the fifth time, in 2016. She was most recently listed as the fifth Most Powerful Women, rising from 35th in 2013.[20]

On May 3, 2014, she delivered the Spring Commencement address for University of Michigan's Ann Arbor campus at Michigan Stadium. She received an honorary degree.[21]

Barra was listed number 1 in Fortune's Most Powerful Women list in 2015, moving from second place the year before.[22]

She remained in the number one spot in Fortune's Most Powerful Women of 2017.[23]

In April 2014, Barra was featured on the cover of *Time*'s "100 Most Influential People in the World."[24]

In December 2016, Barra joined a business forum assembled by then President-Elect Trump to provide strategic and policy advice on economic issues.[25]However, she left the forum in 2017, following Trump's response to the Charlottesville protests.

Personal life

Family

Barra is married to consultant Tony Barra, whom she met while studying at Kettering University, and has two children.[3] The family lives in Northville, a suburb of Detroit.[26]

Interests

She has named the Chevrolet Camaro and the Pontiac Firebird as her favorite cars.[9]

Donald Trump

Donald John Trump (born June 14, 1946) is the 45th and current President of the United States, in office since January 20, 2017. Before entering politics, he was a businessman and television personality.

Trump was born and grew up in the New York City borough of Queens. He earned an economics degree from the Wharton School of the University of Pennsylvania. A third generation businessman, he followed in the footsteps of his grandmother Elizabeth and father Fred in running the family real estate company. He renamed it The Trump Organization, and ran it from 1971 until his 2017 inauguration. Trump's real estate career focused on building or renovating skyscrapers, hotels, casinos, and golf courses. He has also started multiple side ventures, branded and licensed his name for real estate and various products.

Trump gained notoriety for his business deals, branding, and television roles. With the help of ghostwriters, he published several books (most notably *The Art of the Deal*), and from 2003 to 2015 he was a producer and the host of *The Apprentice*, a reality television game show. He also owned the Miss Universe and Miss USA beauty pageants. According to *Forbes* magazine, he was the world's 544th richest person as of May 2017, with an estimated net worth of $3.5 billion.

Trump expressed interest in politics as early as 1987. He entered the 2016 presidential race as a Republican and defeated sixteen opponents in the primaries. Commentators described his political positions as populist, protectionist, and nationalist. His campaign received extensive free media coverage; many of his public statements were controversial or false. Trump won the general election on November 8, 2016 against Democratic opponent Hillary Clinton. He became the oldest and wealthiest person ever to assume the presidency, the first without prior military or government service, and the fifth to have won the election despite losing the popular vote. His election, opinions, comments, and policies have sparked numerous protests.

In domestic policy, Trump appointed Neil Gorsuch to the Supreme Court and nominated many federal judges. Citing security concerns, he ordered a travel ban on citizens from several Muslim-majority countries; a revised version was implemented after legal challenges. In December 2017 he signed tax reform legislation which cut rates and eliminated the Obamacare insurance mandate.

In foreign policy, Trump withdrew the United States from the Trans-Pacific Partnership and from the Paris Agreement on climate change, partially reversed the Cuban Thaw, pressured North Korea over the acceleration of their missile tests and nuclear program, and recognized Jerusalem as the capital of Israel.

After Trump dismissed FBI Director James Comey, the Justice Department appointed a special counsel to continue the investigation into links between Russia and Trump campaign associates and any related matters.

Family and personal life

Ancestry

Trump's ancestors originated from the German village of Kallstadt in the Palatinate on his father's side, and from the Outer Hebrides in Scotland on his mother's side. His grandparents and his mother were born in Europe.[1]

Trump's paternal grandfather, Friedrich Trump, first immigrated to the United States in 1885 at the age of 16 and became a citizen in 1892. He amassed a fortune operating boom-town restaurants and boarding houses in the Seattle area and the Klondike region of Canada during its gold rush.[2] On a visit to Kallstadt, he met Elisabeth Christ and married her in 1902. The couple settled in New York permanently in 1905.[3] Frederick died from influenza during the 1918 pandemic.[4]

Trump's father Fred was born in 1905 in The Bronx. Fred started working with his mother in real estate when he was 15, shortly after his father's death. Their company, Elizabeth Trump & Son, was primarily active in the New York boroughs of Queens and Brooklyn. Fred eventually built and sold thousands of houses, barracks, and apartments.[4][5] The company later became The Trump Organization after Donald Trump took over in 1971.[6]

Trump's mother Mary Anne was born in Tong, Lewis, Scotland. At age 18 in 1930, she immigrated to New York, where she worked as a maid.[7] Fred and Mary were married in 1936 and raised their family in Queens.[7][8]

Trump's uncle John was an electrical engineer, physicist, and inventor. He worked as a professor at MIT from 1936 to 1973. During World War II, he was involved in radar research for the Allies and helped design X-ray machines that were used to treat cancer.[9]

Early life and education

Senior yearbook photo of Trump in 1964 wearing the uniform of his private boarding school, New York Military Academy[10][11]

Donald Trump was born on June 14, 1946, at the Jamaica Hospital Medical Center, Queens, New York City, the fourth of five children.[12] Trump grew up in Jamaica, Queens, and attended the Kew-Forest School from kindergarten through seventh grade. At age 13, he enrolled in the New York Military Academy, a private boarding school, after his parents discovered that he had made frequent trips into Manhattan without their permission.[13][14]

In 1964, Trump began his higher education at Fordham University.[10][15] After two years, he transferred to the Wharton School of the University of Pennsylvania, because it offered one of the few real-estate studies departments in United States academia at the time.[15][16] In addition to his father, Trump was inspired by Manhattan developer William Zeckendorf, vowing to be "even bigger and better".[17] While at Wharton, he worked at the family business, Elizabeth Trump & Son,[18] graduating in May 1968 with a Bachelor of Science degree in economics.[15][19][20]

Trump did not serve in the military during the Vietnam War.[21] While in college from 1964 to 1968, he obtained four student deferments.[22] In 1966, he was deemed fit for service based upon a military medical examination, and in 1968 was briefly classified as fit

by a local draft board. In September of that year, he was given a medical deferment, which he later attributed to heel spurs.[23] In 1969, he received a high number in the draft lottery, which gave him a low probability to be called to military service.[23][24][25]

Family

Donald Trump is sworn in as president on January 20, 2017: Trump, wife Melania, son Donald Jr., son Barron, daughter Ivanka, son Eric, and daughter Tiffany

Trump has had three elder siblings—Maryanne, Fred Jr. (1938–1981), and Elizabeth—as well as a younger brother named Robert. Maryanne is an inactive Federal Appeals Court judge on the Third Circuit.[26]

Trump has five children by three marriages, as well as nine grandchildren.[27][28] His first two marriages ended in widely publicized divorces.[29] He is the second divorced American president, after Ronald Reagan.

In 1977, Trump married his first wife, Czech model Ivana Zelníčková, at the Marble Collegiate Church in Manhattan in a ceremony performed by the Reverend Norman Vincent Peale.[30][31] They had three children: Donald Jr. (b. 1977), Ivanka(b. 1981), and Eric (b. 1984). Ivana became a naturalized

United States citizen in 1988.[32] The couple divorced in 1992, following Trump's affair with actress Marla Maples.[33]

In October 1993, Maples gave birth to Trump's daughter, who was named Tiffany after high-end retailer Tiffany & Company.[34] Maples and Trump were married two months later in December 1993.[35] They divorced in 1999,[36] and Tiffany was raised by Marla in California.[37]

Trump and his wife Melania at the Liberty Ball on Inauguration Day

In 2005, Trump married his third wife, Slovenian model Melania Knauss, at Bethesda-by-the-Sea Episcopal Church in Palm Beach, Florida. The ceremony was followed by a reception at Trump's Mar-a-Lago estate.[38] In 2006, Melania became a United States citizen[39] and gave birth to a son, Barron.[40][41] Melania became First Lady of the United States upon Trump's inauguration as the nation's 45th president in January 2017.[42]

Upon his inauguration as president, Trump delegated the management of his real estate business to his two adult sons, Eric and Don Jr.[43] His daughter Ivanka resigned from The Trump Organization and moved to Washington with her husband Jared Kushner. She serves as an assistant to the president,[44] and he is a Senior Advisor in the White House.[45]

Religion

Trump's ancestors were Lutheran on his father's side in Germany[46] and Presbyterian on his mother's side in Scotland.[47] His parents married in a Manhattan Presbyterian church in 1936.[48] As a child, he attended the First Presbyterian Church in Jamaica, Queens, and had his Confirmation there.[31] In the 1970s, his family joined the Marble Collegiate Church (an affiliate of the Reformed Church in America) in Manhattan.[49] The pastor at that church, Norman Vincent Peale, author of *The Power of Positive Thinking* and *The Art of Living*, ministered to Trump's family and mentored him until Peale's death in 1993.[50][49] Trump, who is Presbyterian,[51][52] has cited Peale and his works during interviews when asked about the role of religion in his personal life.[49]

Trump receives Holy Communion, but he has said that he does not ask God for forgiveness. He stated: "I think if I do something wrong,

I just try and make it right. I don't bring God into that picture....I guess that [Communion] is a form of asking for forgiveness".[53] On the campaign trail, Trump has referred to *The Art of the Deal* as his second favorite book after the Bible, saying, "Nothing beats the Bible."[54] *The New York Times* reported that Evangelical Christians nationwide thought "that his heart was in the right place, that his intentions for the country were pure".[55]

Trump has had associations with a number of Christian spiritual leaders, including Florida pastor Paula White, who has been called his "closest spiritual confidant."[56] In 2015, he received a blessing from Greek Orthodox priest Emmanuel Lemelson[57] and in 2016, he released a list of his religious advisers, including James Dobson, Jerry Falwell Jr., Ralph Reed and others.[58] Referring to his daughter Ivanka's conversion to Judaism before her marriage to Jared Kushner, Trump said: "I have a Jewish daughter; and I am very honored by that."[59]

Health

See also: Physician to the President and White House Medical Unit

In 2016, Trump's personal physician, Harold Bornstein, issued a medical report that showed Trump's blood pressure and liver and thyroid function to be in normal ranges.[60][61] It also showed that he is overweight and takes statins to lower his cholesterol.[61]

Trump does not drink alcohol; this decision arose in part from watching his older brother Fred Jr. suffer from alcoholism that contributed to his early death in 1981.[62][63] He also said that he has never smoked cigarettes or consumed drugs, including marijuana.[64]

Wealth

Trump said that he began his career with "a small loan of one million dollars" from his father.[65] He appeared on the initial *Forbes 400* list of wealthy individuals in 1982 with an estimated $200 million fortune, including an "undefined" share of his parents' estate.[66] During the late 1980s he became a billionaire,[67] and made the *Forbes World's Billionaires* list for the first time in 1989,[68] but he was absent from

the *Forbes 400* list following business losses from 1990 to 1995; he reportedly borrowed from his siblings' trusts in 1993.[66] His father's estate, valued at more than $20 million, was divided in 1999 among

Trump, his three surviving siblings and their children.[69][70]

Trump International Hotel

Las Vegas, with gold infused glass[71]

When Trump announced his candidacy

for the presidency on June 16, 2015, he released a one-page financial summary that stated a net worth of $8,737,540,000.[72] The following month, he filed a 92-page Federal Election Commission (FEC) financial disclosure form[73] and declared his net worth was "in excess of ten billion dollars".[74] In his presidential announcement speech, he said "I'm really rich", and said this would make him less indebted to large campaign donors.[75][76] *Forbes* called his net worth estimate "a whopper", setting their own estimate at $4.1 billion in 2015. Trump valued his "properties under development" at $293 million; *Forbes* said they could not evaluate those deals, and booked them for $0.[77][78] Trump's 2015 FEC disclosure reported $362 million in total income for the year 2014.[74]

After Trump made controversial remarks about illegal immigrants in 2015, he lost business contracts with several companies; this reduced his *Forbes* estimate by $125 million.[79] Consumer boycotts and reduced bookings may have further affected his brand value during the presidential campaign.[80][81][82] Trump's 104-page FEC disclosure in May 2016[83] still claimed a total wealth over $10 billion, unchanged from 2015.[73] The release of the *Access Hollywood* tapes in October 2016 put further pressure on his brand,[84] but real estate experts predicted a positive rebound from being president after he was elected.[85]

In its 2017 billionaires' ranking, *Forbes* estimated Trump's net worth at $3.5 billion (544th in the world, 201st in the U.S.)[86] making him one of the richest politicians in American history. These estimates fluctuate from year to year, and among various analysts. In July 2016 *Bloomberg News* had pegged his wealth at $3 billion, calling it an increase thanks to his presidential nomination,[87] whereas *Forbes* had ranked him 324th in the world (113th in the U.S.) with $4.5 billion just a few months earlier.[88] The discrepancies among these estimates and with Trump's own figures stem mainly from the uncertain values of appraised property and of his personal brand.[89]

Business career

Real estate

The distinctive façade of Trump Tower, the headquarters of The Trump Organization, in Midtown Manhattan

In 1968, Trump began his career at his father's real estate development company, Elizabeth Trump & Son, which owned middle-class rental housing in New York City's outer boroughs, but also had business elsewhere.[90][91] During his undergraduate study, Trump joined his father Fred in revitalizing the foreclosed Swifton Village apartment complex in Cincinnati, Ohio, boosting the occupancy rate from 66% to 100%.[92][93]

When his father became chairman of the board in 1971, Trump was promoted to president of the company and renamed it The Trump Organization.[6][94] In 1973, he and his father drew wider attention when the Justice Department contended that the organization systematically discriminated against African Americans who wished to rent apartments. The Department alleged that the Trump Organization had screened out people based on race and not low income, as the Trumps had stated. Under an agreement reached in 1975, the Trumps made no admission of wrongdoing and made the Urban League an intermediary for qualified minority applicants.[95][96] His adviser and attorney during (and after) that period was Roy Cohn, who responded to attacks by counterattacking with maximum force, who valued both positive and negative publicity, and who Trump emulated.[97]

Manhattan developments

 In 1978, Trump launched his Manhattan real estate business by purchasing a 50% stake in the financially troubled Commodore Hotel. The purchase was largely funded by a $70 million construction loan that was jointly guaranteed by Fred Trump and the Hyatt hotel chain.[98] When the remodeling was finished, the hotel reopened as the Grand Hyatt Hotel, located next to Grand Central Terminal.[99][100]

Also in 1978, Trump finished negotiations to develop Trump Tower, a 58-story, 202-meter (663-foot) skyscraper in Midtown Manhattan, which *The New York Times* attributed to his "persistence" and "skills as a negotiator".[101] To make way for the new building, a crew of undocumented Polish workers demolished an old Bonwit Teller store, including art deco features that had initially been marked for preservation.[102] The building was completed in 1983 and houses both the primary penthouse condominium residence of Trump and the headquarters of The Trump Organization.[103][104] Architectural critic Paul Goldberger said in 1983 that he was surprised to find the tower's atrium was "the most pleasant interior public space to be completed in New York in some years".[105][106] Trump Tower was the setting of the NBC television show *The Apprentice* and includes a fully functional television studio set.[107]

Central Park's Wollman Rink after the Trump renovation

in 1980, a general contractor who was unconnected to Trump began repairs on Central Park's Wollman Rink.

Despite an anticipated two and a half year construction timeframe, the repairs remained incomplete in 1986.

Trump took over the project and completed it in three months for $1.95 million, which was $775,000 less than the initial budget. He operated the rink for a year and gave most of the profits to charity and public works projects[108] in exchange for the rink's concession rights.[109]

In 1988 Trump acquired the Plaza Hotel in Manhattan for a record-setting $407 million and appointed his wife Ivana to manage its operation.[110] Trump invested $50 million to restore the building, which he called "the Mona Lisa".[111] According to hotel expert Thomas McConnell, the Trumps boosted it from a three-star to a four-star ranking and sold it in 1995, by which time Ivana was no longer involved in the hotel's day-to-day operations.[112]

In 1994, Trump got involved with the refurbishing of the Gulf and Western Building on Columbus Circle. The former office building was remodeled with design and structural enhancements to become a luxury residential and hotel property.[113][114] When the job was finished, Trump owned commercial space in a 44-

story mixed-use tower (hotel and condominium) that he named Trump International Hotel and Tower.[115]

In 1996, Trump acquired the Bank of Manhattan Trust Building, which was a vacant seventy-one story skyscraper on Wall Street that had briefly been the tallest building in the world when it was completed in 1930. After an extensive renovation, the high-rise was renamed the Trump Building at 40 Wall Street.[116]

In 1997, he began construction on Riverside South, which he dubbed Trump Place, a multi-building development along the Hudson River. The project encountered delays the following year because a subcontractor had to replace defective concrete.[117][118] He and the other investors in the project ultimately sold their interest for $1.8 billion in 2005 in what was then the biggest residential sale in the history of New York City.[119]

From 1994 to 2002, Trump owned a 50% share of the Empire State Building. He would have renamed it "Trump Empire State Building Tower Apartments" if he had been able to boost his share.[120][121]

In 2001, Trump completed Trump World Tower, which was across from the headquarters of the United Nations. For a while, the structure was the tallest all-residential tower in the world.[122] In 2002, Trump acquired the former Hotel Delmonico, which was renovated and reopened in 2004 as the Trump Park Avenue; the building consisted of 35 stories of luxury condominiums.[123] Meanwhile, he continued to own millions of square feet of other prime Manhattan real estate.[124]

Palm Beach estate

Main article: Mar-a-Lago

Mar-a-Lago in 2009

The Trumps with Chinese President Xi Jinping and wife at Mar-a-Lago in 2017

In 1985, Trump acquired the Mar-a-Lago estate in Palm Beach, Florida for under $8 million.[125] The home was built in the 1920s by heiress and socialite Marjorie Merriweather Post, who envisioned the house as a future winter retreat for American presidents.[126]

Trump's initial offer of $28 million had been rejected, and he was able to get the property at the much lower price by purchasing Jack C. Massey's beachfront property for $2 million[127] and threatening to build a house on it that would block Mar-a-Lago's ocean view. In addition to using the estate as a home, Trump also turned it into a private club open to everyone who could afford the initiation fee of $100,000 plus annual dues.[128]

In 1986, Trump acquired a foreclosed 33-story, twin-tower condominium complex in nearby West Palm Beach for $40 million. Auto CEO Lee Iacocca invested in three of the condos.[129] Trump spruced up the complex's public areas and heavily promoted the property for years, but selling the units proved difficult, and the deal turned out to be unprofitable.[130]

Atlantic City casinos

New Jersey legalized casino gambling in 1977, and Trump went to Atlantic City, New Jersey the following year in order to explore how he might get involved in a new business venture. Seven years later, Harrah's at Trump Plaza hotel and casino opened there; the

project was built by Trump with financing from Holiday Corporation,
which also managed the operation.[131] Renamed "Trump Plaza" soon after it opened, it was at the time the tallest building in Atlantic City.[132] The casino's poor financial results exacerbated disagreements between Trump and Holiday Corp., which led to Trump's paying
$70 million in May 1986 to buy out their interest in the property.[133][134] Trump also acquired a partially completed building in

tlantic City from the Hilton Corporation for $320 million; when completed in 1985, that hotel and casino became Trump Castle, and Trump's wife, Ivana, managed that property until Trump transferred her in 1988 to run the Trump Plaza Hotel in New York.[135][136]

Entrance of the Trump Taj Mahal in Atlantic City

Also in 1988, Trump acquired his third casino in Atlantic City, the Taj Mahal (then halfway through construction), through a complex transaction with television host and entertainer Merv Griffin as well as the resort and casino company Resorts International.[137] In October 1989, three of his top Atlantic City executives were killed in a helicopter accident, which both stymied and delayed the planned opening of the Taj Mahal.[138] The Taj finally opened in April 1990 and was built at a total cost of $1.1 billion, which at the time made it the most expensive casino ever.[139][140] The project was financed with $675 million in junk bonds[141] and was a major gamble by Trump.[142] The project underwent debt restructuring the following year,[143] leaving Trump with 50% ownership.[144] He also sold his 282-foot (86 m) megayacht, the *Trump Princess*, which had been indefinitely docked in Atlantic City while leased to his casinos for use by wealthy gamblers.[145][146]

In 1995, Trump founded Trump Hotels & Casino Resorts (THCR), which assumed ownership of Trump Plaza, Trump Castle, and

the Trump Casino in Gary, Indiana.[147] THCR purchased Taj Mahal in 1996 and underwent bankruptcy restructuring in 2004 and 2009, leaving Trump with 10% ownership in the Trump Taj Mahal and other Trump casino properties.[148] From mid 1995 until early 2009, he served as chairman of the publicly-traded THCR organization—which was renamed Trump Entertainment Resorts—and served as CEO from mid 2000 to mid 2005.[149]

During the 1990s, Trump's casino ventures faced competition from Native American gaming at the Foxwoods casino located on an Indian reservation in Connecticut, where it was exempt from the state's anti-gambling laws. Trump stated in 1993 that the casino owners did not look like real Indians to him or to other Indians.[150] Subsequent to that well-publicized remark about the Mashantucket Pequot Tribe, Trump became a key investor backing the Paucatuck Eastern Pequots, who were also seeking state recognition.[151]

Golf courses

The Trump Organization operates many golf courses and resorts in the United States and around the world. According to *Golfweek*, Trump owns or manages about 18 golf courses.[152] His personal financial disclosure with the Federal Elections Commission stated that his golf and resort revenue for the year 2015 was roughly $382 million,[73][83] while his three European golf courses did not show a profit.[87]

Turnberry Hotel and golf course, Ayrshire, Scotland

In 2006, Trump bought

1,400 acres (570 ha), including the Menie

Estate in Balmedie, Aberdeenshire, Scotland, and created a golf resort there.[153] Scottish supporters emphasized potential economic benefits, and opponents emphasized potential environmental harm to a Site of Special Scientific Interest (SSSI).[154][155][156] A spokesperson for the golf course has said 95% of the SSSI is untouched.[157] A 2011 independent documentary, *You've Been Trumped*, chronicled the golf resort's construction and struggles.[158] In 2015, an offshore windfarm being built within sight of the golf course prompted a legal challenge by Trump, which was dismissed by the U.K. Supreme Court.[159] In the wake of the 2008 recession, Trump greatly scaled back development of this property, and as of December 2016 Scottish officials were pushing for completion of the far larger development as originally approved.[160]

In April 2014, Trump purchased the Turnberry hotel and golf resort in Ayrshire, Scotland, which hosted the Open Championship four times between 1977 and 2009.[161][162] After extensive renovations and a remodeling of the course by golf architect Martin Ebert, Turnberry was re-opened in June 2016.[163]

Hotels outside New York

Trump International Hotel and Tower in Chicago

In the late 2000s and early 2010s, The Trump Organization expanded its footprint beyond New York with the co-development and management of hotel towers in Chicago, Las Vegas, Washington D.C., Panama City, Toronto, and Vancouver. There are also Trump-branded buildings in Dubai, Honolulu, Istanbul, Manila, Mumbai and in Indonesia.[164]

Branding and licensing

Main article: List of things named after Donald Trump

Trump has marketed his name on a large number of building projects that are owned and operated by other people and companies. He has also licensed his name for various commercial products and services. In doing so, he achieved mixed success for himself, his partners, and investors in the projects.[165] In 2011, *Forbes'* financial experts estimated the value of the Trump brand at $200 million. Trump disputed this valuation, saying his brand was worth about $3 billion.[166] According to an analysis by *The Washington Post*, there are more than 50 licensing or management deals involving Trump's name, which have generated at least 59 million dollars in revenue for his companies.[167]

Legal affairs and bankruptcies

As of 2016, Trump and his businesses had been involved in more than 3,500 state and federal legal actions. He or one of his companies was the plaintiff in 1,900 cases and the defendant in 1,450. With Trump or his company as plaintiff, more than half the cases have been against gamblers at his casinos who had failed to pay off their debts. With Trump or his company as a defendant, the most common type of case involved personal injury cases at his hotels. In cases where there was a clear resolution, Trump's side won 451 times and lost 38.[168][169]

Trump has never filed for personal bankruptcy, but his hotel and casino businesses have been declared bankrupt six times between 1991 and 2009 in order to re-negotiate debt with banks and owners of stock and bonds.[170][171] Because the businesses used Chapter 11 bankruptcy, they were allowed to operate while negotiations proceeded. Trump was quoted by *Newsweek* in 2011 saying, "I do play with the bankruptcy laws – they're very good for me" as a tool for trimming debt.[172][173]

The six bankruptcies were the result of over-leveraged hotel and casino businesses in Atlantic City and New York: Trump Taj Mahal (1991), Trump Plaza Hotel and Casino (1992), Plaza

Hotel (1992), Trump Castle Hotel and Casino (1992), Trump Hotels and Casino Resorts (2004), and Trump Entertainment Resorts(2009).[174][175] Trump said, "I've used the laws of this country to pare debt ... We'll have the company. We'll throw it into a chapter. We'll negotiate with the banks. We'll make a fantastic deal. You know, it's like on *The Apprentice*. It's not personal. It's just business."[143]

A 2016 analysis of Trump's business career by *The Economist* concluded that his "... performance [from 1985 to 2016] has been mediocre compared with the stock market and property in New York", noting both his successes and bankruptcies.[176] A subsequent analysis by *The Washington Post* concluded that "Trump is a mix of braggadocio, business failures, and real success", calling his casino bankruptcies the "most infamous flop" of his business career.[177]

Side ventures

After Trump took over the family real estate firm in 1971 and renamed it The Trump Organization, he greatly expanded its real estate operations, and also ventured into numerous other business activities. The company eventually became the umbrella organization for several hundred individual business ventures and partnerships.[178]

Sports events

In September 1983, Trump purchased the New Jersey Generals— an American football team that played in the United States Football League (USFL)—from oil magnate J. Walter Duncan. The USFL played three seasons during the spring and summer. After the 1985 season, the organization folded due to continuous financial difficulties, despite winning an antitrust lawsuit against the NFL.[179] Trump remained involved with other sports after the Generals folded; he operated golf courses in several countries.[179] At the Trump Plaza in Atlantic City, he hosted several boxing matches, which included Mike Tyson's 1988 heavyweight championship fight against Michael Spinks.[180] He also acted as a financial advisor to Mike Tyson.[181] In 1989 and 1990, Trump lent his name to the Tour de Trump cycling stage race, which was an attempt to create an American equivalent of European races such as the Tour de France or the Giro d'Italia.[182]

Miss Universe

From 1996 to 2015, Trump owned part or all of the Miss Universe pageants.[183][184] The Miss Universe Pageants include Miss USA and Miss Teen USA, and his management of this business involved his family members; for example, daughter Ivanka once hosted Miss Teen USA. Trump hired the first female president of the Miss Universe business in 1997.[185] He became dissatisfied with how CBS scheduled the pageants, and took both Miss Universe and Miss USA to NBC in 2002.[186][187]

In his 2015 U.S. presidential campaign kickoff speech, Trump made statements about illegal immigrants who crossed the border from Mexico. NBC then decided to end its business relationship with him and stated that it would no longer air the Miss Universe or Miss USA pageants on its networks.[188] In September 2015, Trump bought NBC's share of the Miss Universe Organization and became its sole owner for three days. He then sold the entire company to the WME/IMG talent agency.[189]

Trump University

Trump University was a for-profit education company that was founded by Trump and his associates, Michael Sexton and Jonathan Spitalny. The company ran a real estate training program and charged between $1,500 and $35,000 per course.[190][191][192] In 2005, New York State authorities notified the operation that its use of the word "university" was misleading and violated state law. After a second such notification in 2010, the name of the company was changed to the "Trump Entrepreneurial Institute".[193] Trump was also found personally liable for failing to obtain a business license for the operation.[194]

In 2013, New York State filed a $40 million civil suit against Trump University; the suit alleged that the company made false statements and defrauded consumers.[193][195] In addition, two class-action civil lawsuits were filed in federal court relating to Trump University; they named Trump personally as well as his companies.[196] During the presidential campaign, Trump criticized presiding Judge Gonzalo P. Curiel, alleging bias in his rulings because of his Mexican heritage.[197][198] Shortly after Trump won the presidency, the parties agreed to a settlement of all three pending cases, whereby Trump paid a total of $25 million and denied any wrongdoing.[199][200]

Foundation

The Donald J. Trump Foundation is a U.S.-based private foundation[201] that was established in 1988 for the initial purpose of giving away proceeds from the book *Trump: The Art of the Deal*.[202][203] The foundation's funds have mostly come from donors other than Trump,[204] who has not given personally to the charity since 2008.[204]

The foundation's tax returns show that it has given to health care and sports-related charities, as well as conservative groups.[205] In 2009, for example, the foundation gave $926,750 to about 40 groups, with the biggest donations going to the Arnold Palmer Medical Center Foundation ($100,000), the New York–Presbyterian Hospital ($125,000), the Police Athletic League ($156,000), and the Clinton Foundation ($100,000).[206][207] From 2004 to 2014, the top donors to the foundation were Vince and Linda McMahon of WWE, who donated $5 million to the foundation after Trump appeared at WrestleMania in 2007.[204] Linda McMahon later became Administrator of the Small Business Administration.[208]

In 2016, *The Washington Post* conducted investigations that revealed how the charity had committed several potential legal and ethical violations; those violations included alleged self-dealing and possible tax evasion.[209] After beginning an investigation into the foundation, the New York State Attorney General's office notified the Trump Foundation that it was allegedly in violation of New York laws regarding charities and ordered it to immediately cease its fundraising activities in New York.[210][211][212] A Trump spokesman called the investigation a "partisan hit job".[210] In response to mounting complaints, Trump's team announced in late December 2016 that the Trump Foundation would be dissolved to remove "even the appearance of any conflict with [his] role as President."[213] According to an IRS filing in November 2017, the foundation intends to shut down and distribute its assets (about $970,000) to other charities.

However, a spokesperson for the New York Attorney General's office said the foundation cannot legally shut down until an ongoing investigation of the charity is completed.[214]

Conflicts of interest

There were questions about how Trump would avoid conflicts of interest between his work in the White House and his business activities. At a press conference on January 10, 2017, Trump said that he and his daughter Ivanka would resign all roles with The Trump Organization, while his two adult sons Don Jr. and Ericwould run the business, together with chief financial officer Allen Weisselberg.[215]

Trump retained his financial stake in the business.[216] His attorney Sherri Dillon said that before the January 20 inauguration, Trump would put those business assets into a trust, which would hire an ethics advisor and a compliance counsel. She added that The Trump Organization would not enter any new foreign business deals, while continuing to pursue domestic opportunities.[217] As of April 2017, Trump companies owned more than 400 condo units and home lots in the United States, valued at over $250 million in total ($200,000 to $35 million each).[218]

Media career

Books

Trump has published numerous books. His first published book in 1987 was *Trump: The Art of the Deal*, written by ghostwriter Tony Schwartz.[219] It reached number 1 on *The New York Times* Best Seller list, stayed there for 13 weeks, and altogether held a position on the list for 48 weeks.[219] According to *The New Yorker*, "The book expanded Trump's renown far beyond New York City, making him an emblem of the successful tycoon."[219] Trump's published writings shifted post-2000, from generally memoirs about himself, to books giving advice about finance.[220]

Professional wrestling

Trump is a World Wrestling Entertainment fan and a friend of WWE

chairman Vince McMahon. In 1988–89 Trump hosted WrestleMania IV and V at Boardwalk Hall (dubbed "Trump Plaza" for storyline

purposes) and has been an active participant in several of the shows.[221] He also appeared in WrestleMania VII, and was interviewed ringside at WrestleMania XX, in 1991 and 2004,

respectively.[222] Trump appeared at 2007's WrestleMania 23 in a match called "The Battle of the Billionaires".[221] In 2013, Trump was inducted into the celebrity wing of the WWE Hall of Fame at Madison Square Garden for his contributions to the promotion. He made his sixth WrestleMania appearance the following night at WrestleMania

29.[223] As president, Trump appointed WWE CEO Linda McMahonto his Cabinet as Administrator of the Small Business Administration.[224]

The Apprentice
Trump posing with former NBA basketball player Dennis Rodman during Rodman's 2009 participation on *Celebrity Apprentice*

In 2003, Trump became the executive producer and host of the NBC reality show *The Apprentice* in which contestants competed for a high-level management job in one of Trump's businesses, and were successively "fired" and eliminated from the game. During the first year of the show, Trump earned $50,000 per episode (roughly $700,000 for the first season), but following the show's initial success, he was paid $1 million per episode.[225] In 2007, Trump received a star on the Hollywood Walk of Fame for his contribution to television on *The Apprentice*.[165][226]

Along with British TV producer Mark Burnett, Trump was hired as host of *The Celebrity Apprentice*, in which celebrities compete to win money for their charities. While Trump and Burnett co-produced the show, Trump stayed in the forefront, deciding winners and "firing" losers. International versions of *The Apprentice* franchise were co-produced by Burnett and Trump.

On February 16, 2015, NBC announced that they would be renewing *The Apprentice* for a 15th season.[227] On February 27, Trump stated that he was "not ready" to sign on for another season because of the possibility of a presidential run.[228] Despite this, on March 18, NBC announced they were going ahead with production.[229] On June 29, after widespread negative reaction stemming from Trump's campaign announcement speech, NBC released a statement saying, "Due to the recent derogatory statements by Donald Trump regarding immigrants, NBCUniversal is ending its business relationship with Mr. Trump."[230] Actor and former California Governor Arnold Schwarzenegger replaced Trump as host for the fifteenth season.[231] Trump is still credited as an executive producer for the show.[232]

Acting

Trump has made cameo appearances in 12 films and 14 television series.[233] He played an oil tycoon in *The Little Rascals*,[234] and had a singing role at the 58th Primetime Emmy Awards in 2006.[235] Trump is a member of the Screen Actors Guild and receives an annual pension of more than $110,000.[236][237] His television reality show *The Apprentice* was twice (2004 and 2005) nominated for an Emmy Award.[238]

Public profile

Racial views

Trump has a history of making racially-charged statements and taking actions perceived as racially motivated.[239][240][241][242] In 1973, the U.S. Department of Justice alleged that his company discriminated against black renters. The suit was settled without any admission of wrongdoing.[91][243][244] In 1989, he was accused of racism for insisting that a group of black and Latino teenagers were guilty of raping a white woman in the Central Park jogger case even after they were exonerated by DNA evidence. He continued to maintain this opinion as late as 2016.[245] Trump launched his 2016 presidential campaign with a speech in which he described Mexican immigrants as criminals and rapists.[246][247] Later, his comments about a Mexican-American judge were criticized as racist.[248] During his first year as president, comments he made following a Charlottesville, Virginia rally were seen as implying a moral equivalence between the white supremacist marchers and those who protested them.[249] In 2018 comments he made during an Oval Office meeting about immigration in which he referred to African countries, El Salvador, and Haiti as "shithole countries" were internationally condemned as racist.[250][251][252] Trump has denied multiple times that he is racist; he has said that he is the "least racist person there is."[253]

Trump's racially insensitive statements[243] have been condemned by many observers in the U.S. and around the world,[254][255] but accepted by his supporters either as a rejection of political correctness[256][257] or because they harbor similar racial sentiments.[258][259] Numerous studies and surveys have shown that since Trump's ascendance in the Republican Party, racist attitudes and racial resentment have become more significant than economic factors in determining voters' party allegiance.[259][260]

Popular culture image

Trump has been the subject of comedians, flash cartoon artists, and online caricature artists. He has been parodied regularly on *Saturday Night Live* by Phil Hartman, *Darrell* Hammond *and* Alec Baldwin, *and* in *South Park* as Mr. Garrison. *The Simpsons* episode "Bart to the Future", written during his 2000 campaign for the Reform party, anticipated a future Trump presidency. A dedicated parody series called *The President Show* debuted in April 2017.[261]

Starting in the 1990s, Trump was a guest about 24 times on the nationally syndicated *Howard Stern Show* on talk radio.[262] Trump also had his own daily talk radio program called *Trumped!*, from 2004 to 2008.[263][264][265] Since the 1980s, Trump's wealth and lifestyle have been a fixture of hip hop lyrics,[266] his name being quoted by more than 50 artists.[267]

Political image

Presidential approval ratings for Trump have shown him to be the least popular U.S. president in the history of modern opinion polling as of the first ten months of the term.[268][269][270] A Pew Research Center global poll conducted in July 2017, found "a median of just 22% has confidence in Trump to do the right thing when it comes to international affairs." This compares to a median of 64% rate of confidence for his predecessor Barack Obama. Trump received a higher rating in only two countries: Russia and Israel.[271] An August 2017 POLITICO/Morning consult poll found on some measures "that majorities of voters have low opinions of his character and competence."[272]

False and misleading statements

As president, Trump has frequently made false statements in public speeches and remarks.[273][274][275] Trump uttered "at least one false or misleading claim per day on 91 of his first 99 days" in office according to *The New York Times*,[273] and 1,318 total in his first 263 days in office according to the "Fact Checker" political analysis column of *The Washington Post*,[276] which also wrote,

"President Trump is the most fact-challenged politician that The Fact Checker has ever encountered... the pace and volume of the president's misstatements means that we cannot possibly keep up."[274]

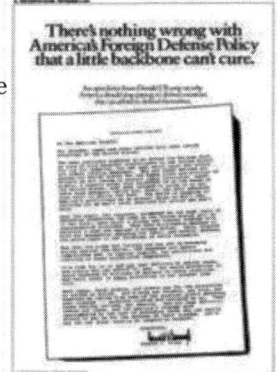

Political career up to 2015

Trump's September 1987 advertisement in *The Boston Globe*, criticizing U.S. defense policy

In 1987 Trump vaguely expressed interest in running for the presidency when he spent almost $100,000 to place full-page advertisements in three major newspapers. In his view at that time, "America should stop paying to defend countries that can afford to defend themselves",[277] and "should present Western Europe and Japan with a bill for America's efforts to safeguard the passage of oil tankers in the Persian Gulf."[278] The advertisements had also advocated for "reducing the budget deficit, working for peace in Central America, and speeding up nuclear disarmament negotiations with the Soviet Union."[279] According to a Gallup poll in December 1988, Trump was the tenth most admired person in America.[280][281]

In 1999, Trump filed an exploratory committee to seek the presidential nomination of the Reform Party in 2000.[282][283] A July 1999 poll matching him against likely Republican nominee George W. Bush and likely Democratic nominee Al Gore showed Trump with seven percent support.[284] Trump eventually dropped out of the race due to party infighting, but still went on to win the party's California and Michigan primaries.[285][286][287] He considered running for president in 2004. [288] In February 2009, Trump appeared on the *Late Show with David Letterman*, and spoke about the automotive industry crisis of 2008–10. He said that "instead of asking for money", General Motors "should go into bankruptcy and work that stuff out in a deal."[289]

Trump publicly speculated about seeking the 2012 Republican presidential nomination, and a *Wall Street Journal* / NBC News poll released in March 2011 found Trump leading among potential contenders; he was one point ahead of former Massachusetts Governor Mitt Romney.[290] A *Newsweek* poll conducted in February 2011 showed Trump within a few points of incumbent president Barack Obama, with many voters undecided in the November 2012 general election for president of the United States.[291] A poll released in April 2011 by Public Policy Polling showed Trump having a nine-point lead in a potential contest for the Republican nomination for president while he was still actively considering a run.[292][293] His moves were interpreted by some media as possible promotional tools for his reality show *The Apprentice*.[294][295][296]

Trump played a leading role in "birther" conspiracy theories that had been circulating since President Obama's 2008 presidential campaign.[297][298] Beginning in March 2011, Trump publicly questioned Obama's citizenship and eligibility to serve as president.[299][300][301] Although the Obama campaign had released a copy of the short-form birth certificate in 2008,[302] Trump demanded to see the original "long-form" certificate.[299] He mentioned having sent investigators to Hawaii to research the question, but he did not follow up with any findings.[299] He also repeated a debunked allegation that Obama's grandmother said she had witnessed his birth in Kenya.[303][304] When the White House later released Obama's long-form birth certificate,[305] Trump took credit for obtaining the document, saying "I hope it checks out."[306] His official biography mentions his purported role in forcing Obama's hand,[307] and he has defended his pursuit of the issue when prompted, later saying that his promotion of the conspiracy made him "very popular".[308] In 2011, Trump had called for Obama to release his student records, questioning whether his grades warranted entry into an Ivy League school.[309]

When asked in 2015 whether he believed Obama was born in the United States, Trump said he did not want to discuss the matter further.[310][311] In September 2016, Trump publicly acknowledged that Obama was born in the United States, and said that the rumors had been started by Hillary Clinton during her 2008 presidential campaign.[300][312][313]

Trump speaking at the Conservative Political Action Conference in 2011

Trump made his first speaking appearance at the Conservative Political Action Conference (CPAC) in February 2011. His appearance at CPAC was organized by GOProud, an LGBT conservative organization, in conjunction with GOProud supporter Roger Stone, who was close with Trump. GOProud pushed for a write-in campaign for Trump at CPAC's presidential straw poll. The 2011 CPAC speech Trump gave is credited for helping kick-start his political career within the Republican Party.[314][315]

In the 2012 Republican primaries, Trump generally had polled at or

below 17 percent among the crowded field of possible candidates.[316] On May 16, 2011, Trump announced he would not run for president in the 2012 election, while also saying he would have become the president of the United States, had he run.[294]

In 2013, Trump was a featured speaker at the Conservative Political Action Conference (CPAC).[317] During the lightly attended early-morning speech, Trump spoke out against illegal immigration, then-President Obama's "unprecedented media protection", and advised against harming Medicare, Medicaid and Social Security.[318][319]

Additionally, Trump spent over $1 million in 2013 to research a possible run for president of the United States.[320] In October 2013, New York Republicans circulated a memo suggesting Trump should run for governor of the state in 2014 against Andrew Cuomo. In response to the memo, Trump said that while New York had problems and that its taxes were too high, running for governor was not of great interest to him.[321] A February 2014 Quinnipiac poll had shown Trump losing to the more popular Cuomo by 37 points in a hypothetical election.[322] In February 2015, Trump told NBC that he was not prepared to sign on for another season of *The Apprentice*, as he mulled his political future.[323]

Political affiliations

Trump meets with
President Ronald Reagan
at a 1987 White House
reception.

Trump's political party affiliation as changed numerous times over
the years. Trump was a Democrat prior to 1987.[324] In 1987,
Trump registered as a Republican in Manhattan.[325] After rumors
of a presidential run, he was then invited by Democratic senators Jim
Wright and John Kerry, and Arkansas congressman Beryl Anthony
Jr., to host a fundraising dinner for Democratic Congressional
candidates – and to switch parties. Anthony told the New York
Times that "the message Trump has been preaching is a Democratic
message," referring to the newspaper advertisements Trump had
bought. Asked whether the rumors were true, Trump denied he was
a candidate and said, "I believe that if I did run for President, I'd
win."[279]

In 1999, Trump switched to the Reform Party and ran a presidential
exploratory campaign for its nomination. After his run, Trump left
the
party in 2001 due to the involvement of David Duke, Pat
Buchanan, and Lenora Fulani.[282]

From 2001 to 2008, Trump identified himself as a Democrat, but in 2008, he endorsed Republican John McCain for president. In 2009, he officially changed his party registration to Republican.[326] In December 2011, Trump became an independent for five months before returning to the Republican Party.[327][328]

In February 2012, Trump endorsed Republican Mitt Romney for president.[329] When asked in 2015 which of the last four presidents he prefers, Trump picked Democrat Bill Clinton over the Republican Bushes.[330][331]

Campaign contributions

According to a New York state report, Trump circumvented corporate and personal campaign donation limits in the 1980s—although no laws were broken—by donating money to candidates from 18 different business subsidiaries, rather than donating primarily in his own name.[332][333] Trump told investigators he did so on the advice of his lawyers. He also said the contributions were not to gain favor with business-friendly candidates, but simply to satisfy requests from friends.[332][334]

Trump has made contributions to campaigns of both Republican Party and Democratic Party candidates, with the top ten recipients of his political contributions being six Democrats and four Republicans.[335] After 2011, his campaign contributions were more favorable to Republicans than to Democrats.[336]

2016 presidential campaign

Trump campaigning in Laconia, New Hampshire, on July 16, 2015

On June 16, 2015, Trump announced his candidacy for President of the United States at Trump Tower in Manhattan. In the speech, Trump drew attention to illegal immigration, offshoring of

American jobs, the U.S. national debt, and Islamic terrorism, which all remained large priorities during the campaign. He also announced his campaign slogan, "Make America Great Again".[337]

Republican primaries

In the 2016 Republican Party presidential primaries, Trump entered a field of 17 major candidates who were vying for the 2016 Republican nomination; this was the largest presidential field in American history.[338]

Trump participated in eleven of the twelve Republican debates, skipping only the January 28 seventh debate, which was the last debate before primary voting began on the first of February. The debates received historically high television ratings, which increased the visibility of Trump's campaign.[339] Republican leaders were hesitant to support him. They doubted his chances of winning the general election and feared that he could harm the image of the Republican Party.[340][341]

By early 2016, the race had focused on Trump and U.S. Senator Ted Cruz.[342] On Super Tuesday, Trump won the plurality of the vote, and he remained the front-runner throughout the remainder of the primaries. By March 2016, Trump became poised to win the Republican nomination.[343] After a landslide win in Indiana on May 3, 2016—which prompted the remaining candidates Ted Cruz and John Kasich to suspend their presidential campaigns—

RNC Chairman Reince Priebus declared Trump the presumptive Republican nominee.[344] With 14,015,993 votes, Trump broke the all-time record in the history of the Republican Party for winning the most primary votes. He also set the record for the largest number of votes cast against the front runner.[345] He won a total of 1441 delegates (58.3% of the total) and 44.9% of the vote versus 25.1% for the runner-up, Ted Cruz.

General election campaign

After becoming the presumptive Republican nominee, Trump shifted his focus to the general election. Trump began campaigning against Hillary Clinton, who became the presumptive Democratic nominee on June 6, 2016.

Clinton had established a significant lead over Trump in national
polls throughout most of 2016. In early July, Clinton's lead narrowed in national polling averages following the FBI's re-opening of its investigation into her ongoing email controversy.[346][347][348]

Trump gives the thumbs up as his running mate Mike
Pence approves at the Republican National Convention, July 20, 2016

On July 15, 2016, Trump announced his selection of Indiana Governor Mike Pence as his running mate.[349] Four days later on July 19, Trump and Pence were officially nominated by the Republican Party at the Republican National Convention.[350] The list of convention speakers and attendees included former presidential nominee

Bob Dole, but the other prior nominees did not
attend.[351][352]

Two days later, Trump officially accepted the nomination in a 76-minute speech that was inspired by Richard Nixon's 1968 acceptance speech.[353] The historically long speech was watched by nearly 35 million people and received mixed reviews, with net negative viewer reactions according to CNN and Gallup polls.[354][355][356]

On September 26, 2016, Donald Trump and Hillary Clinton faced off in their first presidential debate, which was held at Hofstra University in Hempstead, New York and moderated by NBC News anchor Lester Holt.[357] The TV broadcast was the most watched presidential debate in United States history.[358] The second presidential debate was held at Washington University in Saint Louis, Missouri. The beginning of that debate was dominated by references to a recently leaked tape of Trump making sexually explicit comments, which Trump countered by referring to alleged sexual misconduct on the part of Bill Clinton. Prior to the debate, Trump had invited four women who had accused Clinton of impropriety to a press conference. The final presidential debate was held on October 19 at the University of Nevada, Las Vegas. Trump's refusal to say whether he would accept the result of the election, regardless of the outcome, drew particular press attention.[359][360]

Political positions

Trump's campaign platform emphasized renegotiating U.S.–China relations and free trade agreements such as NAFTA and the Trans-Pacific Partnership, strongly enforcing immigration laws, and building a new wall along the U.S.–Mexico border. His other campaign positions included pursuing energy independence while opposing climate change regulations such as the Clean Power Plan and the Paris Agreement, modernizing and expediting services for veterans, repealing and replacing the Affordable Care Act, abolishing Common Core education standards, investing in infrastructure, simplifying
the tax code while reducing taxes for all economic classes, and imposing tariffs on imports by companies that offshore jobs. During the campaign, he also advocated a largely non-interventionistapproach to foreign policy while increasing military spending, extreme vetting or a ban of immigrants from Muslim-majority countries[361] to pre-empt domestic Islamic terrorism, and aggressive military action against Islamic State of Iraq and the Levant (ISIL, also known as ISIS or IS).

Media have described Trump's political positions as

"populist",[362][363] and some of his views cross party lines. For example, his economic campaign plan calls for large reductions in income taxes and deregulation,[364] consistent with Republican Party policies, along with significant infrastructure investment,[365] usually considered a Democratic Party policy.[366][367] According to political writer Jack Shafer, Trump may be a "fairly conventional American populist when it comes to his policy views", but he attracts free media attention, sometimes by making outrageous comments.[368][369]

Trump has supported or leaned toward varying political positions over time.[370][371][372] *Politico* has described his positions as "eclectic, improvisational and often contradictory",[372] while NBC News counted "141 distinct shifts on 23 major issues" during his campaign.[373]

Campaign rhetoric

Trump rally in the U.S. Bank Arena, Cincinnati, Ohio, on October 13, 2016

In his campaign, Trump said that he disdained political correctness; he also stated that the media had intentionally misinterpreted his words, and he made other claims of adverse media bias.[374][375][376] In part due to his fame, and due to his willingness to say things other candidates would not, and because a candidate who is gaining ground automatically provides a compelling news story, Trump received an unprecedented amount of free media coverage during his run for the presidency, which elevated his standing in the Republican primaries.[377]

Fact-checking organizations have denounced Trump for making a record number of false statements compared to other candidates.[378][379][380] At least four major publications – *Politico*, *The Washington Post*, *The New York Times*, and the *Los Angeles Times* – have pointed out lies or falsehoods in his campaign statements.[381] *NPR* said that Trump's campaign statements were often opaque or suggestive.[382] Lucas Graves, an assistant professor of journalism and mass communication at the University of Wisconsin–Madison,[383] opined that Trump "often speaks in a suggestive way that makes it unclear what exactly he meant, so that fact-checkers "have to be really careful" when picking claims to check, "to pick things that reflect what the speaker was clearly trying to communicate."[384]

Trump's penchant for hyperbole is believed to have roots in the New York real estate scene, where Trump established his wealth and where puffery abounds.[385] Trump has called his public speaking style "truthful hyperbole", an effective political tactic that may, however,

backfire for overpromising.[385] Martin Medhurst, a Baylor University professor of communication and political science, analyzed

Trump's frequently used rhetorical devices, such as catchy slogans, hyperbole, insinuations and preterition.[386]

White nationalist support

The alt-right movement coalesced around Trump's candidacy,[387] due in part to its opposition to multiculturalism and immigration.[388][389] Trump personally condemned the alt-right in an interview after the election.[390]

During the campaign, Trump was accused of pandering to white nationalists.[391] He gave an interview to far-right radio host Alex Jones, retweeted open racists, and refused to condemn the support of David Duke—a former Imperial Wizard of the Ku Klux Klan—in a CNN interview with Jake Tapper.[392][393] Trump later said he "disavowed Duke the day before at a major conference."[394] In August 2016, he appointed Steve Bannon—the executive chairman of Breitbart News—as his campaign CEO; the website was described by Bannon as "the platform for the alt-right."[395] Bannon later told the *Wall Street Journal* that he was an "economic nationalist" but not "a supporter of ethno-nationalism."[396] In a CBS interview in 2017, Bannon said "there's no room in American society" for White nationalists, neo-Nazis, and the KKK.[397] According to Michael Barkun, the Trump campaign was remarkable for bringing fringe ideas, beliefs, and organizations into the mainstream.[398]

Financial disclosures

In compliance with FEC regulations of all presidential candidates, Trump published a 92-page financial disclosure form in 2015.[73] He did not release his tax returns,[399] which was contrary to usual practice by every presidential candidate since Gerald Ford in 1976.[400] Although it is tradition to do so, presidential candidates are not required by law to release their returns,[401] and Trump's refusal to do so led to speculation that he was hiding something.[402] Trump said that his tax returns were being audited, and his lawyers had advised him against releasing the returns.[403][404] However, no law prohibits release of tax returns during an audit.[405] Tax attorneys differ about whether such a release is wise legal strategy.[406] Trump has told the news media that his tax rate was none of their business, and that he tries to pay "as little tax as possible".[407][408][409]

In October 2016, portions of Trump's state filings as part of Trump's 1995 tax return were leaked to a reporter from *The New York Times*. They show that using allowed deductions for losses,

Trump claimed a loss of $916 million that year. During the second presidential debate, Trump acknowledged using the deduction, but declined to provide details such as the specific years it was applied.[410] He said that he did use the tax code to avoid paying taxes.[411][412][413]

On March 14, 2017, the first two pages of Trump's 2005 federal income tax returns were leaked to MSNBC's Rachel Maddow. The two pages showed that Trump paid $38 million in federal taxes and had a gross adjusted income of $150 million.[414][415] The White House confirmed the authenticity of the 2005 documents and stated: "Despite this substantial income figure and tax paid, it is totally illegal to steal and publish tax returns."[414][415]

Safra A. Catz

Safra Catz (Hebrew: ץק ארפצ, born December 1, 1961) is an Israeli-born American business executive. She has been an executive at Oracle Corporation since April 1999, and a board member since 2001. In April

2011 she was named co-president and chief financial officer, reporting to founder/CEO Larry Ellison.[3] On September 18, 2014 Oracle announced that Larry Ellison will step down as CEO and that Mark Hurd and Safra Catz have been named as the new CEOs.[4]

Early life

Catz was born in Holon, Israel,[5] to Jewish parents.[6][7] Her father was an immigrant from Romania.[8] She moved from Israel to Brookline, Massachusetts at the age of six.

Catz graduated from Brookline High School.[9] She earned a bachelor's degree from the Wharton School of the University of Pennsylvania in 1983 and a J.D. from the University of Pennsylvania Law School in 1986.[5][10]

Career

Catz was a banker at Donaldson, Lufkin & Jenrette,[11] joining in 1986;[citation needed] Catz served as a managing director from February 1997 to March 1999 and a senior vice president from January 1994 to February 1997 and previously held various investment banking positions since 1986. She has been a non-executive director of Hyperion Solutions since April 14, 2007.[12]

She has been a member of the executive council of TechNet since March 14, 2013. She served as a director of PeopleSoft Inc. since December 30, 2004 and Stellent Inc. since December 12, 2006.

Catz joined Oracle Corporation in April 1999.[3] Catz became a member of the company's Board of Directors in October 2001 and President of Oracle Corporationin early 2004.[3][13] She is credited for having driven Oracle's 2005 efforts to acquire software rival PeopleSoft in a $10.3 billion takeover.[11] Catz is also the company's Chief Financial Officer, serving temporarily in that role from November 2005 to September 2008, and from April 2011 to the present.[3] Mark Hurdjoined her as Co-President in 2010.[3]

In 2009 she was ranked by *Fortune* as the 12th most powerful woman in business.[9] In 2009 she was also ranked by *Forbes* as the 16th most powerful business-woman.[14] In 2014, she was ranked at #24.[15] According to an Equilar analysis published by *Fortune*, she was in 2011 the highest-paid woman among Fortune 1000 companies, receiving an estimated US$51,695,742 in total remuneration.[16] Catz is a lecturer in accounting at the Stanford Graduate School of Business.[17] Catz was a director of HSBC Group from 2008 to 2015.[18]

After the election of Donald Trump, Catz was one of several high-profile CEOs, including, among others, Tim Cook, Sheryl Sandberg and Jeff Bezos, invited to talk with the then president-elect about potentially taking up a position in the incoming administration.[19] According to Bloomberg, she was considered for the post of U.S. Trade Representative or Director of National Intelligence.[19]

Catz is the highest paid female CEO of any U.S. company as of April 2017, earning $40.9 million after a 23% drop in her total compensation relative to 2016.[20]

Catz was elected to the board of directors of The Walt Disney Company on December 7, 2017, effective on February 1, 2018.[21]

Personal life

Catz is married to Gal Tirosh and has two sons, Scott and Gary.[5]

Tony Robbins

Tony Robbins, born Anthony J. Mahavoric (February 29, 1960), is an

American author, entrepreneur, philanthropistand life coach.[1] Robbins is known for his infomercials, seminars, and self-help books including *Unlimited Power*and *Awaken the Giant Within*. Approximately 4 million people have attended his live seminars.[2][3]

Robbins is the founder of several companies that earn approximately $6 billion in annual sales. In 2015 and 2016 he was listed on the *Worth Magazine* Power 100 list.[4][5] He is also a philanthropist, partnering with organizations such as Feeding America.[6]

Early life

Robbins was born Anthony J. Mahavoric in North Hollywood, California, on February 29, 1960.[7] Robbins is the eldest of three children and his parents divorced when he was 7. His mother then had a series of husbands, including Jim Robbins, a former semi-professional baseball player who legally adopted Anthony when he was 12.[8]

Robbins was raised in Azusa and Glendora, California, and attended Glendora High School. He was elected student body president in his senior year. While growing up, Robbins worked as a handyman to help provide for his siblings.[9]

During high school, Robbins grew ten inches, a growth spurt later attributed to a pituitary tumor.[7] He has said his home life was "chaotic" and "abusive". When he was seventeen years old, he left home and never returned.[7] Robbins later worked as a janitor, and did not attend college.[8]

Career

Robbins began his career promoting seminars for motivational speaker and author Jim Rohn when he was 17 years old.[10][11][12]

In the early 1980s, soon after meeting Neurolinguistic Programming co-founder John Grinder, the two became partners. At this time Robbins taught NLP and Ericksonian Hypnosis.[12] In 1983 Robbins learned to firewalk, and incorporated it into his seminars.[13]

In 1988 Robbins released his first infomercial, Personal Power, produced by Guthy Renker,[14] which helped to promote his services as a "peak performance coach". The infomercial helped Robbins gain wide exposure, selling his Personal Power self-help audiotapes. His early infomercials featured celebrities such as Pro Football Hall of Fame quarterback Fran Tarkenton and actor Martin Sheen. By 1991 an estimated 100 million Americans in 200 media markets had seen his infomercials.[15]

In 1997, Robbins began the Leadership Academy seminar.[16][17] He is a speaker on the seminar circuit sponsored by Learning Annex.[18] Robbins was a featured speaker at the 2007 Technology, Entertainment and Design (TED) conference.

Together with Cloé Madanes, Robbins founded the Robbins-Madanes Center for Intervention, an organization that trains life skills coaches to help families and individuals deal with addiction and other issues.[17][19]

In 2014, Robbins, along with a group of investors including Magic Johnson, Mia Hamm, and Peter Guber, acquired rights to launch a Major League Soccerfranchise in Los Angeles, California, currently referred to as the Los Angeles Football Club. The soccer team is scheduled to begin competition in 2018.[20][21][22]

In 2016, Robbins partnered with Golden State Warriors co-owner Peter Guber and Washington Wizards co-owner Ted Leonsis to purchase Team Liquid, an eSports pro gaming organization.[23] In 2017 Team Liquid won The International 7, a Dota 2 tournament with a prize pool of over $24 million.[24]

Robbins has worked on an individual basis with Bill Clinton,[25] Donald Trump,[26] Justin Tuck, Wayne Gretzky,[27] Serena

Williams,[28] Hugh Jackman[29] and Pitbull.[30] He has also counseled American businessmen Peter Guber, Steve Wynn and Marc Benioff.[31] He was named one of the "Top 50 Business Intellectuals" by Accenture[32] and one of the "Top 200 Business Gurus" by the Harvard Business Press,[33] and is ranked on the Forbes Celebrity 100.[34]

Select bibliography

As of 2017 Robbins has written five books, four of them best-sellers, including *Unlimited Power*[35] and *Awaken the Giant Within*.[36] In 2014, inspired by the financial crisis that cost many Americans their retirement savings,[37] he published *Money: Master the Game*, which reached #1 on the New York Times best-selling list in December.[38]

Unlimited Power. Free Press. (1986) ISBN 0-684-84577-6

Awaken the Giant Within. Free Press. (1991) ISBN 0671791540

Giant Steps. Touchstone. (1994) ISBN 0671891049

Money: Master the Game. Simon & Schuster. (2014) ISBN 1476757801

Unshakeable: Your Financial Freedom Playbook. Simon & Schuster. (2017) (co-authored with Peter Mallouk) ISBN 1501164589

Teachings

Personal performance

Throughout his writings, seminars, and speeches, Robbins espouses viewpoints, techniques, and other practices he asserts can help adherents improve their lives.[39] Among these are methods he calls the "controlling state" and "neuro-associative conditioning".[40] He speaks about various "human needs, influences that affect people, the power of making decisions" and the need to achieve "emotional mastery".[41][42]

Seminars

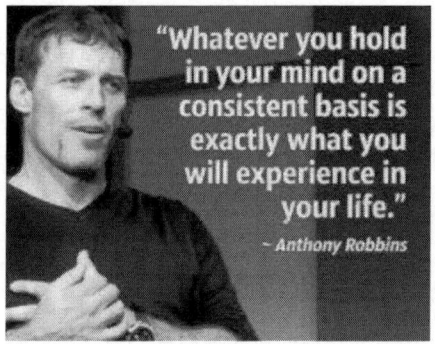
"Whatever you hold in your mind on a consistent basis is exactly what you will experience in your life."
– Anthony Robbins

Robbins holds multiple seminars annually. These seminars include *Unleash the Power Within, Date with Destiny, Life and Wealth Mastery, Business Mastery* and *Leadership Academy.*[43]

Health and energy2

"Energy: The Fuel of Excellence", a chapter in *Unlimited Power*, is dedicated to a discussion of health and energy. It endorses the *Fit For Life* program of Harvey and Marilyn Diamond, food combining and deep breathing. Robbins refers to Harvey and Marilyn Diamond as his "former partners".[44]

Philanthropy

Anthony Robbins Foundation

In 1991, Jay Robbins founded the Anthony Robbins Foundation.[45] The charity helps individuals and organizations to make a difference in the quality of life for youth, homeless, hungry, prisoners, elderly and disabled.[46] The Basket Brigade, one of the programs of the Foundation, brings groups of volunteers across the world together to assemble and deliver baskets of food and household items to needy families.[47]

In 2016 Robbins and his Foundation partnered with Bob Carr and the Give Something Back Foundation on the *ROC 'N Robbins Challenge* event. Carr matched the $1 million Robbins donated at the event, with the proceeds going to send 100 low-income students to medical school.[48]

Independent charity watchdog Charity Navigator gives the Anthony Robbins Foundation a rating of four out of four stars.[49]

Feeding America

In 2014, he donated the profits of his book, *Money: Master the Game*, along with an additional personal donation, through Feeding America to provide meals to people in need.[50] The combined donation fed 100 million needy people in 2014-15, according to the charity.[51][52] Robbins partnered with the charity again in 2016 to provide 100 million more meals.[53] On February 2, 2017, Feeding America announced that the 100 Million More Meals Challenge, conducted in partnership with Robbins, helped provide more than 101.6 million meals to children, families and seniors through Feeding America's network of 200-member food banks in 2016. Robbins also donated profits from *Unshakeable: Your Financial Freedom Playbook* to Feeding America.[54]

Spring Health

Robbins works with a water company called Spring Health, which provides fresh water to small villages in rural eastern India to prevent waterborne diseases.[55]

X-Prize Foundation

He is also a benefactor of the X-Prize Foundation. Robbins joined Elon Musk and donated to the Global Learning X-Prize.[56]

Underground Railroad

Robbins helped raise more than $1 million for Operation Underground Railroad, a non-profit organization that fights against child trafficking and slavery with the assistance of former CIA, Navy SEALs, and Special Ops operatives.[57]

Legal issues

In May 1995, Robbins Research International (R.R.I.) settled with the Federal Trade Commission over alleged violations of the agency's Franchise Rule. Under the settlement, R.R.I. was not found to have violated any law and agreed to pay $221,260 in consumer redress.[58]

Wade Cook sued Robbins for allegedly using copyrighted terms from Cook's book *Wall Street Money Machine* in Robbins' seminars. In 2000, a jury awarded Cook $655,900 judgement, which was appealed.[59][60] Cook and Robbins settled for an undisclosed amount.[61][62]

In 2001, the British Columbia Supreme Court ruled that *The Vancouver Sun* had defamed Robbins when it called him an "adulterous, wife-stealing hypocrite. "The court awarded Robbins $20,000 in damages and his legal costs.[63][64]

In July 2012, the *San Jose Mercury News* published a story reporting that multiple people had been burned and hospitalized during one of Robbins' fire-walking events on July 19, 2012. This story was picked up by other media outlets, including Fox News. These reports were later retracted as inaccurate.[65] A similar corrective article was published by *The Huffington Post.*[66][67]

On June 24, 2016, it was reported that "dozens were burned and required medical attention after attempting to walk on hot coals during

a fire-walking event at a Tony Robbins seminar in Dallas, Texas".[68] Several attendees were transported to medical facilities to treat burns, and a bus was used as a staging-area for between 30 and 40 people who were less seriously hurt.[69] A spokeswoman for the Robbins organization stated, "Someone unfamiliar with the process of

the fire-walk called 911 reporting the need for emergency services vehicles [...] there was no need for emergency personnel [...] only 5 of

7,000 participants requested an examination beyond what was readily available on site."[70]

Television and film

Robbins has played cameo roles in the films *Reality Bites*, *The Cable Guy*[71] and the 2001 film *Shallow Hal*.[72] He also appeared in *The Roseanne Show* and an episode of *The Sopranos*.[73] He plays himself in the 2010 documentary film *The Singularity Is Near: A True Story about The Future*.[74] He was lampooned in the *Family Guy* episode "When You Wish Upon a Weinstein"[75] and the *Beavis and Butt-head* episode "The Miracle That is Beavis".

In July 2010, NBC debuted "Breakthrough with Tony Robbins", a reality show that followed Robbins as he helped the show's participants face their personal challenges.[76][77] NBC canceled the show after airing two of the planned six episodes due to low viewership of 2.8 million.[78] In March 2012, the OWN Networkpicked up the show for another season beginning with the original first season set to re-run and thereafter leading directly into the new 2012 season.[79][80] In April 2012, Robbins began cohosting *Oprah's Lifeclass* on the OWN Network.[81]

In 2015, film maker Joe Berlinger directed and produced the documentary "Tony Robbins: I Am Not Your Guru", about the Tony Robbins event "Date with Destiny" after filming it in Boca Raton,

Florida, in December 2014.[82] It premiered at the South by Southwest film festival in March 2016[83] and opened the American Documentary Film Festival (AmDocs) in Palm Springs in February 2016.[84] The documentary was translated into languages for 190 countries and released by Netflix on July 15, 2016.[82][85]

Personal life

In 1984, he married Rebecca "Becky" Jenkins, after meeting her at a seminar.[86][87][88] Jenkins had three children from two former marriages whom Robbins adopted. Robbins and Jenkins filed for divorce 14 years later.[88]

In 1984, Robbins and former girlfriend Liz Acosta had a son Jairek Robbins, who is also a personal empowerment trainer.[89]

Robbins married Bonnie "Sage" Robbins (née Humphrey) in October 2001.[90] Robbins resides in Palm Beach, Florida.[91]

CHAPTER THIRTEEN

MARKETING INFORMATION SYSTEM

A marketing information system (MkIS) is a management information system (MIS) designed to support marketing decision making. Jobber  (2007) defines it as a "system in which marketing data is formally gathered, stored, analyzed and distributed to managers in accordance with their informational needs on a regular basis." In addition, the online business dictionary defines Marketing Information System (MkIS) as "a system that analyzes and assesses marketing information, gathered continuously from sources inside and outside an organization or a store."[1]

Furthermore, "an overall Marketing Information System can be defined as a set structure of procedures and methods for the regular, planned collection, analysis and presentation of information for use in making marketing decisions." (Kotler, at al, 2006)

Overview

Reid and Bojanic (2010) claimed that, " The term market research informs relatively narrowly than Marketing Information System (MkIS) which is altered from the term management information systemization. Market research indicates that information is not collected for a specific reason or project; the major objective is a one-time use. "[2]

"A marketing information system, which continuously collects the initial, routine and systematic data, is not only used for one particular topic but is designed for monitoring the degree of the marketing success to ensure the achievable of the operation as well."[2]

Importance

Developing a MkIS system is becoming extremely important as the strength of economies rely on services and to better understand the specific needs of customers. Kotler, et al. (2006) defined it more broadly as "people, equipment, and procedures to gather, sort, analyze, evaluate, and distribute needed, timely, and accurate information to marketing decision makers."[3]

Insofar as an economy focuses on services, marketing is important to "monitor the marketing environment for changes in buyer behavior competition, technology, economic conditions, and government policies."[4] In this sense, the role of marketing is becoming pivotal for an organization to "adapt to changes in the market environment." (Harmon, 2003)

As an economy relies on the acquisition of knowledge, MkIS systems are necessary to be able to define and differentiate the value proposition that one organization provides with respect to another, as well as to define their competitive advantage. (Harmon, 2003)

The main benefit of MkIS systems is to integrate market-monitoring systems with strategy development and the strategic implementation of policies and processes that help capture and act on customer management applications with marketing decision support systems. This area constitute Marketing intelligence that supports the analysis and market based activities that support customer relations and customer service with real time formation with real time applications that support market based approaches.

Relevance of MkIS

Shajahan and arya(2004) stated that, "Demands for the MkIS can be expressed by three crucial developments. Firstly, when companies expand and diversify into new markets, both the companies and customer's point of view are needed to be handled by the marketing managers. Therefore, there would be greater need for marketing information. Secondly, when consumers obtain an increment in the level of their income, it causes a tendency for them to be more discriminating during the purchasing procedure. A full awareness of the points that drive a consumer prefer a brand and the points that distinguished his

brand from that of the rivals should be obtained by the marketers. This awareness is possible only with the help of a well-designed effective MkIS. Thirdly, the development of the markets and the movement from price to non-price grounds of competition lead to an increase in the importance of adoption and implementation by the competitors and finding the response of the consumers towards them. Analyzing the needs for MkIS from a third person's angle, three more factors come to the forefront viz., the information explosion, increasing complexity in decision making and the technological developments.
" [5]

Marketing Research(MR)and MkIS

In addition, "Great demand of information gathering for marketing decisions results in the need of attention by themselves. Though marketing research information can be generated by studies, which are normally conducted in the market place whereas marketing information systems are designed to gather, integrate, process and distribute marketing information comprehensively from all sources, including that from marketing research. The contrasting characteristics of MkIS and MR are presented in Table 5.1 as shown below:

Table 5.1 Showing contrasting characteristic of MR and MkIS

Marketing Research	1.Emphasis is on handling external information

2.It is concerned with solving problems.

3.It operates in a fragmented fashion – on a project-to-project basis.

4.It tends to focus on past information.

5.It is a source of input for marketing information system.

4.It tends to be future oriented.

5.It includes other subsystems besides marketing research.

Marketing Information System

1.It handles both internal and external data.

2. It is concerned with preventing as well as solving problems.

3.It operates continuously as a system.

The business function of marketing is concerned more with the planning, promotion and sale of products in existing markets and the development of new products and new markets. Thus marketing performs a vital function in the operation of a business enterprise. Business firms who turned to computers have been able to perform vital marketing function effectively for organizations' growth in the face of global competition."[5]

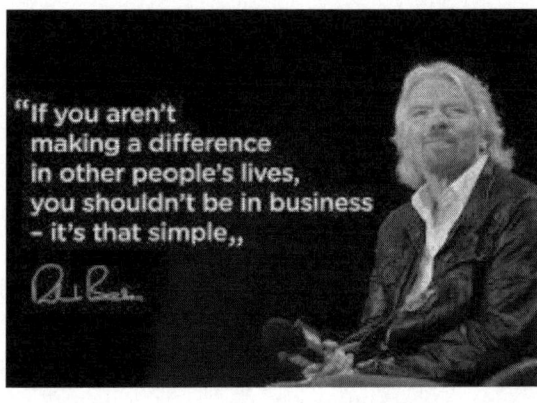

Main Structure

According to Robert Jamon (2003), MkIS systems are decomposed on four components: (1) user interfaces, (2) application software, (3) databases, and (4) system support. The following is a description of each one of these components.

1. User interfaces. The essential element of the MAkINAS is the managers who will use the system and the interface they need to effectively analyze and use marketing information. The design of the system will depend on what type of decision managers need to make.

2. Application software. These are the programs that marketing decision makers use to collect, analyze, and manage data for the purpose of developing the information necessary for marketing decisions.
3. Database marketing. A marketing database is a system in which marketing data files are organized and stored.

4. System support. This component consists of system managers who manage and maintain the system assets including software and hardware network, monitor its activities and ensure compliance with organizational policies.

Along with these components, MkIS systems include Marketing Decision Support Systems (MDSS), which in turn rely on simple systems such as Microsoft Excel, SPSS, and on-line analytical tools that help collect data. Data compiled for analysis is stored and processed from a data warehouse, which is simply a data repository system that helps store and further process data collected internally and externally. (Harmon, 2003)

Databases

From Pride and Ferrell (2010), "Internal database is a part of the most marketing information systems. In addition, it's relatively convenient for access and retrieve of information. A databases allow marketers to tap into an abundance of information useful in making marketing decisions: internal sales reports, newspaper articles, company news releases, government economic reports, bibliographies, and more, often accessed through a computer system."[6]

Internal Data

In with Birn (2004), " internal data is a part of the data that is needed to be collect and handled by the marketing information system.

Furthermore, managers regard this as a command to make effective operation. But getting the information that is really needed from a marketing information system depends on what the information is and how it is used. The following internal operating data are essential:

Sales data, presented in a graphic format, can provide regular sales trend information and highlight whether certain customer types need to be targeted or focused.

Price information by product line, compare with competitors, can monitor market trends; analyzed by customer type, it can check price trends in customer groups.

Stock level data and trends in key accounts or distributors, focusing on whether different outlets need support, provide market share information.

Market support information, coordinating the effects of marketing promotions, through advertising, direct marketing, trade incentives, consumer competitions and so on, helps to determine whether decisions are being made effectively.

Competitive information, reviewing competitors' promotions and communications to see if the company is doing it better or worse than competitors, can improve market targeting."[7]

Environmental scanning

Sandhusen (2000) defined that, environmental scanning is a display of the nature of MIS processed. "It gives assistance for the marketers to develop the strategies, policies, plans and to make programs and budgets through dealing with the ongoing information on trends."[8]

Kotler's Model

According to Philip Kotler, the four components that comprise the MkIS system are Internal Reports (Records) System, Marketing Research System, Marketing Intelligence System, and Marketing Decision Support System.

1.Internal Reports System: It records various data from different department of a company, which is regarded as a major source of information.

2.Marketing Intelligence System: It is a main source used by managers for gaining daily information of the external environment, hence assists the managers to react to the changing rapidly.

3.Marketing Research System: It is used to collect primary and secondary data, and displays the results in forms of reports.

4.Marketing Decision Support System: Compared to the supply of the data by the three previous systems, it focuses more on processing the data.[9]

Advantages , Limitations & Possible Risks[edit]

Advantages

Bhasin stated that,"With an increasingly competitive and expanding market, the amount of information needed daily by an organization is
profound. So they have to establish a Marketing Information system. There are several advantages of marketing information systems

Organized Data collection – MkIS can help the managers to organize loads of data collected from the market, thus results in an increment in the productivity.

A broad perspective – With a proper MkIS in place, the organization can be tracked which can be used to analyze independent processes. This helps in establishing a broader perspective which helps us know which steps can be taken to facilitate improvement.

Storage of Important Data – The storage of important data is essential in execution and thus proves again that MkIS is not important only for information but also for execution.

Avoidance of Crisis – The best way to analyze a stock (share market) is to see its past performance. Top websites like moneycontrol thrive on MIS. Similarly MIS helps you keep tracks of margins and profits. With an amazing information system established, an organizations direction can be analysed and probably crises averted before they place.

Co-ordination – Consumer durables and FMCG companies have huge number of processes which needs to be co-ordinate. These companies depend completely on MIS for the proper running of the organization.

Analysis and Planning – MkIS plays a crucial role in the planning process, considering the planning procedure requires information. For planning, the first thing which is needed is the organizations capabilities, then the business environment and finally competitor analysis. In a proper MkIS, all these are present by default and are continuously updated. Therefore, MkIS is very important for planning and analysis.

Control – Just like MkIS can help in a crisis, in normal times it provides control as you have information of the various processes going on and what is happening across the company."[10]

"You will not find it difficult to prove that battles, campaigns, and even wars have been won or lost primarily because of logistics."
~Dwight D. Eisenhower

Possible risks

"Nevertheless, the collection of marketing information should obey a high-frequent manner due to the rapid change in the external market." The possible risks the business may face if they disobey the manner

according to Bhasin are:[11]

Opportunities may be missed.

There may be a lack of awareness of environmental changes and competitors' actions.

Data collection may be difficult to analyze over several time periods.

Marketing plans and decisions may not be properly reviewed. Data collection may be disjointed.

Previous studies may not be stored in an easy to use format.

Time lags may result if a new study is required.

Actions may be reactionary rather than anticipatory.

Maintenance, complexity and setting up a MkIS are one of the major hindrances to Marketing information systems. Furthermore, wrong information being fed in MkIS can become cumbersome and appropriate filters need to be established. [10]

Limitations

Kotler and Philip have said that "both primary and secondary researches offer loads of the data and information needed for the marketers, whereas the secondary data sources are relatively superior in quick provision of data at lower cost. Simultaneously, a firm cannot find all the data required by itself, but sometimes can be done with the help of secondary research. However, researchers must assess those data collected from both primary and secondary data sources to enable the accuracy, updates and fairness. Each primary data collection method – observational, survey, and experimental – has its own advantages and disadvantages. Similarly, each of the various research contact methods – mail, telephone, personal interview, and online – also has its own advantages and drawbacks." [12]

Rural Marketing Information System (RuMIS)

A RuMIS is necessary not only for corporate organizations engaged in marketing of agricultural goods and manufactured goods intended for sales in rural areas. RuMIS is required also by the agriculturists and farmers who have enormous decis!ion-making to do. [13]

CHAPTER FIFTEEN

LESSONS FROM INFORMATION MILLIONAIRES

Walt Disney

Walter Elias Disney (/ˈdɪzni/;[1] December 5, 1901 – December 15, 1966) was an American entrepreneur, animator, voice actor and film producer. A pioneer of the American animation industry, he introduced several developments in the production of cartoons. As a film producer, Disney holds the record for most Academy Awardsearned by an individual, having

won 22 Oscars from 59 nominations.

He was presented with

two Golden GlobeSpecial Achievement Awards and an Emmy Award, among other honors. Several of his films are included in the National Film Registry by the Library of Congress.

Born in Chicago in 1901, Disney developed an early interest in drawing. He took art classes as a boy and got a job as a commercial illustrator at the age of 18. He moved to California in the early 1920s and set up the Disney Brothers Studio with his brother Roy. With Ub Iwerks, Walt developed the character Mickey Mouse in 1928, his first highly popular success; he also provided the voice for his creation in the early years. As the studio grew, Disney became more adventurous, introducing synchronized sound, full-color three-strip Technicolor, feature-length cartoons and technical developments in cameras. The results, seen in features such as *Snow White and the Seven Dwarfs* (1937), *Fantasia, Pinocchio* (both 1940), *Dumbo* (1941) and *Bambi* (1942), furthered the development of animated film. New animated and live-action films followed after World War II, including the critically successful *Cinderella* (1950) and *Mary Poppins* (1964), the latter of which received five Academy Awards.

In the 1950s, Disney expanded into the amusement park industry, and in 1955 he opened Disneyland. To fund the project he diversified into television programs, such as *Walt Disney's Disneyland* and *The Mickey Mouse Club; he* was also involved in planning the 1959 Moscow Fair, the 1960 Winter Olympics, and the 1964 New York World's Fair. In 1965, he began development of another theme park, Disney World, the heart of which was to be a new type of city, the "Experimental Prototype Community of Tomorrow" (EPCOT). Disney was a heavy smoker throughout his life, and died of lung cancer in December 1966 before either the park or the EPCOT project were completed.

Disney was a shy, self-deprecating and insecure man in private but adopted a warm and outgoing public persona. He had high standards and high expectations of those with whom he worked. Although there have been accusations that he was racist or anti-Semitic, they have been contradicted by many who knew him. His reputation changed in the years after his death, from a purveyor of homely patriotic values to a representative of American imperialism. He nevertheless remains an important figure in the history of animation and in the cultural history of the United States, where he is considered a national cultural icon. His film work continues to be shown and adapted; his studio maintains high standards in its production of popular entertainment, and the

Disney amusement parks have grown in size and number to attract visitors in several countries.

Walt Disney **Biography**

Early life: 1901–1920

was born on December 5, 1901, at 1249 Tripp Avenue, in Chicago's Hermosa neighborhood.[a] He was the fourth son of Elias Disney—born in the Province of Canada, to Irish parents— and Flora (née Call), an American of German and English descent.[3][4][b] Aside from Disney, Elias and Call's sons were Herbert, Raymond and Roy; the couple had a fifth child, Ruth, in December 1903.[7] In 1906, when Disney was four, the family moved to a farm in Marceline, Missouri, where his uncle Robert had just purchased land. In Marceline, Disney developed his interest in drawing when he was paid to draw the horse of a retired neighborhood doctor.[8] Elias was a subscriber to the *Appeal to Reason* newspaper, and Disney practiced drawing by copying the front-page cartoons of Ryan Walker.[9] Disney also began to develop an ability to work with watercolors and crayons.[4] He lived near the Atchison, Topeka and Santa Fe Railway line and became enamored with trains.[10] He and his younger sister Ruth started school at the same time at the Park School in Marceline in late 1909.[11]

In 1911, the Disneys moved to Kansas City, Missouri.[12]

There, Disney attended the Benton Grammar School, where he met fellow-student Walter Pfeiffer, who came from a family of theatre fans and introduced Disney to the world of vaudeville and motion pictures. Before long, he was spending more time at the Pfeiffers' house than at home.[13] Elias had purchased a newspaper delivery route for *The*

Kansas City Star and *Kansas City Times*. Disney and his brother Roy woke up at 4:30 every morning to deliver the *Times* before school and repeated the round for the evening *Star* after school. The schedule was exhausting, and Disney often received poor grades after falling asleep in class, but he continued his paper route for more than six years.[14] He attended Saturday courses at the Kansas City Art Institute and also took a correspondence course in cartooning.[4][15]

In 1917, Elias bought stock in a Chicago jelly producer, the O-Zell Company, and moved back to the city with his family.[16] Disney enrolled at McKinley High School and became the cartoonist of the school newspaper, drawing patriotic pictures about World War I;[17][18] he also took night courses at the Chicago Academy of Fine Arts.[19] In mid-1918, Disney attempted to join the United States Army to fight against the Germans, but he was rejected for being too young. After forging the date of birth on his birth certificate, he joined the Red Cross in September 1918 as an ambulance driver. He was shipped to France but arrived in November, after the armistice.[20] He drew cartoons on the side of his ambulance for decoration and had some of his work published in the army newspaper *Stars and*

Stripes.[21] Disney returned to Kansas City in October 1919,[22] where he worked as an apprentice artist at the Pesmen-Rubin Commercial Art Studio. There, he drew commercial illustrations for advertising,

theater programs and catalogs. He also befriended fellow artist Ub Iwerks.[23]

Early career: 1920–1928
Walt Disney's business envelope featured a self-portrait c. 1921

In January 1920, as Pesmen-Rubin's revenue declined after Christmas, Disney and Iwerks were laid off. They started their own business, the short-lived

Iwerks-Disney Commercial Artists.[24] Failing to attract many customers, Disney and Iwerks agreed that Disney should leave temporarily to earn money at the Kansas City Film Ad Company, run by A. V. Cauger; the following month Iwerks, who was not able to run their business alone, also joined.[25] The company produced commercials using the cutout animation technique.[26] Disney became interested in animation, although he preferred drawn cartoons such as *Mutt and Jeff* and *Koko the Clown*. With the assistance of a borrowed book on animation and a camera, he began experimenting at home.[27][c] He came to the conclusion that cel animation was more promising than the cutout method.[d] Unable to persuade Cauger to try cel animation at the company, Disney opened a new business with a co-worker from the Film Ad Co, Fred Harman.[29] Their main client was the local Newman Theater, and the short cartoons they produced were sold as "Newman's Laugh-O-Grams".[30] Disney studied Paul Terry's *Aesop's Fables* as a model, and the first six "Laugh-O-Grams" were modernized fairy tales.[31]

Newman Laugh-O-Gram (1921)

In May 1921, the success of the "Laugh-O-Grams" led to the establishment of Laugh-O-Gram Studio, for which he hired more
animators, including Fred Harman's brother Hugh, Rudolf Ising and
Iwerks.[32] The Laugh-O-Grams cartoons did not provide enough income to keep the company solvent, so Disney started production
of *Alice's Wonderland*–based on *Alice's Adventures in Wonderland*–
which combined live action with animation; he cast Virginia Davis in the title role.[33]The result, a 12-and-a-half-minute, one-reel film, was completed too late to save Laugh-O-Gram Studio, which went into bankruptcy in 1923.[34]

Disney moved to Hollywood in July 1923. Although New York was the center of the cartoon industry, he was attracted

to Los Angeles because his brother Roy was convalescing from tuberculosis there.[35] Disney's efforts to sell *Alice's Wonderland* were in vain until he heard from New York film distributor Margaret J. Winkler. She was losing the rights to both the *Out of the Inkwell* and *Felix the Cat* cartoons, and needed a new series. In October they signed a contract for six *Alice* comedies, with an option for two further series of six episodes each.[36] Disney and his brother Roy formed the Disney Brothers Studio—which later became The Walt Disney Company—to produce the films;[37][38] they persuaded Davis and her family to relocate to Hollywood to continue production, with Davis on contract at $100 a month. In July 1924

Disney also hired Iwerks, persuading him to relocate to Hollywood from Kansas City.[39]

Early in 1925, Disney hired an ink artist, Lillian Bounds. They married in July of that year, at her brother's house in her hometown of Lewiston, Idaho.[40] The marriage was generally happy, according to Lillian, although according to Disney's biographer Neal Gabler she did

not "accept Walt's decisions meekly or his status unquestionably, and she admitted that he was always telling people 'how henpecked he is'."[41][e] Lillian had little interest in films or the Hollywood social scene and she was, in the words of the historian Steven Watts, "content with household management and providing support for her husband".[42] Their marriage produced two daughters, Diane (born

December 1933) and Sharon (adopted in December 1936, born six

weeks previously).[43][f] Within the family, neither Disney nor his wife

hid the fact Sharon had been adopted, although they became annoyed if people outside the family raised the point.[44] The Disneys were careful to keep their daughters out of the public eye as much as possible, particularly in the light of the Lindbergh kidnapping; Disney

took steps to ensure his daughters were not photographed by the press.[45]

Theatrical poster for *Trolley Troubles* (1927)

By 1926 Winkler's role in the distribution of the *Alice* series had been handed over to her husband, the film producer Charles Mintz, although the relationship between him and Disney was sometimes strained.[46] The series ran until July 1927,[47] by which time Disney had begun to tire of it and wanted to move away from the mixed format to all animation.[46][48] After Mintz requested new material to distribute through Universal Pictures, Disney and Iwerks created Oswald the Lucky Rabbit, a character Disney wanted to be "peppy, alert, saucy and venturesome, keeping him also neat and trim".[48][49]

In February 1928, Disney hoped to negotiate a larger fee for producing the *Oswald* series, but found Mintz wanting to reduce the payments. Mintz had also persuaded many of the artists involved to work directly for him, including Harman, Ising, Carman Maxwell and Friz Freleng. Disney also found out that Universal owned the intellectual property rights to Oswald. Mintz threatened to start his own studio and produce the series himself if Disney refused to accept the reductions. Disney declined Mintz's ultimatum and lost most of his animation staff, except Iwerks, who chose to remain with him.[50][51][g]

Creation of Mickey Mouse to the first Academy Awards: 1928–1933

To replace Oswald, Disney and Iwerks developed Mickey Mouse, possibly inspired by a pet mouse that Disney had adopted while working in his Laugh-O-Gram studio, although the origins of the character are unclear.[53][h] Disney's original choice of name was Mortimer Mouse, but Lillian thought it too pompous, and suggested Mickey instead.[54][i] Iwerks revised Disney's provisional sketches to make the character easier to animate, and Disney provided Mickey's voice until 1947. In the words of one Disney employee, "Ub designed Mickey's physical appearance, but Walt gave him his soul."[56]

The first appearance of Mickey Mouse, in *Steamboat Willie* (1928)

Mickey Mouse first appeared in May 1928 as a single test screening of the short *Plane Crazy*, but it, and the second feature, *The Gallopin' Gaucho*, *failed* to find a distributor.[57] Following the 1927 sensation *The Jazz Singer*, Disney used synchronized sound on the third short, *Steamboat Willie*, to create the first post-produced sound cartoon. After the animation was complete, Disney signed a contract with the former executive of Universal Pictures, Pat Powers, to use the "Powers Cinephone" recording system;[58] Cinephone became the new distributor for Disney's early sound cartoons, which soon became popular.[59]

To improve the quality of the music, Disney hired the professional composer and arranger Carl Stalling, on whose suggestion the *Silly Symphony* series was developed, providing stories through the use of music; the first in the series, *The Skeleton Dance*(1929), was drawn and animated entirely by Iwerks. Also hired at this time were several local artists, some of whom stayed with the company as core animators; the group later became known as the Nine Old

Men.[60][j] Both the Mickey Mouse and *Silly Symphonies* series were successful, but Disney and his brother felt they were not receiving their rightful share of profits from Powers. In 1930, Disney tried to trim costs from the process by urging Iwerks to abandon the practice of animating every separate cel in favor of the more efficient technique of drawing key poses and letting lower-paid assistants sketch the in-between poses. Disney asked Powers for an increase in payments for the cartoons. Powers refused and signed Iwerks to work for him; Stalling resigned shortly afterwards, thinking that without Iwerks, the Disney Studio would close.[61]Disney had a nervous breakdown in October 1931—which he blamed on the machinations of Powers and his own overwork—so he and Lillian took an extended holiday to Cuba and a cruise to Panama to recover.[62]

Disney in 1935

With the loss of Powers as distributor, Disney studios signed a contract with Columbia Pictures to distribute the Mickey Mouse cartoons, which became increasingly popular, including internationally.[63][64][k] Disney, always keen to embrace new technology, filmed *Flowers and Trees* (1932) in full-color three-strip Technicolor;[65] he was also able to negotiate a deal giving him the sole right to use the three-strip process until August 31, 1935.[66] All subsequent *Silly Symphony* cartoons were in color.[67] *Flowers and Trees* was popular with audiences [65] and won the Academy Award for best Short Subject (Cartoon) at the 1932 ceremony. Disney had been nominated for another film in that category, *Mickey's Orphans*, and received an Honorary Award "for the creation of Mickey Mouse".[68][69]

In 1933, Disney produced *The Three Little Pigs*, a film described by the media historian Adrian Danks as "the most successful short animation of all time".[70] The film won Disney another Academy Award in the Short Subject (Cartoon) category. The film's success led to a further increase in the studio's staff, which numbered nearly 200 by the end of the year.[71] Disney realized the importance of telling emotionally gripping stories that would interest the audience,[72] and he invested in a "story department" separate from the animators, with storyboard artists who would detail the plots of Disney's films.[73]

Golden age of animation: 1934–1941

Walt Disney introduces each of the seven dwarfs in a scene from the original 1937 *Snow White* theatrical trailer.

By 1934, Disney had become dissatisfied with producing formulaic cartoon shorts,[74] and began a four-year production of a feature-length

cartoon, *Snow White and the Seven Dwarfs, based* on the fairy tale. When news leaked out about the project, many in the film industry predicted it would bankrupt the company; industry insiders nicknamed it "Disney's Folly".[75] The film, which was the first animated feature made in full color and sound, cost $1.5 million to produce—three times over budget.[76] To ensure the animation was as realistic as possible, Disney sent his animators on courses at the Chouinard Art Institute;[77] he brought animals into the studio and hired actors so that the animators could study realistic movement.[78] To portray the changing perspective of the background as a camera moved through a scene, Disney's animators developed a multiplane camera which allowed drawings on pieces of glass to be set at various distances from the camera, creating an illusion of depth. The glass could be moved to create the impression of a camera passing through the scene. The first work created on the camera—a *Silly Symphony* called *The Old Mill* (1937)—won the Academy Award for Animated Short Film because of its impressive visual power. Although *Snow White* had been largely finished by the time the multiplane camera had been completed, Disney ordered some scenes be re-drawn to use the new effects.[79]

Snow White premiered in December 1937 to high praise from critics and audiences. The film became the most successful motion picture of 1938 and by May 1939 its total gross of $6.5 million made it the most successful sound film made to that date.[75][l] Disney won another Honorary Academy Award, which consisted of one full-sized and seven miniature Oscar statuettes.[81][m] The success of *Snow White* heralded one of the most productive eras for the studio; the Walt Disney Family Museum calls the following years "the 'Golden Age of Animation' ".[82][83] With work on *Snow White* finished, the studio began producing *Pinocchio* in early 1938 and *Fantasia* in November of the same year. Both films were released in 1940, and neither performed well at the box office—partly because revenues from Europe had dropped following the start of World War II in 1939. The studio made a loss on both pictures and was deeply in debt by the end of February 1941.[84]

In response to the financial crisis, Disney and his brother Roy started the company's first public stock offering in 1940, and implemented heavy salary cuts. The latter measure, and Disney's sometimes high-handed and insensitive manner of dealing with staff, led to a 1941 animators' strike which lasted five weeks.[85]While a federal mediator from the National Labor Relations Board negotiated with the two sides, Disney accepted an offer from the Office of the Coordinator of Inter-American Affairs to make a goodwill trip to South America, ensuring he was absent during a resolution he knew would be unfavorable to the studio.[86][n] As a result of the strike—and the financial state of the company—several animators left the studio, and Disney's relationship with other members of staff was permanently strained as a result.[89] The strike temporarily interrupted the studio's next production, *Dumbo* (1941), which Disney produced in a simple and inexpensive manner; the film received a positive reaction from audiences and critics alike.[90]

World War II and beyond: 1941–1950

Disney drawing Goofy for a group of girls in Argentina, 1941

Shortly after the release of *Dumbo* in October 1941, the U.S. entered World War II. Disney formed the Walt Disney Training Films Unit within the company to produce instruction films for the military such as *Four Methods of Flush Riveting* and *Aircraft Production Methods.*[91] Disney also met with Henry Morgenthau, Jr., the Secretary of the Treasury, and agreed to produce short Donald Duck cartoons to promote war bonds.[92] Disney also produced several propaganda productions, including shorts such as *Der Fuehrer's Face*—which won an Academy Award—and the 1943 feature film *Victory Through Air Power.*[93] The military films generated only enough revenue to cover costs, and the feature film *Bambi*—which had been in production since 1937— underperformed on its release in April 1942, and lost $200,000 at the box office.[94] On top of the low earnings from *Pinocchio* and *Fantasia*, the company had debts of $4 million with the Bank of America in 1944.[95][o] At a meeting with Bank of America executives to discuss the future of the company, the bank's chairman and founder, Amadeo Giannini, told his executives, "I've been watching the Disneys' pictures quite closely because I knew we were lending them money far above the financial risk. ... They're good this year, they're good next year, and they're good the year after. ... You have to relax and give them time to market their product."[96] Disney's production of short films decreased in the late 1940s, coinciding with increasing competition in the animation market from Warner Bros. and Metro-Goldwyn-Mayer. Roy Disney, for financial reasons, suggested more combined animation and live-action productions.[58][p] In 1948, Disney initiated a series of popular live-action nature films, titled

True-Life Adventures, with *Seal Island* the first; the film won the Academy Award in the Best Short Subject (Two-Reel) category.[97]

Disney grew more politically conservative as he got older. A Democratic Party supporter until the 1940 presidential election, when he switched allegiance to the Republicans,[98] he became a generous donor to Thomas E. Dewey's 1944 bid for the presidency.[99] In 1946 he was a founding member of the Motion Picture Alliance for the Preservation of American Ideals, an organization who stated they "believ[ed] in, and like, the American Way of Life ... we find ourselves in sharp revolt against a rising tide of Communism, Fascism and kindred beliefs, that seek by subversive means to undermine and change this way of life".[100] In 1947, during the Second Red Scare, Disney testified before the House Un-American Activities Committee (HUAC), where he branded Herbert Sorrell, David Hilbermanand William Pomerance, former animators and labor union organizers, as communist agitators; Disney stated that the 1941 strike led by them was part of an organized communist

effort to gain influence in Hollywood.[101][102]

Disney family at Schiphol Airport (1951)

In 1949, Disney and his family moved to a new

home in the Holmby Hills district of Los Angeles. With the help of his friends Ward and Betty Kimball, who already had their

own backyard railroad, Disney developed blueprints and immediately set to work on creating a miniature live steam railroad for his backyard. The name of the railroad, Carolwood Pacific Railroad, came from his home's location on Carolwood Drive. The miniature working steam locomotive was built by Disney Studios engineer Roger E. Broggie, and Disney named it *Lilly Belle* after his wife;[103] after three years Disney ordered it into storage due to a series of accidents involving his guests.[104]

Theme parks, television and other interests: 1950–1966

In early 1950, Disney produced *Cinderella*, his studio's first animated feature in eight years. It was popular with critics and theater audiences. Costing $2.2 million to produce, it earned nearly $8 million in its first year.[105][q] Disney was less involved than he had been with previous pictures because of his involvement in his first entirely live-action feature, *Treasure Island* (1950), which was shot in Britain, as was *The Story of Robin Hood and His Merrie Men* (1952).[106] Other all-live-action features followed, many of which had patriotic themes.[58][r] He continued to produce full-length animated features too, including *Alice in Wonderland* (1951) and *Peter Pan* (1953). From the early to mid-1950s, Disney began to devote less

attention to the animation department, entrusting most of its operations to his key animators, the Nine Old Men, although he was always present at story meetings. Instead, he started concentrating on other ventures.[107] Disney shows the plans of Disneyland to officials from Orange County in December 1954 For several years Disney had been considering building a theme park. When he visited Griffith Park in Los Angeles with his daughters, he wanted to be in a clean, unspoiled park, where both children and their parents could have fun.[108] He visited the Tivoli Gardens in Copenhagen, Denmark, and was heavily influenced by the cleanliness and layout of the park.[109]

In March 1952 he received doning permission to build a theme park in Burbank, near the Disney studios.[110]This site proved too small, and a larger plot in Anaheim, 35 miles (56 km) south of the studio, was purchased. To distance the project from the studio—which might attract the criticism of shareholders—Disney formed WED Enterprises (now Walt Disney Imagineering) and used his own money to fund a group of designers and animators to work on the plans;[111][112] those involved became known as "Imagineers".[113] After obtaining bank funding he invited other stockholders, American Broadcasting-Paramount Theatres—part of American Broadcasting Company (ABC)—and Western Printing and Lithographing Company.[58] In mid-1954, Disney sent his Imagineers to every amusement park in the U.S. to analyze what worked and what pitfalls or problems there were in the various locations and incorporated their findings into his design.[114] Construction work started in July 1954, and Disneyland opened in July 1955; the opening ceremony was broadcast on ABC, which reached 70 million viewers.[115] The park was designed as a series of themed lands, linked by the central Main Street, U.S.A.—a replica of the main street in his hometown of Marceline. The connected themed areas were Adventure land, Frontier land, Fantasyland and Tomorrowland. The park also contained the narrow gauge Disneyland Railroad that linked the lands; around the outside of the park was a high berm to separate the park from the outside world.[116][117] An editorial in *The New York Times* considered that Disney had "tastefully combined some of the pleasant things of yesterday with fantasy and dreams of tomorrow".[118] Although there were early minor problems with the park, it was a success, and after a month's operation, Disneyland was receiving over 20,000 visitors a day; by the end of its first year, it attracted 3.6 million guests.[119]

The money from ABC was contingent on Disney television programs.[120] The studio had been involved in a successful television special on Christmas Day 1950 about the making of *Alice in Wonderland*. Roy believed the program added millions to the box

First, **think**. Second, **dream**.
Third, **believe**. And finally, **dare**.

- Walt Disney

office takings. In a March 1951 letter to shareholders, he wrote that "television can be a most powerful selling aid for us, as well as a source of revenue. It will probably be on this premise that we enter television when we do".[58] In 1954, after the Disneyland funding had been agreed, ABC broadcast *Walt Disney's Disneyland*, an anthology consisting of animated cartoons, live-action features and other material from the studio's library. The show was successful in terms of ratings and profits, earning an audience share of over 50%.[121][s] In April 1955, *Newsweek* called the series an "American institution".[122] ABC was pleased with the ratings, leading to Disney's first daily television program, *The Mickey Mouse Club*, a variety show catering specifically to children.[123] The program was accompanied by merchandising through various companies (Western Printing, for example, had been producing coloring books and comics for over 20 years, and produced several items connected to the show).[124] One of the segments of *Disneyland* consisted of the five-part miniseries *Davy Crockett* which, according to Gabler, "became an overnight sensation".[125] The show's theme song, "The Ballad of Davy Crockett", became internationally popular, and ten million records were sold.[126] As a result, Disney formed his own record production and distribution entity, Disneyland Records.[127]

As well as the construction of Disneyland, Disney worked on other projects away from the studio. He was consultant to the 1959 American National Exhibition in Moscow; Disney Studios' contribution

was *America the Beautiful*, a 19-minute film in the 360-degree Circarama theater that was one of the most popular attractions.[58] The following year he acted as the chairman of the Pageantry Committee for the 1960 Winter Olympics at Squaw Valley, California, where he designed the opening, closing and medal ceremonies.[128]

Disney in 1954

Despite the demands wrought by non-studio projects, Disney continued to work on film and television projects. In 1955 he was involved in "Man in Space", an episode of the *Disneyland* series, which was made in collaboration with NASA rocket designer Wernher von Braun.[t] Disney also oversaw aspects of the full-length features *Lady and the Tramp* (the first animated film in CinemaScope) in 1955, *Sleeping Beauty* (the first animated film in Technirama 70 mm film) in 1959, *One Hundred and One Dalmatians* (the first animated feature film to use Xerox cels) in 1961 and *The Sword in the Stone* in 1963.[130]

In 1964, Disney produced *Mary Poppins*, based on the book series by P. L. Travers; he had been trying to acquire the rights to the story since the 1940s.[131] It became the most successful Disney film of the 1960s, although Travers disliked the film intensely and regretted having sold the rights.[132] The same year he also became involved in plans to expand the California Institute of the Arts (colloquially called CalArts), and had an architect draw up blueprints for a new building.[133]

Disney provided four exhibits for the 1964 New York World's Fair, for which he obtained funding from selected corporate sponsors.

For PepsiCo, who planned a tribute to UNICEF, Disney developed It's a Small World, a boat ride with audio-animatronic dolls depicting children of the world; Great Moments with Mr. Lincoln contained an animatronic Abraham Lincolngiving excerpts from his speeches; Carousel of Progress promoted the importance of electricity; and Ford's Magic Skyway portrayed the progress of mankind. Elements of all four exhibits—principally concepts and technology— were re-installed in Disneyland, although It's a Small World is the ride that most closely resembles the original.[134][135]

During the early to mid-1960s, Disney developed plans for a ski resort in Mineral King, a glacial valley in California's Sierra Nevada. He hired experts such as the renowned Olympic ski coach and ski-area designer Willy Schaeffler.[136][137][u] With income from Disneyland accounting for an increasing proportion of the studio's income, Disney continued to look for venues for other attractions. In late 1965, he announced plans to develop another theme park to be called "Disney World" (now Walt Disney World), a few miles southwest of Orlando, Florida. Disney World was to include the "Magic Kingdom"—a larger and more elaborate version of Disneyland—plus golf courses and resort hotels. The heart of Disney World was to be the "Experimental Prototype

Community of Tomorrow" (EPCOT),[139] which he described as: an experimental prototype community of tomorrow that will take its cue from the new ideas and new technologies that are now emerging from the creative centers of American industry. It will be a community of tomorrow that will never be completed, but will always be introducing and testing and demonstrating new materials and systems. And EPCOT will always be a showcase to the world for the ingenuity and imagination of American free enterprise.[140] During 1966, Disney cultivated businesses willing to sponsor EPCOT.[141]

He increased his involvement in the studio's films, and was heavily involved in the story development of *The Jungle Book*, the live-action musical feature *The Happiest Millionaire* (both 1967) and the animated short *Winnie the Pooh and the Blustery Day*.[142]

Illness, death and aftermath

Grave of Walt Disney at Forest Lawn, Glendale

Disney had been a heavy smoker since World War I. He did not use cigarettes with filters, and had smoked a pipe as a young man. In November 1966, he was
diagnosed with lung cancer and was treated with cobalt
therapy. On November 30 he felt unwell and was taken to St. Joseph
Hospital where, on December 15, ten days after his 65th birthday, he died of circulatory collapsecaused by lung cancer.[143] Disney's

remains were cremated two days later, and his ashes interred at the Forest Lawn Memorial Park in Glendale, California.[144][v]

His estate included a 14 percent holding in Walt Disney Productions worth $20 million.[w][x] He left 45 percent of his estate to his wife and children—much in a family trust—and 10 percent to his sister, nieces and nephews.[147] The remaining 45 percent went into a charitable trust, 95 percent of which was designated for CalArts, to build a new campus (a figure of around $15 million); he also donated 38 acres (0.154 km^2) of the Golden Oaks ranch in Valencia for construction of that school. The university moved there in November 1971.[148]

The release of *The Jungle Book* and *The Happiest Millionaire* in 1967 raised the total number of feature films that Disney had been involved in to 81.[17] When *Winnie the Pooh and the Blustery Day* was released in 1968, it earned Disney an Academy Award in the Short Subject (Cartoon) category, awarded posthumously.[149] After Disney's death, his studios continued to produce live-action films prolifically but largely abandoned animation until the late 1980s, after which there was what *The New York Times* describes as the "Disney Renaissance" that began with *The Little Mermaid* (1989).[150] Disney's companies continue to produce successful film, television and stage entertainment.[151]

Roy O. Disney finished the building of Disney World

Disney's plans for the futuristic city of EPCOT did not come to fruition. After Disney's death, his brother Roy deferred his retirement to take full control of the Disney companies. He changed the focus of the project from a town to an attraction.[152] At the inauguration in 1971, Roy dedicated Walt Disney World to his brother.[153][y] Walt Disney World expanded with the opening of Epcot Center in 1982; Walt Disney's vision of a functional city was replaced by a park more akin to a permanent world's fair.[155] In 2009, the Walt Disney Family Museum, designed by Disney's daughter Diane and her son Walter E. D. Miller, opened in the Presidio of San Francisco.[156] Thousands of artifacts from Disney's life and career are on display, including numerous awards that he received.[157] In 2014, the Disney theme parks around the world hosted approximately 134 million visitors.[158]

Disney has been portrayed numerous times in fictional works. H. G. Wells references Disney in his 1938 novel *The Holy Terror*, in which World Dictator Rud fears that Donald Duck is meant to lampoon the dictator.[159] Disney was portrayed by Len Cariou in the 1995 made-for-TV film *A Dream Is a Wish Your Heart Makes: The Annette Funicello Story*,[160] and by Tom Hanks in the 2013 film Saving Mr. Banks.[161] In 2001, the German author Peter Stephan Jungk published *Der König von Amerika* (trans: *The King of America*), a fictional work of Disney's later years that re-imagines him as a power-hungry racist. The composer Philip Glasslater adapted the book into the opera *The Perfect American* (2013).[162]

Honors

Display case in the lobby of The Walt Disney Family Museum showing many of the Academy Awards won by Disney

Disney received 59 Academy Award nominations, including 22 awards: both totals are records.[163] He was nominated for three Golden Globe Awards, but did not win, but he was presented with two Special Achievement Awards—for *Bambi* (1942) and *The Living Desert* (1953)—and the Cecil

B. DeMille Award.[164] He also received four Emmy Award nominations, winning once, for Best Producer for

the *Disneyland* television series.[165] Several of his films are included in the United States National Film Registry by the Library of Congress as "culturally, historically, or aesthetically significant": *Steamboat Willie*, *The Three Little Pigs*, *Snow White and the Seven Dwarfs*, *Fantasia*, *Pinocchio*, *Bambi* and *Mary Poppins*.[166] In 1998, the American Film Institutepublished a list of the 100 greatest American films, according to industry experts; the list included *Snow White and the Seven Dwarfs* (at number 49), and *Fantasia* (at 58).[167]

In February 1960, Disney was inducted to the Hollywood Walk of Fame with two stars, one for motion pictures and the other for his television work;[168] Mickey Mouse was given his own star for motion pictures in 1978.[169] Disney was also inducted into the Television Hall of Fame in 1986,[170] the California Hall of Fame in December 2006,[171] and was the inaugural recipient of a star on the Anaheim walk of stars in 2014.[172] The Walt Disney Family Museum records that he "along with members of his staff, received more than 950 honors and citations from throughout the world".[17] He was made a *Chevalier* in the French *Légion d'honneur* in 1935,[173] and in 1952 he was awarded the country's highest artistic decoration, the *Officer d'Academie*.[174]

Other national awards include Thailand's Order of the Crown; Brazil's Order of the Southern Cross and Mexico's Order of the Aztec Eagle.[175] Inthe United States, he received the Presidential Medal of Freedom on

September 14, 1964[176] and, in 1969, he was posthumously awarded the Congressional Gold Medal.[177] He received the Showman of the

World Award from the National Association of Theatre Owners,[175] and, in 1955, the National Audubon Society awarded

Disney its highest honor, the Audubon Medal, for promoting the

"appreciation and understanding of nature" through his *True-Life Adventures* nature films.[178] A minor planet *discovered* in 1980 by astronomer Lyudmila Karachkina, was named 4017 Disneya,[179] and he was also awarded honorary degrees from Harvard, Yale, the University of Southern California and the University of California, Los Angeles.[17]

Personality and reputation\

1968 U.S. postage stamp

Disney's public persona was very different from his actual

personality.[180] Playwright Robert E. Sherwood described him as "almost painfully shy ... diffident" and self-deprecating.[181] According to his biographer Richard Schickel, Disney hid his shy and insecure personality behind his public identity.[182] Kimball argues that Disney "played the role of a bashful tycoon who was embarrassed in public" and knew that he was doing so.[183] Disney acknowledged the façade, and told a friend that "I'm not Walt Disney. I do a lot of things Walt Disney would not do. Walt Disney does not smoke. I smoke. Walt Disney does not drink. I drink."[184] Critic Otis Ferguson, in *The New Republic*, called the private Disney: "common and everyday, not inaccessible, not in a foreign language, not suppressed or sponsored or anything. Just Disney."[183]

Many of those with whom Disney worked commented that he gave his staff little encouragement due to his exceptionally high expectations. Norman recalls that when Disney said "That'll work", it was an indication of high praise.[185] Instead of direct approval, Disney gave high-performing staff financial bonuses, or recommended certain individuals to others, expecting that his praise would be passed on.[186]

Views of Disney and his work have changed over the decades, and there have been polarized opinions.[187] Mark Langer, in the *American Dictionary of National Biography*, writes that "Earlier evaluations of Disney hailed him as a patriot, folk artist, and popularizer of culture. More recently, Disney has been regarded as a paradigm of American imperialism and intolerance, as well as a debaser of culture."[58] Steven Watts wrote that some denounce Disney "as a cynical manipulator of cultural and commercial formulas",[187] while PBS records that critics have censured his work because of its "smooth façade of sentimentality and stubborn optimism, its feel-good re-write of American history".[188] Although Disney's films have been highly praised, very popular and commercially successful over time,[58][189] there were criticisms by reviewers. Caroline Lejeune comments in *The Observer* that *Snow White* (1937) "has more faults than any earlier Disney cartoon. It is vulnerable again and again to the barbed criticisms of the experts. Sometimes it is, frankly, badly drawn."[190]

Robin Allen, writing for *The Times*, notes that *Fantasia* (1940) was "condemned for its vulgarity and lurches into bathos",[191] while Lejeune, reviewing *Alice in Wonderland* (1951), feels the film "may drive lovers of Lewis Carroll to frenzy".[192] *Peter Pan* (1953) was criticized in *The Times* as "a children's classic vulgarized" with "Tinker Bell ... a peroxided American cutie".

The reviewer opined that Disney "has slaughtered good Barrie and has only second-rate Disney to put in its place".[193]

Disney has been accused of anti-semitism,[194][z] although none of his employees—including the animator Art Babbitt, who disliked Disney intensely—ever accused him of making anti-semitic slurs or taunts.[196] The Walt Disney Family Museum acknowledges that ethnic stereotypes common to films of the 1930s were included in some early cartoons.[aa] Disney donated regularly to Jewish charities, he was named "1955 Man of the Year" by the B'nai B'rith chapter in Beverly Hills,[197][198] and his studio employed a number of Jews, some of whom were in influential positions.[199][ab] Gabler, the first writer to gain unrestricted access to the Disney archives, concludes that the available evidence does not support accusations of anti-semitism and that Disney was "not [anti-semitic] in the conventional sense that we think of someone as being an anti-Semite". Gabler concludes that "though Walt himself, in my estimation, was not anti-Semitic, nevertheless, he willingly allied himself with people who were anti-Semitic [meaning some members of the MPAPAI], and that reputation stuck. He was never really able to expunge it throughout his life".[200] Disney distanced himself from the Motion Picture Alliance in the 1950s.[201]

Disney has also been accused of racism because some of his productions released between the 1930s and 1950s contain racially insensitive materials.[202][ac] The feature film *Song of the South* was criticized by contemporary film critics, the National Association for the Advancement of Colored People, and others for its perpetuation of black stereotypes,[203] but Disney later campaigned successfully for an Honorary Academy Award for its star, James Baskett, the first black actor so honored.[204][ad] Gabler argues that "Walt Disney was no racist. He never, either publicly or privately, made disparaging remarks about blacks or asserted white superiority. Like most white Americans of his generation, however, he was racially insensitive."[202] Floyd Norman, the studio's first black animator who worked closely with Disney during the 1950s and 1960s, said, "Not once did I observe a hint of the racist behavior Walt Disney was often accused of after his death. His treatment of people—and by this I mean all people—can only be called exemplary."[205]

Watts argues that many of Disney's post World War II films "legislated a kind of cultural Marshall Plan. They nourished a genial cultural imperialism that magically overran the rest of the globe with the values, expectations, and goods of a prosperous middle-class United States."[206] Film historian Jay P. Telotte acknowledges that many see Disney's studio as an "agent of manipulation and repression", although he observes that it has "labored throughout its history to link its name with notions of fun, family, and fantasy".[207] John Tomlinson, in his study *Cultural Imperialism*, examines the work of Ariel Dorfman and Armand Mattelart, whose 1971 book *Para leer al Pato Donald* (trans: *How to Read Donald Duck*) *identifies* that there are "imperialist ... values 'concealed' behind the innocent, wholesome façade of the world of Walt Disney"; this, they argue, is a powerful tool as "it presents itself as harmless fun for consumption by children."[208] Tomlinson views their argument as flawed, as "they simply *assume* that reading American comics, seeing adverts, watching pictures of the affluent ... ['Yankee'] lifestyle has a direct pedagogic effect".[209]

Several commentators have described Disney as a cultural icon.[210] On his death, journalism professor Ralph S. Izard comments that the values in Disney's films are those "considered valuable in American Christian society", which include "individualism, decency, ... love for our fellow man, fair play and toleration".[211]Disney's obituary in *The Times* calls the films "wholesome, warm-hearted and entertaining ... of incomparable artistry and of touching beauty".[212] Journalist Bosley Crowther argues that Disney's "achievement as a creator of entertainment for an almost unlimited public and as a highly ingenious merchandiser of his wares can rightly be compared to the most successful industrialists in history."[4] Correspondent Alistair Cooke calls Disney a "folk-hero ... the Pied Piper of Hollywood",[213] while Gabler considers Disney "reshaped the culture and the American consciousness".[189] In the *American Dictionary of National Biography*, Langer writes:

Disney remains the central figure in the history of animation. Through technological innovations and alliances with governments and corporations, he transformed a minor studio in a marginal form of communication into a multinational leisure industry giant. Despite his critics, his vision of a modern, corporate utopia as an extension of traditional American values has possibly gained greater currency in the years after his death.[58]

David Ogilvy (businessman)

David Mackenzie Ogilvy CBE (/ˈoʊɡəlviː/; 23 June 1911 – 21 July 1999) was an advertising tycoon, founder of Ogilvy & Mather, and known as the father of advertising[1][2]. Trained at the Gallup research organisation, he attributed the success of his campaigns to meticulous research into consumer habits.

Early life (1911–1938)[edit] David Mackenzie Ogilvy was born on 23 June 1911 at West Horsley, Surrey in England. His mother was Dorothy Blew Fairfield (1881-1942), daughter of Arthur Rowan Fairfield, a civil servant from Ireland. His father, Francis John Longley Ogilvy, (c. 1867 - 1943) was born in Argentina and a self-taught Gaelic-speaker who was a classics scholar and a failed financial broker.[3][4] He married Sophie Louise Blew Jones. He was a first cousin once removed of the writer Rebecca West and of Douglas Holden Blew Jones, who was the brother-in-law of Freda Dudley Ward and the father-in-law of Antony Lambton, 6th Earl of Durham.[5]

Ogilvy attended St Cyprian's School, Eastbourne, on reduced fees because of his father's straitened circumstances and won a scholarship at age thirteen to Fettes College, in Edinburgh. In 1929, he again won a scholarship, this time in History to Christ Church, Oxford. Without the scholarships, Ogilvy would not have been able to attend Fettes or Oxford University because his father's business was badly hit by the depression of the mid-1920s. His studies were not successful, however, and he left Oxford for Paris in 1931 where he became an apprentice chef in the Hotel Majestic. After a year, he returned to Scotland and started selling AGA cooking stoves, door-to-door. His success at this marked him out to his employer, who asked him to write an instruction manual, *The Theory and Practice of Selling the AGA Cooker,*[6] for the other salesmen. Thirty years later, *Fortune* magazine editors called it the finest sales instruction manual ever written.

After seeing the manual, Ogilvy's older brother Francis Ogilvy—the father of actor Ian Ogilvy—showed the manual to management at the London advertising agency Mather & Crowther where he was working. They offered the younger Ogilvy a position as an account

executive.

At Gallup (1938–1948)

In 1938, Ogilvy persuaded his agency to send him to the United
States for a year, where he went to work for George Gallup's *Audience Research Institute* in New Jersey. Ogilvy cites Gallup as one of the major influences on his thinking, emphasizing meticulous research methods and adherence to reality.

During World War II, Ogilvy worked for the British Intelligence Service at the British embassy in Washington, DC. There he analyzed and made recommendations on matters of diplomacy and security. According to a biography produced by Ogilvy & Mather, "he extrapolated his knowledge of human behaviour from consumerism to nationalism in a report which suggested 'applying the Gallup technique to fields of secret intelligence.'"[7] Eisenhower's *Psychological Warfare Board* picked up the report and successfully put Ogilvy's suggestions to work in Europe during the last year of the war.

Also during World War II David Ogilvy was a notable alumnus of the secret Camp X, located near the towns of Whitby and Oshawa in Ontario, Canada. According to an article on the:[8] "It was there he mastered the power of propaganda before becoming king of Madison Avenue. Although Ogilvy was trained in sabotage and close combat, he was ultimately tasked with projects that included successfully ruining the reputation of businessmen who were supplying the Nazis with industrial materials."[9]

After the war, Ogilvy bought a farm in Lancaster County, Pennsylvania and lived among the Amish. The atmosphere of "serenity, abundance, and contentment" kept Ogilvy and his wife in Pennsylvania for several years, but eventually he admitted his limitations as a farmer and moved to Manhattan.

The Ogilvy & Mather years (1949–1973)

Having worked as a chef, researcher, and farmer, Ogilvy now started his own advertising agency with the backing of Mather and Crowther, the London agency being run by his elder brother, Francis, which later acquired another London agency, S.H. Benson. The new agency in New York was called Ogilvy, Benson, and Mather. David Ogilvy had just $6,000 ($59,726.72 in 2016 dollars) in his account when he started the agency. He writes in *Confessions of an Advertising Man* that, initially, he struggled to get clients. Ogilvy also admitted (referring to the pioneer of British advertising Bobby Bevan, the chairman of Benson): "I was in awe of him but Bevan never took notice of me!" They would meet later, however. [10]

Ogilvy & Mather was built on David Ogilvy's principles; in particular, that the function of advertising is to sell and that successful advertising for any product is based on information about its consumer. He disliked advertisements that had loud patronizing voices, and believed a customer should be treated as intelligent. In 1955, he coined the phrase, "The customer is not a moron, she's your wife" based on these values. [11]

His entry into the company of giants started with several iconic advertising campaigns: former First Lady, Eleanor Roosevelt, did a commercial for Good Luck Margarine in 1959. In his autobiography, Ogilvy On Advertising, he said it had been a mistake to persuade her to do the ad – not because it was undignified, but because he had grown to realize that putting celebs in ads is a mistake.

"The man in the Hathaway shirt" with his aristocratic eye patch which used George Wrangel as model; *"The man from Schweppes is here"* introduced Commander Edward Whitehead, the elegant bearded Brit, bringing Schweppes (and "Schwep pervescence") to the U.S.; a famous headline in the automobile business, *"At 60 miles an hour the loudest noise in this new Rolls-Royce comes from the electric clock"*, *"Pablo Casals is coming home – to Puerto Rico"*, a campaign which Ogilvy said helped change the image of a country, and was his proudest achievement.

One of his greatest successes was *"Only Dove is one-quarter moisturizing cream"*. This campaign helped Dove become the top selling soap in the U.S.

Ogilvy believed that the best way to get new clients was to do notable work for his existing clients. Success in his early campaigns helped Ogilvy get big clients such as Rolls-Royce and Shell. New clients followed and Ogilvy's company grew quickly. He was widely hailed as "The Father of Advertising".[12] In 1962, *Time* called him "the most sought-after wizard in today's advertising industry".[13]

In 1973, Ogilvy retired as Chairman of Ogilvy & Mather and moved to Touffou, his estate in France. While no longer involved in the agency's day-to-day operations, he stayed in touch with the company. His correspondence so dramatically increased the volume of mail handled in the nearby town of Bonnes that the post office was reclassified at a higher status and the postmaster's salary raised.

Ogilvy & Mather linked with H.H.D Europe in 1972.

Life with WPP and afterward (1989–1999)

Ogilvy came out of retirement in the 1980s to serve as chairman of Ogilvy, Benson, & Mather in India. He also spent a year acting as temporary chairman of the agency's German office, commuting weekly between Touffou and Frankfurt. He visited branches of the company around the world, and continued to represent Ogilvy & Mather at gatherings of clients and business audiences.

In 1989, *The Ogilvy Group* was bought by WPP Group, a British parent company, for US$864 million in a hostile takeover made possible by the fact that the company group had made an IPO as the first company in marketing to do so.

During the takeover procedures, Sir Martin Sorrell, the founder of WPP, who already had a tarnished reputation in the advertising industry following a similar successful takeover of J. Walter Thompson, was described by Ogilvy as an "odious little shit",[14] and he promised to never work again. (Reports softened it to "odious little jerk", and when Martin Sorrell signed his next company report, he followed the signature with the letters OLJ.) Two events followed simultaneously, however: WPP became the largest marketing communications firm in the world, and David Ogilvy was named the company's non-executive chairman (a position he held for three years). Eventually he became a fan of Sorrell. A letter of apology from Ogilvy adorns Sorrell's office, which is said to be the only apology David Ogilvy ever offered in any form during his adult life. Only a year after his derogatory comments about Sorrell, he was quoted as saying, 'When he tried to take over our company, I would like to have killed him. But it was not legal. I wish I had known him 40 years ago. I like him enormously now.'

At age seventy-five, Ogilvy was asked if anything he'd always wanted had somehow eluded him. His reply was, "Knighthood. And a big family - ten children." His only child, David Fairfield Ogilvy, was born during his first marriage, to Melinda Street. That marriage ended in divorce (1955) as did a second marriage to Anne Cabot. Ogilvy married Herta Lans in France during 1973.

He didn't achieve knighthood, but he was made a Commander of the Order of British Empire (CBE) in 1967. He was elected to the U.S. Advertising Hall of Fame in 1977 and to France's Order of Arts and Letters in 1990. He chaired the Public Participation Committee for Lincoln Center in Manhattan and served as a member of the Metropolitan Museum of Art's 100th

Anniversary Committee.[15] He was appointed Chairman of the United Negro College Fund in 1968, and trustee on the Executive Council of the World Wildlife Fund in 1975. Mr. Ogilvy was inducted into the Junior Achievement U.S. Business Hall of Fame in 1979. David Ogilvy died on 21 July 1999 at his home, the Château de Touffou, in Bonnes, France. Ogilvy remains one of the most famous names in advertising and is considered one of its dominant thinkers.

Works

His book *Ogilvy on Advertising* is a general commentary on advertising and not all the ads shown in the book are his. In early 2004, *Adweek* magazine asked people in the business "Which individuals - alive or dead - made you consider pursuing a career in advertising?", and Ogilvy topped the list. The same result came when students of advertising were surveyed. His best-selling book *Confessions of an Advertising Man* (ISBN 1-904915-01-9) is one of the most popular and famous books on advertising. Based on this book, there is a strong suspicion that Ogilvy is the inspiration for Don Draper in the popular series *Mad Men*.

Ogilvy's advertising philosophy followed these four basic principles:

Creative brilliance: had a strong emphasis on the "BIG IDEA".

Research: coming, as he did, from a background in research, he never underestimated its importance in advertising. In fact, in 1952, when he opened his own agency, he billed himself as research director.

Actual results for clients: "In the modern world of business, it is useless to be a creative, original thinker unless you can also sell what you create." Professional discipline: "I prefer the discipline of knowledge to the anarchy of ignorance." He codified knowledge into slide and film presentations he called Magic Lanterns. He also instituted several training programs for young advertising professionals.

Mary Kay Ash

From Wikipedia, the free encyclopedia

Mary Kay Ash (May 12, 1918 – November 22, 2001) was an American businesswoman and founder of Mary Kay Cosmetics, Inc.

Early life

Mary Kay Ash, born Mary

Kathlyn
Wagner in Hot Wells, Harris County, Texas,
was the daughter of Edward Alexander and
Lula Vember Hastings Wagner.[1] Her
mother
was trained as a nurse and later became a manager of a
restaurant in Houston.[2] Ash attended Dow Elementary School
and Reagan High School in Houston, and graduated in 1934.[3]

Ash married Ben Rogers at age 17. They had three children, Ben Jr., Marylin Reed and Richard Rogers. While her husband served in

World War II, she sold books door-to-door. After her husband's return in 1945, they divorced. (missing reference)

Career

Ash went to work for Stanley Home Products.[4] Frustrated when passed over for a promotion in favor of a man that she had trained, Ash retired in 1963 and intended to write a book to assist women in business. The book turned into a business plan for her ideal company, and in the summer of 1963, Mary Kay Ash and her new husband, George Hellenbeck,[1] planned to start Mary Kay Cosmetics. However, one month before Mary Kay and George started Beauty by Mary Kay, as the company was then called, George died of a heart attack.[1] One month after George's death on September 13, 1963 when she was 45 years old[2] with a $5,000 investment from her oldest son, Ben Rogers, Jr. and with her young son, Richard Rogers taking her late husband's place, Ash started Mary Kay Cosmetics.[2] The company started its original storefront operation in Dallas.[2]

She died in Dallas, Texas on November 22, 2001.[5]

Awards

Both during her life and posthumously, Ash received numerous honors from business groups, including the Horatio Alger Award. Ash was inducted into the Junior Achievement U.S. Business Hall of Fame in 1996. A long-time fundraiser for charities, she founded the Mary Kay Ash Charitable Foundation to raise money to combat domestic violence and cancers affecting women. Ash served as Mary Kay Cosmetics' chairman until 1987, when she was named Chairman Emeritus. Fortune magazine recognized Mary Kay Inc. with inclusion in "The 100 best companies to work for in America." The company was also named one of the best 10 companies for women to work. Her most recent acknowledgements were the "Equal Justice Award" from Legal Services of North Texas in 2001, and "Most Outstanding Woman in Business in the 20th Century" from Lifetime Television in 1999.[4]

Mary Kay Cosmetics, Inc.

Ash and her partners, which included her son, Richard, took the company public in 1968. In 1985, the company's board decided to take the company private again after seventeen years as a public company. Ash remained active in Mary Kay Cosmetics, Inc. until suffering a stroke in 1996. Richard Rogers was named CEO of Mary Kay Cosmetics, Inc. in 2001. At the time of Ash's death, Mary Kay Cosmetics had over 800,000 representatives in 37 countries, with total annual sales over $200 million. As of 2014, Mary Kay Cosmetics has more than 3 million consultant's worldwide and wholesale volume in excess of 3 billion. Mary Kay herself was honored as a leading female entrepreneur in American history.

Books

Ash was the author of several books, including "Mary Kay", an autobiography in 1994, "Miracles Happen" and *You Can Have It All* in 1995. Her first book called "Mary Kay on People Management" was published in 1984 and the publisher Nightingale Conant produced an audio program written by Ash with the same title as the book.

Tim Ferriss

Timothy Ferriss (born July 20, 1977) is an American author, entrepreneur, self-proclaimed "human guinea pig", and public speaker.[1][2][3]

He has written a number of self-help books on the "4-hour" theme, some of which have appeared on the *New York Times*, *Wall Street Journal*, and *USA Today* bestseller lists, starting with *The 4-Hour Workweek*.[12]

Ferriss is also an angel investor and an advisor to Facebook, Twitter, StumbleUpon, Evernote, and Uber, among other companies.[13][14]

Early life

Ferriss grew up in East Hampton, New York and graduated from St. Paul's School, Concord, New Hampshire. He received a degree in East Asian Studies from Princeton University in 2000.[15][16] After graduation, Ferriss worked in sales at a data storage company.[17] Ferriss began building his own Internet business, BrainQUICKEN, while still employed at the company.[17]

Career

In 2001, Ferriss founded BrainQUICKEN and sold the company to a London-based private equity firm in 2010.[18][19][20][21][22] He said *The 4-Hour Workweek* was based on this period.[3]

In December 2008, Ferriss had a pilot on the History Channel called Trial by Fire, where he had one week to attempt to learn a skill normally learned over the course of many years. In the pilot episode he practiced yabusame, the Japanese art of horseback archery.[23]

In December 2013, his television series *The Tim Ferriss Experiment* debuted on HLN. Although there were 13 episodes shot, only a portion of those were shown on television. The show was released in its entirety on iTunes.[24]

In November 2013, Ferriss began an audiobook publishing venture, Tim Ferriss Publishing.[25] The first book published was *Vagabonding* by Rolf Potts.[25] Other books include *The Obstacle Is The Way* by Ryan Holiday, *Daily Rituals* by Mason Currey, and *What I Learned Losing A Million Dollars* by Jim Paul and Brendan Moynihan.[26]

Investor and advisor

Ferriss is an angel investor and advisor to startups.[27]

He has invested or advised in startups such as StumbleUpon, Posterous, Evernote, DailyBurn, Shopify, Reputation. com, Trippy, and TaskRabbit.[28] He is a pre-seed money advisor to Uber, a company co-founded by Garrett Camp, the founder of StumbleUpon, which Ferriss also advises.[29][30]

In September 2013, Ferriss raised $250,000 in under an hour to invest in Shyp by forming a syndicate on AngelList.[31] Ferriss ended up raising over $500,000 through his backers and Shyp raised a total of $2.1 million.[32]

The New York Times listed Ferriss among their "Notable Angel Investors" while CNN said he was "one of the planet's leading angel investors in technology."[33][34]

In 2015, Ferriss declared a long vacation from new investing, citing the stress of the work, and a feeling his impact was minimal in the long run, preferring to spend the time on his writing and media projects.[35]

Author

Ferriss is the author of five books, *The 4-Hour Workweek*, *The 4-Hour Body*, *The 4-Hour Chef*, *Tools of Titans*, and *Tribe of Mentors*; the first two were No. 1 New York Times bestsellers and the third was a No. 1 *Wall Street Journal* bestseller.[4][9][36]

The 4-Hour Workweek

Main article: The 4-Hour Workweek

Ferriss developed the ideas present in *The 4-Hour Workweek* while working 14-hour days at BrainQUICKEN.[3][37] In 2007, Random House, the 26th publisher, released the book through its Crown imprint.[38] Before release, Ferriss was an unknown.[39] He marketed the book heavily through bloggers with whom he created personal relationships.[39][39][40][41] *The 4-Hour Workweek* would reach No. 1 on the New York Times bestseller list, No. 1 on the *Wall Street Journal* bestseller list, and No. 1 on the *BusinessWeek* bestseller list.[42] It has currently sold over 1,350,000 copies and has spent nearly 4 years on the *New York Times* bestseller list.[4][5][43][44]

The book received both positive and negative reviews. Leslie Garner of *The Telegraph* noted that, "With a punchy writing style and a higher literacy level than most flash-in-the-pan gurus, Ferriss has struck a chord with his critique of workers's slavish devotion to corporations...

Ferriss' book skillfully compartmentalises, then pathologises, workers's unhealthy relationships with office life."[45] Dylan Tweney of *Wired* wrote, "Nearly every idea taken to extreme. No sense of work being anything more than a paycheck."[46]

In 2009, *The 4-Hour Workweek, Expanded and Updated* was released by Random House and included multiple case studies authored by people who have utilized Ferriss's methods.[47]

The 4-Hour Body

In December 2010, Ferriss's second book, *The 4-Hour Body: An Uncommon Guide to Rapid Fat-Loss, Incredible Sex, and Becoming Superhuman*, was published by Crown.[48] The book covers more than 50 topics, including rapid fat

loss, increasing strength, boosting endurance, and polyphasic sleep.[49] Ferriss introduces his version of the Slow-Carb Diet, which involves the elimination of starches and anything sweet (including fruit and all artificial sweeteners) and a strong preference for lean protein, legumes, and vegetables.[50]

For the book, Ferriss interviewed more than 200 experts over a three-year period. The experts ranged from doctors to athletes to black-market drug salesmen.[51] He said that he had recorded every workout he had done since the age of 18, and from 2004 (three years before his first book was published) he had tracked a variety of blood chemistry measurements, including insulin levels, hemoglobin A1c, and free testosterone.[48] In the book, Ferriss wrote about using anabolic steroids, specifically "a number of low-dose therapies, including testosterone cypionate," under medical supervision following shoulder surgery, as well as using "stacks" consisting of testosterone enanthate, Sustanon 250, HGH, Deca-Durabolin, Cytomel, and other unnamed ingredients while training.[52]

The 4-Hour Body debuted at No. 1 on *The New York Times* Best Seller list.[9] It peaked at No. 4 on both the *Wall Street Journal* and *USA Today*'s lists, and was one of Amazon.com's top 5 bestselling books for December 2010 and January 2011.[53][54][55]

As part of the press for the book, Ferriss appeared as a guest on *The Dr. Oz Show* and ABC's *The View*.[56][57]

The 4-Hour Chef[

Ferriss's third book, *The 4-Hour Chef: The Simple Path to Cooking Like a Pro, Learning Anything, and Living the Good Life* was released by Amazon Publishing in November 2012.[58] *The 4-Hour*

Chef contains practical cooking and recipe tips and uses the skill of cooking to explain his methods for accelerated learning, which he calls "meta-learning".[59][59][60]

The book reached No. 1 on the *Wall Street Journal* bestseller list in its first week of issue.[11] However, many brick and mortar bookstores including independents and Barnes & Noble chose to not stock the book due to their objections to the business practices of Amazon Publishing.[61]

This required Ferriss to make arrangements with non-conventional partners, including BitTorrent, Panera Bread, and TaskRabbit in order to distribute the book.[62][63][64] In particular, Ferriss teamed up with BitTorrent to distribute an exclusive bundle of *4-Hour Chef* content including excerpts from the book, photos, interviews and unpublished content,[65] which was downloaded over 300,000 times the first week after release.[66][67] The audiobook featured guest narration by Neil Gaiman.[63][68][69][70][71][72]

Tools of Titans

Ferriss' fourth book *Tools of Titans* was released on December 6, 2016 by Houghton Mifflin Harcourt.[73] The book's content consists of tactics and routines from some of the most popular guests on The Tim Ferriss Show podcast.[74]

Tools of Titans debuted at #1 on the New York Times Bestseller list.[75][76] The book was the first podcast-based book to debut on the New York Times list.[77]

Tribe of Mentors

Ferriss's fifth book, *Tribe of Mentors: Short Life Advice from the Best in the World* was released on November 21, 2017 by Houghton Mifflin Harcourt.[78]

The Tim Ferriss Show[edit]

Ferriss has been called the "Oprah of Audio" due to the influence and reach of his podcast "The Tim Ferriss Show" which as of 2016 had over 80 million downloads.[73][79] It covers topics ranging from personal and character development, to exercise routines, acting, venture capital and metaphysics.[80] The show was voted "Best Podcast Episode of 2015" by users of Product Hunt in their "Golden Kitty Awards."[81]

Fear(Less) with Tim Ferriss

Ferriss is the host of the 2017 TV show *Fear(Less) with Tim Ferriss*.[82] The show uncovers the tactics and strategies of famous icons to lesser-known phenoms that work in the real world. The show is filmed in front of a live audience and is executive produced by Vince Vaughn's Wild West Productions.

Influence

The New Yorker described Ferriss as this generation's self-help guru, comparing Ferriss and his books to authors of similar influence of previous generations—Napoleon Hill, Norman Vincent Peale, Stephen Covey, and Spencer Johnson.[83] *Wired* called Ferriss "The Superman of Silicon Valley".[84] *The New York Times* said Ferriss was "somewhere between [retired General Electric chairman and CEO] Jack Welch and a Buddhist monk."[17] In 2011, *Newsweek* declared Ferriss "The World's Best Guinea Pig".[85]

He has been named among *Newsweek*'s Digital Power Index 100 as the seventh most powerful online personality, *Fortune*'s "40 Under 40", one of *Fast Company*'s "Most Innovative Business People of 2007", and a Henry Crown Fellow by the Aspen Institute.[86][87][88][89]

Both *The 4-Hour Body* and *The 4-Hour Workweek* are in the "10 Most Highlighted Books of All Time" on Amazon Kindle.[90][91]

In 2008, he was named *Wired*'s "Greatest Self-Promoter of All Time."[92]

"The Tim Ferriss Effect"

In 2012, author Michael Ellsberg coined the phrase "The Tim Ferriss Effect" in a *Forbes* profile.[93] The phrase was used to describe the influence a blog post on Ferriss' site had on the sales of Ellsberg's

book.[93][94]

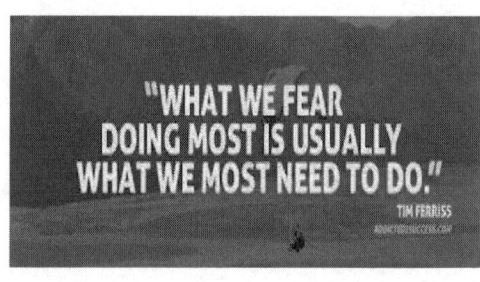

Ellsberg foun6d that his post on Ferriss' blog sold more books than a piece in *The New York Times* and a three-minute segment on CNN.[93] Ryan Holiday, who had previously been hired by Ferriss to assist with the promotion of *The 4-Hour Body* and *The 4-Hour Chef,*[95] said this effect helped to sell 30,000 copies of his own book in the weeks following its release.[96] The clothing brand Mizzen+Main wrote about the effect on their clothing sales, stating that a mention on the podcast boosted exposure and sales for the brand more than a profile in *The New York Times*, an announcement in *The Wall Street Journal*, or a full page ad in *Esquire.*[97]

ilanthropy

Ferriss is a charity advocate and a member of the National Advisory Council of the public school nonprofit DonorsChoose.[98][99] His projects and donations have raised more than $250,000 for underfunded public school teachers and classroom projects, and his campaigns, such as dedicating his birthday to raising funds and heading LitLiberation to increase literacy worldwide, have impacted more than 60,000 students.[100][101][102][103] In March 2016, Ferriss flash funded 145 school projects posted on DonorsChoose.org in coordination with Stephen Colbert.[104][105]

In October 2014, BUILD Boston, a not-for-profit organization that uses entrepreneurship to equip Boston youth for high school and college success, honored Ferriss with the annual BUILDer Award for Innovation and Entrepreneurship for his work in education reform.[106][107]

Ferriss is also on the advisory board of the non-profit QuestBridge, along with LinkedIn Founder Reid Hoffman, David Sze, and others.[108] QuestBridge was created in 2003 to connect disadvantaged students with elite colleges and helps place over 2,000 students per year.[108]

Psychedelic research

Ferriss has raised funds for psychedelic studies at institutions such as Johns Hopkins University School of Medicine.[109] In 2016, Ferriss donated at least $100,000 to research psychedelic drugs for the treatment of major depression.[109]

Personal life

In 2017 Ferriss moved to Austin, Texas.[110] after living for 17 years in Silicon Valley. According to an interview to the Business Insider, he moved because of the "intellectual smugness" and "closed-mindedness masquerading as opened-mindedness." "For the last few years I've witnessed what appears to be the forming of an echo chamber that is even more hermetically sealed than it usually is in Silicon Valley."

He holds a Guinness World Record in Argentine tango.[111] Ferriss has stated that prior to his writing career he won in the 165 lb (75 kg) weight class at the 1999 USAWKF national Sanshou (Chinese kickboxing) championship through a process of shoving opponents out of the ring and by dramatically dehydrating himself before weigh in, and then rehydrating before the fight in order to compete

several classes below his actual weight – a practice known as weight cutting.[112][112][113]

Ferriss is a practitioner of the Transcendental Meditation technique.[114]

10 Lessons Every Entrepreneur Must Learn

As entrepreneurs, we all follow our own path. For some, the rise to financial success is a long, slow, painful process. For others, things just seem to magically fall into place. I believe that the latter isn't a result of magic, however, but is the sure sign of an entrepreneur who understands the importance of learning from, adapting to and growing with their business.

The following are 10 lessons every entrepreneur must learn in order to build a long-term, healthy and sustainable business.

1. The customer is not always right. From day one, we're told that "the customer is always right." We're expected to bend over backwards to please every single customer, even when they're clearly and painfully wrong. This maxim, however, can do a serious disservice to ourselves, our employees and our customers. Give your customers the benefit of the doubt, but not at the expense of your (or your employees') dignity.
2. Time is money. Money, customers, ideas: all resources you can potentially gain more of. *Time*, however, is the one commodity you'll always have a finite amount of. One way to ensure you make the most of your time is to assign an hourly dollar amount to your tasks.

Ask yourself: What would be a fair wage for the tasks I perform? If someone else can competently accomplish these tasks for less money, let them do it so you can focus on higher level, revenue-generating tasks. As a business owner, you should only do the tasks that only you can do.

3. Not all money is good money. This is a lesson many entrepreneurs struggle with early in their career. When you're getting your business off the ground, it's easy to fall into the

trap of taking money from anyone who offers it. The problem is, not all customers or clients are worth it.

Avoid clients who take up too much of your time, who consistently have unrealistic expectations or who you just generally dread working with. It's just not worth it!

4. There are no cheap shortcuts in marketing. I often speak to business owners who want marketing advice, but who then shun my recommendations as being "too expensive." The truth is, cheap marketing can make your brand look cheap.

Low-quality content, cheap ads and "budget" SEO may save you money in the short term, but the damage they do to your brand's reputation can last far longer. For insight on how to market the right way, see my eBook.

5. Outsource as much as possible. If you don't have in-house staff to share the workload, consider outsourcing. Many entrepreneurs find that hiring an overseas virtual assistant significantly reduces the time they need to spend on routine tasks, freeing them up to work on revenue-generating tasks.

6. Build your personal brand as well as your company brand. Many entrepreneurs make the mistake of focusing on building their company brand to the exclusion of building their personal brand. However, your personal brand will differentiate you from your

competitors, give you authority and credibility in your field, and stick with you in the event your company ultimately experiences failure.

For some practical tips, see my article, How to Grow Your Personal Brand with Your Content Strategy.

And while there's been a lot of talk over the years about work-life separation or work-life balance, our whole thing is about work-life integration. Because it's just life – and the ideal would be if you can be the same person at home as you are in the office and vice versa. -- Tony Hsieh, CEO of Zappos.com

7. Work is life, and life's too short to hate your work. Work-life balance is something many entrepreneurs struggle with, which is why I'm such a huge fan of Tony Hsieh's approach. When you're passionate about what you do, and when you focus on happiness (both your own and that of your employees'), work isn't just something you do to fund your "real life." It becomes infinitely more enjoyable and meaningful, and significantly reduces your chances of experiencing burnout.

My philosophy is to always find the smartest people you can. Hire people smarter than you. – Donny Deutsch

8. Hire people who are smarter than you. Face it: There will always be people who are smarter than you. If you're lucky enough to find these people, hire them. Focus on the things that you're best at, and give them the freedom to do the same.

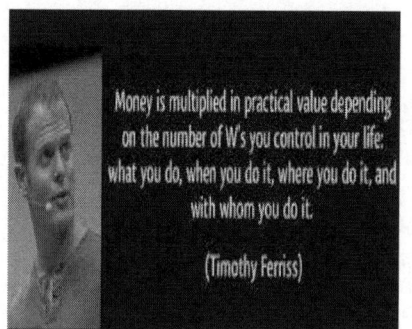

Money is multiplied in practical value depending on the number of W's you control in your life: what you do, when you do it, where you do it, and with whom you do it.

(Timothy Ferriss)

9. Best practices may not be best for your customers. Particularly when you're just starting a business, it's easy to get caught up in doing what others tell you is the "best way" to do something. Problem is, "they" don't know *your* customers or clients. Use best practices as a starting point, but adapt them to meet the unique needs of your business and customers.

10. Just do it. Planning, strategizing and weighing options all have important roles within a business. But there comes a point in time when you just have to do it. You know the quote: *"Better to do something imperfectly than to do nothing perfectly."*

Analysis paralysis or simply the lack of ability to execute a plan will stifle growth, innovation and progress in any business. Even if the payoff for work done now won't come for years. Successful people do the work anyway because they know how to delay gratification, and this ability is what separates successful people from unsuccessful people, according to renowned physicist and author Michio Kaku.

There you have it: 10 lessons every entrepreneur must learn in order to build a profitable and sustainable business. Not easy lessons, to be sure, but ones that ensure the best possible chance of long-term success.

Forget buzzwords like influencer marketing, augmented reality or artificial intelligence. The big topic at Advertising Week this year was "control." From brands to agencies and platforms, everyone wants more, but in the amorphous stew that is digital marketing, can any one ingredient ever truly dominate the rest?

There was a lot of talk about brands grabbing control by creating in-house shops and asserting themselves with digital platforms to ensure brand safety and clearer results. At the same time, marketers pondered how to release more creative control to social influencers, who were repeatedly pointed to last week as one of the only tactics that can break through in today's cluttered media landscape.

Story continues below

Amidst the expected sessions on trends like AR and AI at the annual gathering in NYC, there was a lot of hand-wringing as attendees discussed a slew of concerns that have plagued marketing this year, including brand safety and a lack of transparency, as well as issues with agencies and programmatic. One particular area of concern is how big brands are increasingly putting their money where their mouths are when it comes to dissatisfaction with digital marketing by decreasing budgets.

Unfortunately, there were no easy answers presented at Advertising Week. But what did emerge was a series of stepping stones brands can and must try to traverse in the months ahead so they can stay on the path of building awareness and engaging consumers while the industry continues to sort out the bigger issues. Here, in no particular order, are seven lessons from Advertising Week that will impact the marketing industry in the months ahead:

1.) Influencer marketing's role for brands evolves

Not surprisingly, influencer marketing was a hot topic at this year's event, with platforms, brands, agencies and influencers themselves discussing how the space is evolving now that it's moving past a period of testing and toward being an established part of the marketing mix, often being included as a specific ask in brands' RFPs.

The big trends in the months ahead are likely to include influencers translating their success into creating their own brands available in stores and online; more brands partnering with influencers to create content to be featured alongside in-house creative as part of a multichannel campaign, often then investing in paid social to broaden the reach of this content; influencers being used to bring local flavor to global campaigns; and agencies embracing influencers as a way to boost the creative output for a specific campaign.

"For American Rag, we found that our influencer content far and away outperforms our professional shoots," said Sarah Anne Spaulding, social media manager for private brands at Macy's, during an Advertising Week session.

2.) Snapchat finds its place

Despite getting a bad rap this year thanks to slowing user growth and the fact that Instagram and others continue to copy its most innovative features, agency and brand executives still see a place for Snapchat, particularly when brands are looking to reach younger consumers with customized content. As social media matures, individual platforms are developing their own unique personalities: Instagram is a popularity contest while Facebook puts brands in front of the widest possible audience.

Snapchat increasingly is being embraced for its ability to create unique experiences for a specific audience.

"Snapchat is the most personal of all the platforms," Greg Meyer, director of client partnerships at Hyfn, told Marketing Dive.

HBO's CEO Richard Plepler, speaking at Advertising Week in a session with Snapchat's Chief Strategy Officer Imran Khan, pointed to the two platform's shared ideologies around building passionate fans and committing to excellence as one reason for the success of a "Game of Thrones" Snapchat lens that fans could unlock to transform anyone into a White Walker ahead of the show's season 7 premiere. The lens was unlocked by more than 45 million fans and averaged 23 seconds of gameplay.

"People want to get engaged emotionally, and that's why there has been so much catalytic success working together," Plepler said.

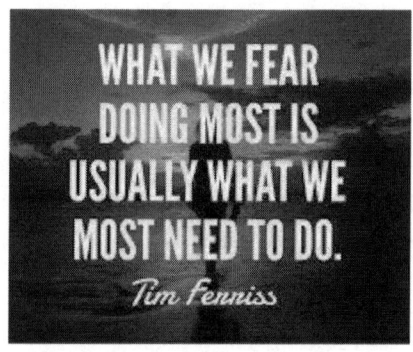

WHAT WE FEAR DOING MOST IS USUALLY WHAT WE MOST NEED TO DO.
Tim Ferriss

3.) Brand safety's in the hot seat, but it still has a spot at the table

This year, marketers have developed a healthy concern for the perception of their brands across digital channels after major companies like McDonald's and L'Oreal saw their advertisements appear alongside hateful and violent videos on YouTube. Many brands immediately pulled their media buys, which led to a short boycott of the video platform. Though YouTube quickly bounced back as the majority of companies returned to the highly valuable platform, the heart of the problem execs discussed at Advertising Week lies in whether the automated and algorithm-driven industry has become too focused on uber-precise targeting of audiences and has subsequently let the context in which their ads appear fall to the wayside.

To navigate the murky landscape, marketers should understand this potential pitfall of the industry and aim to work with agencies to take more control of where ads are placed — or alternatively explore opportunities to leverage earned media, user-generated content and influencers, which all come with their own set of challenges. But despite brand safety being thrown into the spotlight, eMarketer estimates that digital ad spend across the industry will jump nearly 16% in 2017 to reach $83 billion, which was supported by statements from several execs at Advertising Week.

"If quality and transparency remain key, there's no reason why programmatic won't grow a much larger share of the digital ad ecosystem," said CEO of OpenX Tim Cadogan, during a session last week. "Programmatic will continue to capture spend as publishers and buyers instill trust in the companies that can [provide] them with the greatest value — we're already starting to see the industry consolidate around the highest quality tech solutions available."

4.) Experiences will beat out screens

As marketers continue to experiment with how to add value to consumers via the Internet of Things, opportunities of connectedness are often in experiences, not screens, Shel Kimen, global user experience practice manager of Ford Motor Co., said at the Mobile Marketing Association's SM2 Innovation Summit the same day Advertising Week kicked off.

Now with devices like voice assistants, beacons and location-based tools that brands can tap to connect with consumers, marketers are faced with a range of platforms to explore beyond ones that require text and visuals. This means strategies should focus on experiences rather than specific screens as they, along with all devices, will continue to get smarter in the "age of ask."

Look for brands to build strong digital experiences as a way to address the inefficiencies with programmatic buying that marketers like JPMorgan Chase and P&G have brought to light. While advancements like AI could make programmatic more precise, Andy Main, principal with Deloitte Digital, told Marketing Dive that brands should be thinking about building a strategy around owned media, something they can accomplish with strong digital experiences and the data that comes with them.

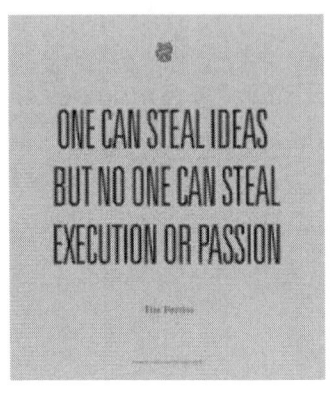

5.) Getting 'good' data is no longer a problem for marketers — what to do with it is

One question that surfaced at several talks across Advertising Week pertained to data: Not whether marketers can collect it, but instead what constitutes "good" data and the ways in which brands can most strategically apply it as it grows more vast in volume.

"You can enter into a kind of boiling the ocean mentality," Brigitte King, chief consumer officer at L'Oreal, warned on a panel. "You can put a lot of tax on your system.

"You have to start with clarity of what you're going after — use cases are really key," she added. "It's important when you're doing anything within the realm of CRM to have a quick-win mentality."

Andy Fisher

Chief Analytics Officer, Merkle

AI was frequently positioned as a solution that will let marketers accrue, analyze and apply their data more efficiently, but some cautioned against completely handing over the reins to technology even as they urged the industry to clean up its house.

"You have to be very careful with AI in a lot of decision-making because what AI does is it looks at the past," said Andy Fisher, chief analytics officer at Merkle, on the panel with King. "It looks at the past, and if that response function has been bad or has been biased, the AI can optimize to the bad or biased response.

"That's why for a lot of things you need the human-AI pair," he said. "[That] will be the model going forward."

6.) In creativity and technology, don't count China out

China's growing presence in the industry was underscored by WPP CEO Martin Sorrell, who, in a talk with journalist Ken Auletta, called out Alibaba and Tencent along with Huawei, as companies that the "Fearsome Five" — Google, Apple, Microsoft, Amazon and Facebook — will need to fear in the future.

"The West basically doesn't want China to succeed," Sorrell said, noting that he doesn't include himself in that group. He and another WPP executive had recently spent two weeks visiting firms around China, and Sorrell called out the size and scale of the campuses of some these companies as indicators of the powerhouses they could become.

"We want to out-compete them," Sorrell said. "They are going to win."

A race to watch now, Sorrell said, will be how Alibaba fares against Amazon as they go head-to-head competing for business in Singapore. While this was just one flashpoint highlighted, Sorrell hinted at other significant areas where the two will clash.

"I was at Alibaba [headquarters] in Hangzhou just days before they launched [TMall] Genie," Sorrell said, referring to the company's Alexa-like digital assistant. "This battle is a major, major battle, and the AI significance of all this is very important."

Perhaps looking to get ahead, WPP's GroupM agency last week announced a partnership with Alibaba. China will also continue to emerge as a significant source of mobile marketing innovation in the months ahead. Brand Yasmin and agency PHD China took home several Golds last week for their "Sex-Ed Revolution" campaign at the Mobile Marketing Association's 2017 Global Smarties Awards.

It was one of several efforts from China to be recognized last week at the group's SM2 Innovation Summit. The effort reached more than 18 million university students in China with educational videos on a taboo topic by inserting them in a popular app for students.

7.) Global marketers must prepare for GDPR now

One elephant in the room last week was the EU's current regulatory crackdown and the looming approach of the General Data Protection Regulation (GDPR). The policy, which is now just eight months away from going into effect, could slap brands and platforms with millions in fines if they don't comply with its standards.

"The GDPR will materially increase the burden placed on marketing and product teams when collecting and processing data on EU citizens by simultaneously expanding the definition of personal data, increasing restrictions for the way data is used and adding explicit consent requirements before data is collected," Bill Magnuson, CEO and co-founder of Appboy — soon to be Braze — explained in a follow-up statement.

"With fines for non-compliance valued at the greater of €20 million or 4% of worldwide business turnover, being good stewards of user data is more important than ever," he said.

Though global marketers must start prepping for GDPR, WPP's Sorrell noted that the ramp-up in pressure from governing bodies like the EU on major ad platforms like Google and Facebook does have its benefits.

In fact, he suggested it might be one of the factors making these platforms keen to deepen their relationships with advertisers.

"I think Google and Facebook have become friendlier frenemies or flexible friends," the exec, a frequent and vocal critic of the duopoly, said. "Because with scale and size comes responsibility."

Elon Musk

Elon Reeve Musk (/ˈiːlɒn ˈmʌsk/; born June 28, 1971) is a South African-born American business magnate, investor,[9][10] engineer,[11] and inventor.[16] He is the founder, CEO, and CTO of SpaceX; a co-founder,[17] Series A investor, CEO, and product architect of Tesla Inc.; co-chairman of OpenAI; founder and CEO of Neuralink, and founder of The Boring Company (2016). Musk is also a co-founder and former chairman

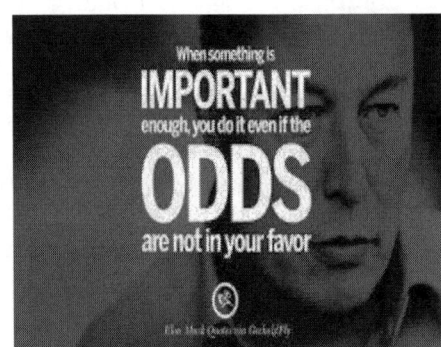

of SolarCity, co-founder of Zip2, and founder of X.com, which merged with Confinity and took the name PayPal.[22]

As of October 2017, Musk has an estimated net worth of $20.8 billion, ranking in the 2017 Forbes 400 as the 21st wealthiest person in America. In March 2016, he was listed by Forbes as the 80th-wealthiest person in the world.[23] In December 2016, Musk was ranked 21st on the *Forbes* list of The World's Most Powerful People.[24]

Musk has stated that the goals of SolarCity, Tesla, and SpaceX revolve around his vision to change the world and humanity.[25] His goals include reducing global warming through sustainable energy production and consumption, and reducing the "risk of human extinction" by "making life multiplanetary"[26][27] by establishing a human colony on Mars.

In addition to his primary business pursuits, he has envisioned a high-speed transportation system known as the Hyperloop, and has proposed a vertical take-off and landing supersonic jet aircraft with electric fan propulsion, known as the Musk electric jet.[28][29]

Musk was born on June 28, 1971, in Pretoria, Transvaal, South Africa,[30] the son of Maye Musk (*née* Haldeman), a model and dietician from Regina, Saskatchewan, Canada,[31] and Errol Musk, a South African electromechanical engineer, pilot, and sailor. He has a younger brother, Kimbal (born 1972), and a younger sister, Tosca (born 1974).[35] His paternal grandmother was British, and he also has Pennsylvania Dutch ancestry.[36][37] His maternal grandfather was American, from Minnesota.[38] After his parents divorced in 1980, Musk lived mostly with his father in the suburbs of Pretoria,[36] which Musk chose two years after his parents split up, but now says was "not a good idea."[39] As an adult, Musk has severed relations with his father.[39]

During his childhood he was an avid reader.[40] At age 10, he developed an interest in computing with the Commodore VIC-20.[41] He taught himself computer programming at the age of 12, sold the code for a BASIC-based video game he created called *Blastar*, to a magazine called *PC and Office Technology*, for approximately $500.[42][43] A web version of the game is available online.[42][44] His childhood reading included Isaac Asimov's *Foundation* series from which he drew the lesson that "you should try to take the set of actions that are likely to prolong civilization, minimize the probability of a dark age and reduce the length of a dark age if there is one."[39]

Musk was severely bullied throughout his childhood,[39] and was once hospitalized when a group of boys threw him down a flight of stairs and then beat him until he lost consciousness.[40]

Musk was initially educated at private schools, attending the English-speaking Waterkloof House Preparatory School. Musk later graduated from Pretoria Boys High School and moved to Canada in June 1989, just before his 18th birthday,[45] after obtaining Canadian citizenship through his Canadian-born mother.[46][47]

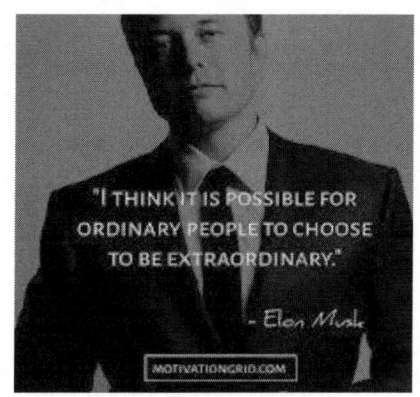

Education

At the age of 17, Musk was accepted into Queen's University in Kingston, Ontario, for undergraduate study. In 1992, after spending two years at Queen's University, Musk transferred to the University of Pennsylvania, where in May 1997 he received a Bachelor of Science degree in physics from its College of Arts and Sciences, and a Bachelor of Science degree in economics from its Wharton School of Business. Musk extended his studies for one year to finish the second bachelor's degree.[40][48] While at the University of Pennsylvania, Musk and fellow Penn student Adeo Ressi rented a 10-bedroom fraternity house, using it as an unofficial nightclub.[40]

In 1995, at age 24, Musk moved to California to begin a PhD in applied physics and materials science at Stanford University, but left the program after two days to pursue his entrepreneurial aspirations in the areas of the internet, renewable energy and outer space.[43][49] In 2002, he became a U.S. citizen.[50][51]

Career

Zip2

In 1995, Musk and his brother, Kimbal, started Zip2, a web software company, with money raised from a small group of angel investors.[39] The company developed and marketed an Internet "city guide" for the newspaper publishing industry.[52] Musk obtained contracts with *The New York Times* and the *Chicago Tribune*[53] and persuaded the board of directors to abandon plans for a merger with CitySearch.[54] While at Zip2, Musk wanted to become CEO; however, none of the board members would allow it.[40] Compaq acquired Zip2 for US$307 million in cash and US$34 million in stock options in February 1999.[55] Musk received US$22 million for his 7 percent share from the sale.[53]

X.com and PayPal

In March 1999, Musk co-founded X.com, an online financial services and e-mail payment company, with US$10 million from the sale of Zip2.[45][52][54] One year later, the company merged with Confinity,[53][56] which had a money transfer service called PayPal. The merged company focused on the PayPal service and was renamed PayPal in 2001. PayPal's early growth was driven mainly by a viral marketing campaign where new customers were recruited when they received money through the service.[57] Musk was ousted in October 2000 from his role as CEO (although he remained on the board) due to disagreements with other company leadership, notably over his desire to move PayPal's Unix-based infrastructure to Microsoft Windows.[58] In October 2002, PayPal was acquired by eBay for US$1.5 billion in stock, of which Musk received US$165 million.[59] Before its sale, Musk, who was the company's largest shareholder, owned 11.7% of PayPal's shares.[60]

In July 2017, Musk purchased the domain x.com from PayPal for an undisclosed amount stating that it has "great sentimental value" to him.[61]

SpaceX

In 2001, Musk conceptualized "Mars Oasis"; a project to land a miniature experimental greenhouse on Mars, containing food crops growing on Martian regolith, in an attempt to regain public interest in space exploration.[62][63] In October 2001, Musk travelled to Moscow with Jim Cantrell (an aerospace supplies fixer), and Adeo Ressi (his best friend from college), to buy refurbished Dnepr Intercontinental ballistic missiles (ICBMs) that could send the envisioned payloads into space. The group met with companies such as NPO Lavochkin and Kosmotras; however, according to Cantrell, Musk was seen as a novice and was consequently spat on by one of the Russian chief designers,[64] and the group returned to the United States empty-handed. In February 2002, the group returned to Russia to look for three ICBMs, bringing along Mike Griffin. Griffin had worked for the CIA's venture capital arm, In-Q-Tel, as well as NASA's Jet Propulsion Laboratory, and was just leaving Orbital Sciences, a maker of satellites and spacecraft.

The group met again with Kosmotras, and were offered one rocket for US$8 million, however, this was seen by Musk as too expensive; Musk consequently stormed out of the meeting. On the flight back from Moscow, Musk realized that he could start a company that could build the affordable rockets he needed.[64] According to early Tesla and SpaceX investor Steve Jurvetson,[65] Musk calculated that the raw materials for building a rocket actually were only 3 percent of the sales price of a rocket at the time. It was concluded that theoretically, by applying vertical integration and the modular approach from software engineering, SpaceX could cut launch price by a factor of ten and still enjoy a 70-percent gross margin.[66] Ultimately, Musk ended up founding SpaceX with the long-term goal of creating a "true spacefaring civilization".[67]

Musk and President Barack Obama at the Falcon 9 launch site in 2010

With US$100 million of his early fortune,[68] Musk founded Space Exploration Technologies, or SpaceX, in May 2002.[69] Musk is chief executive officer (CEO) and chief technology officer (CTO) of the Hawthorne, California-based company. SpaceX develops and manufactures space launch vehicles with a focus on advancing the state of rocket technology. The company's first two launch vehicles are the Falcon 1 and Falcon 9 rockets (a nod to Star Wars' *Millennium Falcon*), and its first spacecraft is the Dragon (a nod to *Puff the Magic Dragon*).[70] In seven years, SpaceX designed the family of Falcon launch vehicles and the

Dragon multipurpose spacecraft. In September 2008, SpaceX's Falcon 1 rocket became the first privately funded liquid-fueled vehicle to put a satellite into Earth orbit.[40] On May 25, 2012, the SpaceX Dragon vehicle berthed with the ISS, making history as the first commercial company to launch and berth a vehicle to the International Space Station.[71]

In 2006, SpaceX was awarded a contract from NASA to continue the development and test of the SpaceX Falcon 9 launch
vehicle and Dragon spacecraft in order to transport cargo to the International Space Station,[72] followed by a US$1.6
billion NASA Commercial Resupply Services program contract on
December 23, 2008, for 12 flights of its Falcon 9 rocket and Dragon spacecraft to the Space Station, replacing the US Space Shuttle after it retired in 2011.[73] Astronaut transport to the ISS is currently handled
solely by the Soyuz, but SpaceX is one of two companies awarded a contract by NASA as part of the Commercial Crew Development program, which is intended to develop a US astronaut transport capability by 2018.[74] On December 22, 2015, SpaceX successfully landed the first stage of its Falcon rocket back at the launch pad. This was the first time in history such a feat had been achieved by an orbital rocket and is a significant step towards

rocket reusability lowering the costs of access to space.[75] This first stage recovery was replicated several times in 2016 by landing on an Autonomous spaceport drone ship, an ocean-based recovery platform,[76] and by the end of 2017, SpaceX had landed and recovered the first stage on 16 missions in a row where a landing and recovery were attempted, including all 14 attempts in 2017. 20 out of 42 first stage Falcon 9 boosters have been recovered overall since the Falcon 9 maiden flight in 2010.[77] In the most recent full year—2017— SpaceX launched 18 successful Falcon 9 flights, more than doubling their highest previous year of 8.[78]

SpaceX is both the largest private producer of rocket engines in the world, and holder of the record for highest thrust-to-weight ratio for a rocket engine.[79] SpaceX has produced more than 100 operational Merlin 1D engines, currently the world's most powerful engine for its weight.[80] The relatively immense power to weight ratio allows each Merlin 1D engine to vertically lift the weight of 40 average family cars. In combination, the 9 Merlin engines in the Falcon 9 first stage produce anywhere from 5.8 to 6.7 MN (1.3 to 1.5 million pounds) of thrust, depending on altitude.[81]

Musk was influenced by Isaac Asimov's *Foundation* series[82] and views space exploration as an important step in preserving and expanding the consciousness of human life.[83] Musk said that multiplanetary life may serve as a hedge against threats to the survival of the human species.

An asteroid or a super volcano could destroy us, and we face risks the dinosaurs never saw: an engineered virus, inadvertent creation of
a micro black hole, catastrophic global warming or some as-yet-unknown technology could spell the end of us. Humankind evolved over millions of years, but in the last sixty years atomic weaponry created the potential to extinguish ourselves. Sooner or later, we must expand life beyond this green and blue ball—or go extinct.

Musk's goal is to reduce the cost of human spaceflight by a factor of 10.[84] In a 2011 interview, he said he hopes to send humans to Mars'
surface within 10–20 years.[85] In Ashlee Vance's biography, Musk
stated that he wants to establish a Mars colony by 2040, with a population of 80,000.[41] Musk stated that, since Mars' atmosphere lacks oxygen, all transportation would have to be electric (electric cars, electric trains, Hyperloop, electric aircraft).[86] Musk stated in June 2016 that the first unmanned flight of the larger Mars Colonial Transporter (MCT) spacecraft is aimed for departure to the red planet
in 2022, to be followed by the first manned MCT Mars flight departing
in 2024.[87] In September 2016, Musk revealed details of

his architecture to explore and colonize Mars.[88] By 2016, Musk's private trust holds 54% of SpaceX stock, equivalent to 78% of voting shares.[89]

In late 2017, SpaceX unveiled the design for its next-generation launch vehicle and spacecraft system—BFR—that would support all SpaceX launch service provider capabilities with a single set of very large vehicles: Earth-orbit, Lunar-orbit, interplanetary missions, and even intercontinental passenger transport on Earth, and totally replace the Falcon 9, Falcon Heavy and Dragon vehicles in the 2020s. The BFR will have a 9-meter (30 ft) core diameter. Significant development on the vehicles began in 2017, while the new rocket engine development began in 2012.[90][91]

Tesla

Tesla, Inc. (originally Tesla Motors) was incorporated in July 2003 by Martin Eberhard and Marc Tarpenning, who financed the company until the Series A round of funding.[92] Both men played active roles in the company's early development prior to Elon Musk's involvement.[93] Musk led the Series A round of investment in February 2004, joining Tesla's board of directors as its chairman.[94] Musk took an active role within the company and oversaw Roadster product design at a detailed level, but was not deeply involved in day-to-day business operations.[95]

Following the financial crisis in 2008,[96] Musk assumed leadership of the company as CEO and product architect, positions he still holds today. Tesla Motors first built an electric sports car, the Tesla Roadster in 2008, with sales of about 2,500 vehicles to 31 countries.

Tesla began delivery of its four-door Model S sedan on June 22, 2012. It unveiled its third product, the Model X, aimed at

the SUV/minivan market, on February 9, 2012; however, the Model X launch was delayed until September 2015.[97][98][99] In addition to its own cars, Tesla sells electric powertrain systems to Daimler for the Smart EV, Mercedes B-Class Electric Drive and Mercedes A Class, and to Toyota for the RAV4 EV. Musk was able to bring in both companies as long-term investors in Tesla.[100]

Musk observing an assembly demo at the reopening of

the NUMMIplant, now known as the Tesla Factory (Fremont, California) in 2010

Musk standing in front of a Tesla Model S in 2011

Musk has favored building a sub-US$30,000 compact Tesla model and building and selling electric vehicle powertrain components so that other automakers can produce electric vehicles at affordable prices without having to develop the products in-house; this led to the Model 3 that is planned to have a base price of US$35,000.[101] several mainstream publications have compared him with Henry Ford for his work on advanced vehicle powertrains.[102]

Musk and Senator Dianne Feinstein next to a Tesla Model S (2010) In a May 2013 interview with All Things Digital, Musk said that to overcome the range limitations of electric cars, Tesla is "dramatically accelerating" its network of supercharger stations, tripling the number on the East and West coasts of the U.S. that June, with plans for more expansion across North America, including Canada, throughout the year.[103] As of January 29, 2016, Musk owns about 28.9 million Tesla shares, which equates to about 22% of the company.[104][105]

As of 2014, Musk's annual salary is one dollar, similar to that of Steve Jobs and other CEOs; the remainder of his compensation is in the form of stock and performance-based bonuses.[106][107]

In 2014, Musk announced that Tesla would allow its technology patents to be used by anyone in good faith in a bid to entice automobile manufacturers to speed up development of electric cars. "The unfortunate reality is electric car programs (or programs for any vehicle that doesn't burn hydrocarbons) at the major manufacturers are small to non-existent, constituting an average of far less than 1% of their total vehicle sales", Musk said.[108]

In February 2016, Musk announced that he had acquired the Tesla.com domain name from Stu Grossman, who had owned it since 1992, and changed Tesla's homepage to that domain.[109]

SolarCity

Musk provided the initial concept and financial capital for SolarCity, which was then co-founded in 2006 by his cousins Lyndon and Peter Rive.[110][111] By 2013, SolarCity was the second largest provider of solar power systems in the United States.[112] SolarCity was acquired by Tesla, Inc. in 2016 and is currently a wholly owned subsidiary of Tesla.[113][114][115]

The underlying motivation for funding both SolarCity and Tesla was to help combat global warming.[116] In 2012, Musk announced that SolarCity and Tesla are collaborating to use electric vehicle batteries to smooth the impact of rooftop solar on the power grid, with the program going live in 2013.[117]

On June 17, 2014, Musk committed to building a SolarCity advanced production facility in Buffalo, New York, that would triple the size of the largest solar plant in the United States. Musk stated the plant will be "one of the single largest solar panel production plants in the world", and it will be followed by one or more even bigger facilities in subsequent years.[118][*needs update*]

Hyperloop

On August 12, 2013, Musk unveiled a concept for a high-speed transportation system incorporating reduced-pressure tubes in which pressurized capsules ride on an air cushion driven by linear induction motors and air compressors.[119] The mechanism for releasing the concept was an alpha-design document that, in addition to scoping out the technology, outlined a notional route where such a transport system might be built: between the Greater Los Angeles Area and the San Francisco Bay Area.[120]

After earlier envisioning Hyperloop, Musk assigned a dozen engineers from Tesla and SpaceX who worked for nine months, establishing the conceptual foundations and creating the designs for the transportation system.[121][122] An early design for the system was then published in a whitepaper posted to the Tesla and SpaceX blogs.[123][124][125] Musk's proposal, if technologically feasible at the costs he has cited, would make Hyperloop travel cheaper than any other mode of transport for such long distances. The alpha design was proposed to use a partial vacuum to reduce aerodynamic drag, which it is theorized would allow for high-speed travel with relatively low power, with certain other features like air-bearing skis and an inlet compressor to reduce freestream flow. The document of alpha design estimated the total cost of an LA-to-SF Hyperloop system at US$6 billion, but this amount is speculative.[126]

In June 2015, Musk announced a design competition for students and others to build Hyperloop pods to operate on a SpaceX-sponsored mile-long track in a 2015–2017 Hyperloop pod competition. The track was used in January 2017, and Musk also started building a tunnel.[127]

Hyperloop One, a company unaffiliated with Musk, had announced that it had done its first successful test run on its DevLoop track in Nevada on July 13, 2017. It was on May 12, 2017 at 12:02 a.m. and

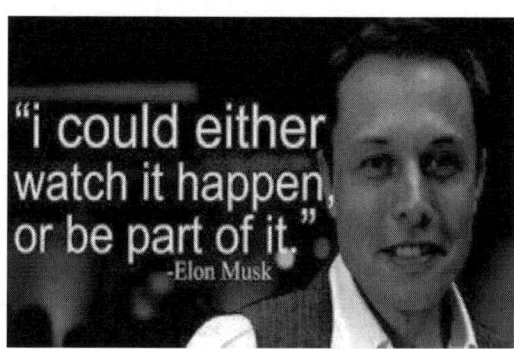

had lasted 5.3 seconds, reaching a top speed of 70 mph.[128]

On July 20, 2017, Elon Musk announced that he had gotten "verbal government

approval" to build a hyperloop from New York City to Washington D.C, stopping in both Philadelphia and Baltimore.[129] However, the New York City Transit Authority, Southeastern Pennsylvania Transportation Authority, Washington Metropolitan Area Transit Authority, Maryland Transit Administration, United States Department of Homeland Security, as well as the mayors of New York, Philadelphia, Baltimore, and Washington D.C. stated that they are unaware of any such agreement.[130]

OpenAI

In December 2015, Musk announced the creation of OpenAI, a not-for-profit artificial intelligence (AI) research company.

OpenAI aims to develop artificial general intelligence in a way that is safe and beneficial to humanity.[131]

By making AI available to everyone, OpenAI wants to "counteract large corporations who may gain too much power by owning super-intelligence systems devoted to profits, as well as governments which may use AI to gain power and even oppress their citizenry".[132] Musk has stated he wants to counteract the concentration of power.[39]

Neuralink

In 2016, Musk co-founded Neuralink, a neurotechnology startup company, to integrate the human brain with artificial intelligence. The company, which is still in the earliest stages of existence, is centered on creating devices that can be implanted in the human brain, with the eventual purpose of helping human beings merge with software and keep pace with advancements in artificial intelligence. These enhancements could improve memory or allow for more direct interfacing with computing devices.[133] Musk sees Neuralink and OpenAI as related: "OpenAI is a nonprofit dedicated to minimizing the dangers of artificial intelligence, while Neuralink is working on ways to implant technology into our brains to create mind-computer interfaces. ... Neuralink allows our brains to keep up in the intelligence race. The machines can't outsmart us if we have everything the machines have plus everything we have. At least, that is if you assume that what we have is actually an advantage."[39]

The Boring Company

On December 17, 2016, while stuck in traffic, Musk tweeted "Am going to build a tunnel boring machine and just start digging..." The company was named 'The Boring Company'.[134] On January 21, 2017, Musk tweeted "Exciting progress on the tunnel front. Plan to start digging in a month or so."[135] The first tunnel will start on the SpaceX campus,[136] and will probably go to a nearby parking garage. As of January 26, 2017, discussions with regulatory bodies have begun,[137] but no requests for permits to dig in the Los Angeles area had been filed with the California Department of Transportation bylate-January 2017.[138]

In February 2017, the company began digging a 30-foot-wide, 50-foot-long, and 15-foot-deep "test trench" on the premises of Space X's offices in Los Angeles, since the construction requires no permits.[139][140] Musk has said that a 10-fold decrease in tunnel boring cost per mile is necessary for economic feasibility of the proposed tunnel network.[141]

Political views

 Musk speaking alongside Irish Taoiseach (Prime Minister) Enda Kenny

Politically, Musk has described himself as "half Democrat, half Republican". In his own words: "I'm somewhere in the middle, socially liberal and fiscally conservative."[142] In December 2016, Musk became a member of two of then President-elect Donald Trump's presidential advisory committees (the Strategic and Policy Forum[143][144][145][146] and Manufacturing Jobs Initiative)[147] but resigned from both in June 2017, in protest at Trump's decision to withdraw the United States from the Paris Agreement on climate change.[148][149]

Musk has described himself as "nauseatingly pro-American". According to Musk, the United States is "[inarguably] the greatest country that has ever existed on Earth", describing it as "the greatest force for good of any country that's ever been." Musk believes outright that there "would not be democracy in the world if not for the United States", arguing there were "three separate occasions in the 20th-century where democracy would have fallen with World War I, World War II and the Cold War, if not for the United States." Musk also stated that he thinks "it would be a mistake to say the United States is perfect, it certainly is not. There have been many foolish things the United States has done and bad things the United States has done."[150]

Prompted by the emergence of self-driving cars and Artificial Intelligence, Musk has voiced support for a universal basic income.[151]

Prior to the election of Donald Trump as President of the United States, Musk criticized candidate Trump by saying: "I feel a bit stronger that he is probably not the right guy. He doesn't seem to have the sort of character that reflects well on the United States."[152] Following Donald Trump's inauguration, Musk expressed approval of Trump's choice of Rex Tillerson as Secretary of State and accepted an invitation to appear on a panel advising President Trump. Regarding his cooperation with Trump, Musk has subsequently commented: "The more voices of reason that the President hears, the better."[153]

Lobbying

In an interview with the *Washington Post*, Musk stated he was a "significant (though not top-tier) donor to Democrats", but that he also gives heavily to Republicans. Musk further stated, "in order to have your voice be heard in Washington, you have to make some little contribution."[154][155]

A recent report from the Sunlight Foundation (a nonpartisan group that tracks government spending), found that "SpaceX has spent over US$4 million on lobbying Congress since it was established in 2002 and doled out more than US$800,000 in political contributions" to Democrats and Republicans. The same report noted that "SpaceX's campaign to win political support has been systematic and sophisticated", and that "unlike most tech-startups, SpaceX has maintained a significant lobbying presence in Washington almost since day 1." The report further noted that "Musk himself has donated roughly US$725,000 to various campaigns since 2002. In 2004, he contributed US$2,000 to President George W. Bush's reelection campaign, maxing out (over US$100,000)[156] to Obama's reelection campaign and donated US$5,000 to Republican Sen. Marco Rubio, who represents Florida, a state critical to the space industry. (...) All told, Musk and SpaceX gave out roughly US$250,000 in the 2012 election cycle."[154][157] Additionally, SpaceX hired former Republican Senate Majority Leader Trent Lott to represent the company, via the Washington-based lobbying group Patton Boggs LLP. Alongside Patton Boggs LLP, SpaceX uses several other outside lobbying firms, who work alongside SpaceX's own lobbyists.[158]

Musk had been a supporter of the U.S. political action committee (PAC) FWD.us, which was started by fellow high-profile entrepreneur Mark Zuckerberg and advocates for immigration reform. However, in May 2013, Musk publicly withdrew his support in protest of advertisements the PAC was running that supported causes like the

Keystone Pipeline. Musk and other members, including David O. Sacks, pulled out, criticizing the strategy as "cynical".[159] Musk further stated, "we shouldn't give in to the politics. If we give in to that, we'll get the political system we deserve."[160]

In December 2013, Sean Becker of the media/political website Mic called Musk a "complete hypocrite", stating that "[for] the 2014 election cycle, Musk has contributed to the Longhorn PAC and the National Republican Congressional Committee – both of which have funded the campaigns of anti-science, anti-environment candidates such as Rep. Michelle Bachman (R-Minn.)."[160] Musk has directly contributed to Republican Sen. Marco Rubio, who has been accused of holding similar positions regarding climate change.[157]

Subsidies

Success doesn't bring happiness, Happiness brings success

~?~

CkvDay.com

Musk has stated that he does not believe the U.S. government should provide subsidies to companies but should instead use a carbon tax to price in the negative externality of air pollution and discourage "bad behavior". Musk argues that the free market would achieve the "best solution", and that producing environmentally unfriendly vehicles should come with its own consequences.[161] Musk's statements have been widely criticized, with Stanford University Professor Fred Turner noting that "if you're an entrepreneur like Elon Musk, you will take the money where you can get it, but at the same time believe as a matter of faith that it's entrepreneurship and technology that are the sources of social change, not the state. It is not quite self-delusion, but there is a habit of thinking of oneself as a free-standing, independent agent, and of not acknowledging the subsidies that one received. And this goes on all the time in Silicon Valley."[162] Author Michael Shellenberger argued that "in the case of Musk, it is hard not to read that as a kind of defensiveness. And I think there is a business reason for it. They are dealing with a lot of investors for whom subsidies are not the basis for a long-term viable business, and they often want to exaggerate the speed with which they are going to be able to become independent." Shellenberger continues, "We would all be better off if these entrepreneurs were a bit more grateful, a bit more humble." While journalist and author Jim Motavalli, who interviewed Musk for *High Voltage*, his 2011 book about the electric vehicle industry, speculated that "Elon is now looking at it from the point of view of a winner, and he doesn't want to see other people win because they get government money – I do think there is a tendency of people, once they have succeeded, to want to pull the ladder up after them."[163]

In 2015, Musk's statements were subject to further scrutiny when an *LA Times* article claimed that SpaceX, Tesla, SolarCity and buyers of their products had or were projected to receive together an estimated

US$4.9 billion in government subsidies over twenty years. One example given is New York State, which is spending $750 million to build a solar panel factory in Buffalo which will be leased to SolarCity for $1 a year. The deal also includes no property taxes for a decade, an estimated $260 million valuation. Musk employs a former U.S. State Department official as the chief negotiator for Tesla.[164]

Opinions

Destiny and religion

When asked whether he believed "there was some kind of destiny involved" in humanity's transition to a multi-planetary species, rather than "just physics", Musk responded:

Well, I do. Do I think that there's some sort of master intelligence architecting all of this stuff? I think probably not because then you have to say: "Where does the master intelligence come from?" So it sort of begs the question. So I think really you can explain this with the fundamental laws of physics. You know it's complex phenomenon from simple elements.[165]

Musk has stated that he does not pray, or worship any being, although previously admitted to praying before an important Falcon 1 launch, asking "any entities that [were] listening" to "bless [the] launch". When asked whether he believed "religion and science could co-exist", Musk replied "probably not".[166]

Extraterrestrial life

Although Musk believes "there is a good chance that there is simple life on other planets", he "questions whether there is other intelligent life in the known universe".[166]

Musk later clarified his "hope that there is other intelligent life in the known universe", and stated that it is "probably more likely than not, but that's a complete guess."[167]

Musk has also considered the simulation hypothesis as a potential solution to the Fermi paradox:

The absence of any noticeable life may be an argument in favour of us being in a simulation.... Like when you're playing an adventure game, and you can see the stars in the background, but you can't ever get there. If it's not a simulation, then maybe we're in a lab and there's some advanced alien civilization that's just watching how we develop, out of curiosity, like mould in a petri dish.... If you look at our current technology level, something strange has to happen to civilizations.

After the internet became a mainstream phenomenon in the late 1990s, it changed life as we know it. Communications, travel, music, government... shopping. Yes, retailers large and small have embraced the Internet as a way sell to customers across the country... and around the world.

E-commerce has grown exponentially over the last decade and shows no signs of slowing down. Consider that 40 percent of the world's internet users, that's more than 1 billion people, have shopped online at least once.

And worldwide business-to-consumer online sales were $1.7 trillion in 2015... and that grew to $2.35 trillion at the end of 2016.

Large e-tailers like Amazon and eBay, as well as traditional retailers like Walmart, have embraced the online business model wholeheartedly. But even though they may dominate the industry, that doesn't mean there isn't room for small operators like you.

In fact, there's never been a better time to get involved in selling online as a solo entrepreneur. It's so much easier to make money with an online business than have a bricks-and-mortar store. The risk, the investment, and time spent is so much smaller.

Along with all this e-commerce activity has grown a whole new way to create and sell products. And it happens to be the easiest, most cost-effective, and oftentimes most profitable way to operate an online business. I'm talking about selling information products.

What Are Digital Information Products?

An information product can come in all sorts of formats, but at its heart a product like this must pass on useful advice to the consumer.

Despite the name, people don't want simply information. They crave tips and strategies for making their life better. They want guidance. And that's what the best information products provide, whether it's a video, an ebook, an audio, a webinar, a membership website...

Keep in mind that in this case, although a CD or DVD or a printed book is technically an information product, we want to focus solely on those products that are delivered electronically, usually via download or some secure membership website.

For example, an ebook in PDF format, a video on a password-protected site, or an audio recording downloaded from your website. The reason for this is because this way your customers can order products anytime day or night, from anywhere in the world, and get their product instantly, without you being involved in the transaction. It's money while you sleep. Sure, you will have to handle customer service and keep an eye on sales. But it's much less hassle than having to keep track and send out orders.

Why You Should Sell Digital Information Products Online

There are several more advantages with digital information products.

1. They are easy and cheap to create. You can make a digital information product using nothing but your time and mental energy. That's free when it comes to your investment money-wise. You just need ideas. Then you write your ebook, film your video, record your audio, create your webinar... whatever you plan to do. This also means that if the product doesn't sell as well as you like, you haven't sunk any

money into the project. That reduces your risk and financial exposure.

2.   It's virtually free to store them. Because these products are digital, they are simply space on a server, on your computer (make sure to back it up), or on the cloud. For people with physical products, if they're not doing online drop shipping, they have to carry large inventories. That costs money to store and manage all that product if you have a warehouse and have hired a fulfillment house or other provider to oversee it. And don't even think about doing it at home — you'll quickly become overwhelmed. Much better to stick with digital in which your products take up basically no space.

At this point, you might be worried. You're thinking that if you have digital products being sent to customers... what's to stop them from sending copies to their friends or selling it on their own? Nothing really. But rest assured that 99.9 percent of your customers won't do this. And for the most part information marketers aren't too concerned about this issue cannibalizing sales.

How to Find a Profitable Market for Information Products

So how do create your own information products... and make sure they'll be bestsellers?

The first step is research. You need to follow the trends and figure out what the most profitable niche markets online are right now and what format would work best to meet that need. A great place to start is with your own interests. If you can match a profitable business with a passion, you're all set.

So start with an interest you have. Then start checking around online to see whether you are the only one who loves... online poker, for example. Look for blogs, Facebook groups, and online forums for discussions about this niche. Look at the mainstream news — is it mentioned? Look at retailers like Amazon or eBay to see what products they have for sale in this niche.

For information products in particular, you should check out the site Clickbank.com, which used to specialize in information products although it has branched out into other areas.

You'll find many categories in all of these places, from yoga to dog training to travel planning to weight loss and fitness... there's sure to be something that you're interested in.

From all these sources you'll get a good sense of whether or not this a viable trend with sales potential. You should also research what sorts of products are offered, the topics they cover, the prices... this is also vital market data you can use to guide as you create and sell your own similar information products. You're not plagiarizing or ripping off — you're getting inspiration.

It may seem counterintuitive to seek out thriving markets and then try to join in. But that simply means that there is a ready market for your products. It's not good to be a pioneer and try to create a market from scratch — that's often a recipe for failure. Your prospect's follow trends and latch on to fads... you should too. At least until the next trend comes along.

How to Create Digital Information Products

"Technology is the key to helping the company achieve its goals. It's exciting to work on projects that directly impact our growth."

- Pinneer

As far as creating your information products, that's easy too. Remember that the content, whatever the format, should be useful advice. You could create how-to guides, strategies, tips, and tricks... provide something the prospect can't get on their own.

For ebooks, magazines, and similar products, you can create them in Microsoft Word and then save them as a PDF. For the cover, find a freelancer on a site like Fiverr.com to create a professional looking cover for you for very little money — as little as $5.

To film videos you can use your smartphone or a simple point-and-click camera. Once you have the "raw" movie file, you can use an intuitive video editing software like iMovie (if you have a Mac) or Windows Movie Maker to create your own cleanly edited video.

Audios are simple too. Just use GarageBand (if you have a Mac) or the Sound Recorder app on Windows Media Player to record your voice. You will need a microphone.

If you want to interview others, you could use something like Skype or GoToWebinar.

Another option, if you're showing people something your computer screen, like explaining the features of a piece of software, you can use the screen capture program like Camtasia to film every second of what you do to playback later.

How to Market Your Information Products

In many ways, no matter how far we've come when it comes to technology and online selling... the same principles of marketing and consumer psychology hold true. And that's definitely the case with your online venture.

The name of the game here is direct-response marketing. Back in the day, this was done with snail mail flyers, letters, magalogs, catalogs, and other printed material. Yes, so-called "junk mail." But they wouldn't send it out by the millions if it didn't work. These days this sort of content is sent out electronically. And it still works like a charm

to get customers to open their wallets.

The good news is that you don't have to spend a ton of money when you engage in direct-response marketing online. Email marketing is a virtually free method to reach sell your products. And that will be the basis of your marketing efforts.

The basic idea is create a list of email subscribers. You send them both useful content — free valuable information related to your product/niche, as well as offers to buy products. Sending them the free content will speed up the process of them knowing, liking, and trusting you enough to buy your paid products. The novelty of buying stuff online wore off years ago and now people have a lot to choose from — you must give them a warm fuzzy feeling to be the one they buy from.

Yes, only a small percentage of people will actually respond. But that's how direct response works. You should have enough prospects coming in that even a small percentage of conversions will result in a profit.

To build an email list, you can employ a variety of methods.
1. Search Engine Optimization: In a nutshell, you use valuable content on your website or blog to catch the attention of Google and get listed high in the search results.

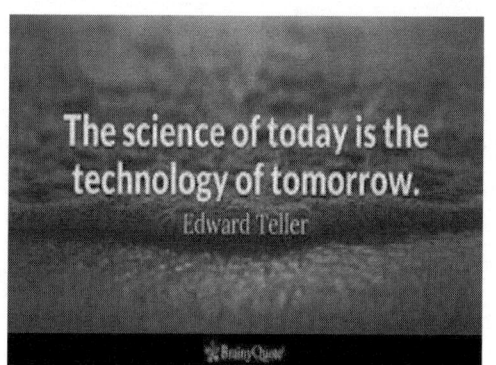

The science of today is the technology of tomorrow.

Edward Teller

BrainyQuote

2. Paid ads: Whether you use Google's own pay-per-click ads or banner ads or run ads on a blog network, this can be a viable option, albeit expensive.

Social Media: Networks like Facebook are invaluable at reaching a targeted customer base these days.

So how do you take it to the next level? You tap into that small amount of people who buy your introductory product, also known as a front-end product. You contact those people differently than your normal subscribers.

Because they have bought something, they are more likely to buy similar products. So you offer them more in-depth, higher-priced products, known as "back end products." That's where the big money is. A back end product could be one-on-one coaching or an event, for example.

Putting It All Together

As you can see information products make for the perfect online business. They're digital, easy to create and deliver. And the profit margins are huge.

So next steps...

1. Find your niche – make sure it has bestselling potential.

2. Figure out which format works best for your niche: audio, video, ebook, etc.

3. Create your information product(s).

4. Create an email list and then market to that list.

5. Profit!

Online Business

      Affiliate Marketing

      Basics

      Web Hosting

      Daily Operations

      Social Media Marketing

      Email Marketing

      Driving Traffic

Blogging

Shortly after the creation of the World Wide Web (WWW), a new breed of business entrepreneurship took hold in America and throughout the world. Pioneering affiliate networks like *ClickBank* saw the potential of a new type of product that with time could rival oil, coffee, gold and any other commodity known to humanity. The product in question is *information*, and thanks to the Internet anyone anywhere in the world has the potential to become an information entrepreneur; i.e. an *infopreneur.*

The Selling of Information Products Over and Over Again A large percentage of

people starting an affiliate marketing business choose to market and sell *information products*, loosely defined as information packed in a specific format (e.g. text, audio, video, etc.) and meant to be sold and delivered to end customers. The best

example of information being sold today is the highly lucrative "How to" category that can be found everywhere, literally in any niche in existence.

Of particular interest to infopreneurs on the Internet are *digital information products*, information products that are sold in digital format of some sort. As opposed to hardcover or softcover books, CDs, manuals or reports, an infopreneur can deliver these items as PDF files, audio files, streaming video and other emerging media. This substantially reduces delivery and transportation costs for businesses and gives customers immediate access to highly coveted information. See also: How to Make Money Publishing Digital Books on Amazon Kindle Thanks to the Internet, passive income can become a reality, thanks to the "create it once, get paid over and over again" model of digital information product-based affiliate marketing. Distinguishing Infopreneurs from Hardcore Sellers.

At this stage as an affiliate, you may not be prepared to create your own information products. However, that does not mean you should discount your ability to offer a value-added service to prospects looking for ways to save money, learn a new skill, or become more time efficient.

Online infopreneurs distinguish themselves from traditional salespeople in that they take a *relationship-oriented marketing* approach *to* doing business. Through various contact
methods like e-mail marketing and social media, they establish their expert status *a priori* as well as a persona suitable for their intended (ideal) audience

Just because you are not the author of the affiliate product does not mean you are not a valuable part of this e-commerce chain. You are offering information in suitable form to prospects looking to solve a problem, and you are holding the key to improving their lives via your affiliate offers.

Benefits of Being an Affiliate Marketing Infopreneur

Making a real commitment to affiliate marketing entails great responsibility and great opportunities at the same time. The following themes are discussed in more detail in other affiliate marketing articles found here, but for now, just accept the following advantages of this type of business:

Direct, relationship-based marketing to potential, "warm" customers looking for an excuse to spend money on your offers.

Less pressure to recruit an endless stream of "tire- clickers". Keeping loyal customers loyal for the benefit of all. Greater opportunities to demonstrate your expertise and trustworthiness to a welcoming audience.

Offering different levels of engagement to people at different stages of purchase comfort.

Various media options to choose from to make information enticing enough to buy!

The Sales Funnel Approach to Infopreneurship

Traditional book authors working through a publishing house, even the successful ones, generally have no idea who buys their books, nor do they possess their customers' contact information. Affiliate marketers following the infopreneurial business approach, on the other hand, are blessed with business channels and opportunities that permit them to build long-term, profitable relationships based on the needs and desires of each customer beyond the "one-shot" sale.

This sales funnel approach to affiliate marketing has proven itself time and time again and is used by the biggest and richest entrepreneurs in the world. For our purposes, it lets you ease your prospects into increasing levels of price, time and product engagement depending on their circumstances.

So, still think that offering free reports to skeptical e-mail subscribers is a waste of time? It could lead to thousands of dollars in sales later on, either through a lifetime of small purchases (e.g. e-books, study guides), the occasional purchase of a complete package, or permission to access a continuity program (a paid monthly subscription to a website, coaching program, etc.) of some sort oI hope you leant a few things in this material. I wisjh you all the best in your endaevours.

Cheers!!!

REFERENCES

1. https://www.entrepreneur.com/article/234833 ACCESSED 28/09/2017
2. https://www.wealthresult.com/darlinton-omeh accessed 28/09/2017
3. http://businessforts.com/blog/about-efe-imiren-and-serviceforts Accessed 28/09/2017
4. https://vimeo.com/blog/post/just-take-my-money-nine-rules-for-creating-killer
   a. Accessed 28/09/2017
5. https://lifehacker.com/how-to-start-your-own-podcast-1709798447 Accessed 28/09/2017
6. https://www.biznessapps.com/blog/app-reseller-tip-what-makes-a-successful-white-label-mobile-app/
   a. https://lists.gnu.org/archive/html/dotgnu-general/2005-09/msg00037.html

   b. Jump up^ *"Research on the MacroEconomic Effects of Patents".*

   c. Jump up^ *"All Registered Sites". demo.ffii.org/online_supporters. FFII. Archived from the original on 2005-03-10. Retrieved 2014-02-13.*

   d. Jump up^ *FFII. "Donors of the FFII". Ffii.org. Retrieved 2012-07-09.*

e. Jump up^ *"Foundation for a Free Information Infrastructure". Retrieved 11 August 2013.*

f. Jump up^ *"FFII France".* Retrieved *11 August 2013.*

External links

7. *Murray, James (2011-12-18). "Cloud network architecture and ICT - Modern Network Architecture". TechTarget =ITKnowledgeExchange. Retrieved 2013-08-18.*

8. Jump up^ *"Information and Communication Technology from". FOLDOC. 2008-09-19.*

9. Jump up^ *"ICT - What is it?". www.tutor2u.net. Retrieved 2015-09-01.*

10. Jump up^ *Zuppo, Colrain M. "Defining ICT in a Boundaryless World: The Development of a Working Hierarchy" (PDF). International Journal of Managing Information Technology (IJMIT). p. 19. Retrieved 2016-02-13.*

11. Jump up^ https://www.computer.org/web/pressroom/framework

12. Jump up^ William Melody et al., *Information and Communication Technologies: Social Sciences Research and Training: A Report by the ESRC Programme on Information and Communication Technologies*, ISBN 0-86226-179-1, 1986. Roger Silverstone et al., "Listening to a long conversation: an ethnographic approach to the study of information and communication technologies in the home", *Cultural Studies*, 5(2), pages 204–227, 1991.

13. Jump up^ The Independent ICT in Schools Commission, *Information and Communications Technology in UK Schools: An Independent Inquiry, 1997.* Impact noted in Jim Kelly, What the Web is Doing for Schools, Financial Times, 2000.

14. Jump up^ Royal Society, Shut down or restart? The way forward for computing in UK schools, 2012, page 18.

15. Jump up^ Department for Education, *"National curriculum in England: computing programmes of study".*

16. Jump up^ United Nations Office of Information and Communications Technology, About

17. ^ Jump up to: [a] [b] [c] *"IT Costs – The Costs, Growth And Financial Risk Of Software Assets".* OMT-CO

Operations Management Technology Consulting GmbH. Retrieved 26 June 2011.

18. Jump up^http://www.whitehouse.gov/sites/default/files/omb/assets/egov_docs/2014_budget_priorities_20130410.pdf

19. ^Jump up to:[a] [b] [c] [d] "The World's Technological Capacity to Store, Communicate, and Compute Information", Martin Hilbert and Priscila López (2011), Science (journal), 332(6025), 60-65; see also "free access to the study" and "video animation".

20. Jump up^ " Information in the Biosphere: Biological and Digital Worlds ", Gillings, M. R., Hilbert, M., & Kemp, D. J. (2016), Trends in Ecology & Evolution, 31(3), 180–189; free access to the article http://escholarship.org/uc/item/38f4b791

21. Jump up^ [http:// 10.1016/j.telpol.2016.01.006 "The bad news is that the digital access divide is here to stay: Domestically installed bandwidths among 172 countries for 1986–2014"], Martin Hilbert (2016), Telecommunications Policy; free access to the article http://escholarship.org/uc/item/2jp4w5rq

22. *Jump up^ "Figure 1.9 Share of ICT sector in total value added, 2013". doi:10.1787/888933224163.*

23. Jump up^ *"Measuring the Information Society"* (PDF). *International Telecommunication Union. 2011. Retrieved 25 July 2013.*

24. ^ Jump up to: ^a b *"ITU releases annual global ICT data and ICT Development Index country rankings - librarylearningspace.com"*. *Retrieved 2015-09-01.*

25. Jump up^ *"Basic information : about wsis"*. International *Telecommunication Union. 17 January 2006. Retrieved 26 May 2012.*

26. ^ Jump up to: ^a b *"ICT Facts and Figures – The world in 2015"*. *ITU. Retrieved 2015-09-01.*

27. Jump up^ *"ICT in Education"*. Unesco. *Unesco. Retrieved 10 March 2016.*

28. Jump up^ Blackwell, C.K., Lauricella, A.R. and Wartella, E., 2014. Factors influencing digital technology use in early childhood education. Computers & Education, 77, pp.82-90.

29. ^ Jump up to: ^a b *"ITU releases annual global ICT data and ICT Development Index country rankings"*. *www.itu.int.*
Retrieved 2015-09-01.

30. Jump up^ *"Survey: 1 In 6 Internet Users Own A Smartwatch Or Fitness Tracker"*. *ARC. Retrieved 2015-09-01.*

31. Jump up^ *"ITU releases annual global ICT data and ICT Development Index country rankings"*. *www.itu.int. Retrieved 2015-09-01.*

32. Jump up^ Bimber, Bruce (1998-01-01). "The Internet and Political Transformation: Populism, Community, and Accelerated Pluralism". Polity. 31 (1): 133–160. doi:10.2307/3235370. JSTOR 3235370.

33. Jump up^ Hussain, Muzammil M.; Howard, Philip N. (2013-03-01). "What Best Explains Successful Protest Cascades? ICTs and the Fuzzy Causes of the Arab Spring". International Studies Review. 15 (1): 48–66. doi:10.1111/misr.12020. ISSN 1521-9488.

34. Jump up^ Kirsh, David (2001). "The Context of Work". Human Computer Interaction.

35. "How celebrity coach Tony Robbins spends his millions". Business Insider. Retrieved 2017-06-29.

36. Jump up^ Schnall, Marianne (2014-11-20). "Interview with Tony Robbins on His New Book, 'Money: Master the Game'". Huffington Post. Retrieved 2017-06-29.

37. Jump up^ Inc., NASDAQ,. "Feeding America to Ring The Nasdaq Stock Market Opening Bell". GlobeNewswire News Room. Retrieved 2017-06-29.

38. Jump up^ FOX. "Tony Robbins: "Money: Master the Game"". KTTV. Retrieved 2017-06-29.

39. Jump up^ "The Power 100 | 2016". Worth. 2016-10-17. Retrieved 2017-10-18.

40. Jump up^ "The Power 100 | 2016". Worth. Retrieved 2017-06-

41. ^ Jump up to: [a] [b] [c] O'Keefe, Brian (October 31, 2014). "Tony Robbins, The CEO Whisperer". Fortune. Retrieved November 1, 2014.

42. ^ Jump up to: [a] [b] O'Keefe, Brian. "Tony Robbins, The CEO Whisperer". Fortune. Retrieved 2017-06-29

1. Jump up^ GRANBERRY, MICHAEL (1991-10-01). "A True Believer : Tony Robbins Has Attracted Converts–and Critics–to His Positive-Thinking Empire". Los Angeles Times. ISSN 0458-3035. Retrieved 2017-06-29.

2. Jump up^ Rolando Ponce de Leon. "Anthony Robbins: A true motivation life". MotivationLife. Archived from the original on October 16, 2009. Retrieved December 31, 2009.

3. Jump up^ "Tony Robbins tribute to Jim Rohn - Success Guide". www.success-guide.com. Retrieved 2017-07-02.

4. ^ Jump up to: [a] [b] "Who Inspires Tony Robbins?". SUCCESS. 2016-11-17. Retrieved 2017-07-02.

5. Jump up^ *Robbins, Tony (2007). Awaken the Giant Within: How to Take Immediate Control of Your Mental, Emotional, Physical and Financial Destiny. Free Press.* ISBN 0-671-79154-0.

6. Jump up^ *Brynildssen, Shawna; Smith, Dawn M. (2011). "Guthy-Renker Corporation," International Directory of Company Histories. 119 (Karen Hill ed.). Detroik: St. James Press.*

7. Jump up^ *GRANBERRY, MICHAEL (1991-10-01). "A True Believer : Tony Robbins Has Attracted Converts–and Critics–to His Positive-Thinking Empire". Los Angeles Times.* ISSN 0458-3035. *Retrieved 2017-07-02.*

8. Jump up^ *Robbins, Anthony (2005). Leadership Academy Manual. San Diego, California: Robbins Research International, Inc. p. 3.*

9. ^ Jump up to:[a][b] *"Who is Tony Robbins? • AISUCCES". AISUCCES (in Romanian). Retrieved 2017-07-02.*

10. Jump up^ *"The Learning Annex / Online Classes / Adult Education / About Us". www2.learningannex.com. Retrieved 2017-07-02.*

11. Jump up^ *"From addict to leader". Israel National News. Retrieved 2017-07-02.*

12. Jump up^ *Baxter, Kevin (2014-10-30). "Magic Johnson, Mia Hamm among owners of new L.A. pro soccer team". Los Angeles Times.* ISSN 0458-3035. *Retrieved 2017-07-02.*

13. Jump up^ *"Will Ferrell joins Magic Johnson and Mia Hamm as an owner of new MLS team LAFC". For The Win. 2016-01-08. Retrieved 2017-07-02.*

14. Jump up^ *O'Keefe, Brian. "Deep-pocketed owners bet big on new MLS soccer team in Los Angeles". Fortune. Retrieved 2017-07-02.*

15. Jump up^ *"eSports powerhouse Team Liquid picked up by new investor group". Engadget. Retrieved 2017-10-18.*

16. Jump up^ *Allen, Eric Van. "Team Liquid Wins Over $10 Million At International Dota 2 Tournament". Compete. Retrieved 2017-10-18.*

17. Jump up^ *"Why Bill Clinton Has Tony Robbins on Speed Dial". Inc.com. 19 March 2015. Retrieved 2017-07-02.*

18. Jump up^ http://thepowerofideas.ideapod.com/tony-robbins-former-business-coach-donald-trump-explains-makes-trump-successful/

19. Jump up^ *"Slump buster: Giants' Tuck walks on hot coals". ESPN.com. Retrieved 2017-07-02.*

20. Jump up^ *"Tony Robbins has taught this productivity trick to clients ranging from Bill Clinton to Serena Williams". Business Insider. Retrieved 2017-07-02.*

21. Jump up^ *"Hugh Jackman on His Surprising Hollywood BFFs and Mother's Abandonment". The Hollywood Reporter. Retrieved 2017-07-02.*

22. Jump up^ *Addicted2SuccessTV (2013-05-26), Pitbull Motivated For Success By Tony Robbins, retrieved 2017-10-18*

23. Jump up^ *O'Keefe, Brian. "Tony Robbins, The CEO Whisperer". Fortune. Retrieved 2017-07-02.*

24. Jump up^ *"Accenture Study Yields Top 50 'Business Intellectuals' Ranking of Top Thinkers and Writers on*

Management Topics / Accenture Newsroom".
newsroom.accenture.com. Retrieved 2017-07-02.

25. Jump up^ *Caprino, Kathy. "Tony Robbins Reveals The Top 6 Leadership Blind Spots That Cripple Business Success". Forbes. Retrieved 2017-07-02.*

26. Jump up^ *"The Celebrity 100 - Forbes.com". www.forbes.com. Retrieved 2017-10-18.*

27. Jump up^ *"No. 1 best-selling author Tony Robbins gives a deeply personal interview for Jan. 2015 SUCCESS magazine". SUCCESS. December 12, 2014. Archived from the original on August 4, 2017. Retrieved July 5, 2017.*

28. Jump up^ *Ellin, Abby (2010-08-06). "With Tony Robbins, Self-Help Author". The New York Times. ISSN 0362-4331. Retrieved 2017-07-05.*

29. Jump up^ *Channick, Robert. "Self-help guru Tony Robbins tackles financial advice". chicagotribune.com. Retrieved 2017-07-05.*

30. Jump up^ *Israel, Ira (2014-12-24). ""Money: Master The Game:" Book Review". Huffington Post. Retrieved 2017-07-05.*

31. Jump up^ *Ellin, Abby (2010-08-06). "With Tony Robbins, Self-Help Author". The New York Times. ISSN 0362-4331. Retrieved 2017-07-18.*

32. Jump up^ *"Neuro Associative Conditioning". www.sportshealth4u.com. Archived from the original on January 30, 2009. Retrieved July 18, 2017.*

33. Jump up^ *Schnall, Marianne (2012-04-29). "An In-depth Interview With Life Coach Tony Robbins". Huffington Post. Retrieved 2017-07-18.*

34. Jump up^ *Tony Robbins (2016-01-21), Science of Achievement & Art of Fulfillment / Tony Robbins, retrieved 2017-07-18*

35. Jump up^ *Heller, Karen (1 December 2014). "Tony Robbins, Self-Help Guru, is Larger Than Life". Washington Post. Retrieved 18 July 2017.*

36. Jump up^ *Robbins, Tony (1987). Unlimited Power. Fawcett Columbine (Ballantine Books). ISBN 0-449-90280-3.*

37. Jump up^ *"Our History - Anthony Robbins Foundation". anthonyrobbinsfoundation.org. Retrieved 2017-07-16.*

38. Jump up^ *"Our Mission". Anthony Robbins Foundation. Retrieved 15 July 2015.*

39. Jump up^ *"Basket Brigade - Anthony Robbins Foundation". anthonyrobbinsfoundation.org. Retrieved 2017-07-16.*

40. Jump up^ *Schnall, Marianne (2016-05-28). "Tony Robbins and Bob Carr Join Forces to Change the World One Child at a Time". Huffington Post. Retrieved 2017-10-18.*

41. Jump up^ *Charity Navigator (2013). "Anthony Robbins Foundation". Charity Navigator Ratings. Retrieved January 4, 2014.*

42. Jump up^ *Hellmich, Nanci (10 December 2014). "Tony Robbins' 7 steps to financial freedom in retirement". USA Today. Retrieved 15 July 2015.*

43. Jump up^ *"Tony Robbins Provides Millions More Meals To Feeding America® To Help Families In Need". Feeding America. Retrieved 2017-07-16.*

44. Jump up^ *"Tony Robbins on The Profound Moment That Inspired Him To End Hunger Nationwide". Woman's Day. 2015-08-08. Retrieved 2017-07-16.*

45. Jump up^ *"Reports from Feeding America - GlobalGiving". www.globalgiving.org. Retrieved 2017-07-16.*

46. Jump up^ *America, Feeding. "Tony Robbins and Feeding America® Exceed Goals and Provide Millions of Meals to Help Families in Need". www.prnewswire.com. Retrieved 2017-07-16.*

47. Jump up^ *"Tony Robbins: The Day I Became (Truly) Wealthy – Thrive Global". Thrive Global. 2016-11-30. Retrieved 2017-07-16.*

48. Jump up^ *"Benefactors".* Global *Learning XPRIZE. 2016-04-19. Retrieved 2017-10-18.*

49. Jump up^ *Shinneman, Shawn (21 March 2017). "After a-ha moment, Dallas CEO leads charge against sex trafficking". www.bizjournals.com. Retrieved 2017-10-18.*

50. Jump up^ *"Robbins Research International, Inc".* Federal *Trade Commission. 1995-05-16. Retrieved 2017-07-03.*

51. Jump up^ *Hoffman, Ivan. "Fair Use: Further, Further Issues". www.ivanhoffman.com. Retrieved 2017-07-05.*

52. Jump up^ *"Wade Cook Jury Award vs. Tony Robbins Upheld by 9th Circuit Court. - Free Online Library". www.thefreelibrary.com. Retrieved 2017-07-05.*

53. Jump up^ *"Casetext".* casetext.com. *Retrieved 2017-10-18.*

54. Jump up^ *Hoffman, Ivan. "Fair Use: Further, Further Issues". www.ivanhoffman.com. Retrieved 2017-10-18.*

55. Jump up^ *"News > News Item"*. Stockwatch. *Archived from the original on April 27, 2006. Retrieved October 17, 2011.*

56. Jump up^ *"2005 BCSC 1634 Robbins v. Pacific Newspaper Group Inc. et al"*. Courts.gov.bc.ca. *Retrieved October 17, 2011.*

57. Jump up^ Doocy, Steve (August 8, 2012). *"Fox News"*. *Archived from the original on August 9, 2012.*

58. Jump up^ Schnall, Marianne (July 31, 2012). *"Tony Robbins Sets the Record Straight About Fire Walk 'Controversy'"*. *Huffington Post. Retrieved August 7, 2012.*

59. Jump up^ Kurhi, Eric; Gomez, Mark (July 21, 2012). *"San Jose: 21 people treated for burns after firewalk at Tony Robbins appearance"*. *San Jose Mercury News. Retrieved July 22, 2012.*

60. Jump up^ *"Robbins Seminar Continues Despite Dozens Burned At Fire-Walking Event"*.

61. Jump up^ *"Robbins Seminar Continues Despite Dozens Burned At Fire-Walking Event"*. *Retrieved 2017-07-05.*

62. Jump up^ *"False Alarm at Tony Robbins's Dallas Seminar"*. Inc.com. *24 June 2016. Retrieved 2017-07-05.*

63. Jump up^ Ramirez, Cesar (18 March 2010). *"Tony Robbins. Do You Really Know Him?"*. *Cesar Ramirez. Retrieved 10 July 2017.*

64. Jump up^ Flanagan, Graham (28 March 2015). *"Tony Robbins reveals the real story behind his unforgettable 'Shallow Hal' cameo"*. *Business Insider. Retrieved 10 July 2017.*

65. Jump up^ *"Tony Robbins Net Worth"*. The *Celeb Worth. 26 July 2013. Retrieved 10 July2017.*

66. Jump up^ *"The SIngularity Is Near (2010)"*. wn.com. *4 May 2014. Retrieved 10 July2017.*

67. Jump up^ *"Tony Robbins Hungry". YouTube. 2012-06-13. Retrieved 2013-09-28.*

68. Jump up^ *Schneider, Michael (February 9, 2009). ""Variety": "NBC Picks Up "Breakthrough with Tony Robbins"""". Variety.com. Retrieved October 17, 2011.*

69. Jump up^ *"Breakthrough with Tony Robbins to Debut July 27". TVGuide.com.*

70. Jump up^ *Press, The Associated. "Tony Robbins' series pulled from NBC schedule". sandiegouniontribune.com. Retrieved 2017-07-10.*

71. Jump up^ *"Tony Robbins, Parts 1 and 2". Oprah.com. 2012-02-19.*

72. Jump up^ *"First Look: Breakthrough with Tony Robbins". Oprah.com. Retrieved 2017-07-10.*

73. Jump up^ *Gallo, Carmine (February 24, 2012). "How Tony Robbins Gets in Peak State for Presentations". Forbes.com.*

74. ^ Jump up to: [a] [b] *Catsoulis, Jeannette (2016-07-12). "Review: 'Tony Robbins: I Am Not Your Guru' Depicts a Self-Help Prophet". The New York Times. ISSN 0362-4331. Retrieved 2017-07-10.*

75. Jump up^ *Gallo, Carmine. "How Tony Robbins Gets in Peak State for Presentations". Forbes. Retrieved 2017-07-10.*

76. Jump up^ *Sharf, Zack. "Joe Berlinger's Tony Robbins Documentary to Open 2016 AmDocs Film Festival | IndieWire". www.indiewire.com. Retrieved 2017-07-10.*

77. Jump up^ *"Netflix Premiers New Joe Berlinger Documentary – Tony Robbins: I am Not Your Guru Exclusively to Members Worldwide on July 15". Netflix. March 9, 2016. Retrieved 2017-07-10.*

78. Jump up^ *"Tony Robbins: An Awakened Giant Within... Life &*

Lessons". One Life Success. 1 May 2014. Retrieved 11 August 2015.[dead link]

79. Jump up^ *Geoffrey Brewer (November 1993). "Is this guy for real?". Sales & Marketing Management. p. 92.*

80. ^ Jump up to:[a] [b] *Robbins, Anthony J. (2002). "Business Leader Profiles for Students". pp. 390–394.*

81. Jump up^ *"About - Tony Robbins". Tony Robbins.*

82. Jump up^ *"Tony Robbins' True Love". Oprah.com. Retrieved 2017-07-03.*

83. Jump up^ *Neal Hall (30 June 2005). "Robbins posed as waiter to meet future in-laws, court told: Father-in-law says his daughter, millionaire were 'really good friends' in August 2000". Vancouver Sun.*

84. Jump up^ *"How you can better influence people".*

85. *Carroll, Roy (July 17, 2013). "Elon Musk's mission to Mars". The Guardian. London, UK. Retrieved July 23, 2013.*

86. ^ Jump up to:[a] [b] *"75 most influential people: Elon Musk".* Esquire. *October 1, 2008.*

87. Jump up^ *"Space Exploration Technologies Corporation Press Release". SpaceX. Retrieved December 15, 2012.*

88. Jump up^ *"Elon Musk: I'll Put a Man on Mars in 10 Years".* Market *Watch. New York. April 22, 2011. Archived from the original on December 1, 2011. Retrieved December 1, 2011.*

89. Jump up^ *Elon Musk speaks at the Hyperloop Pod Award Ceremony (2016.1.30). January 31, 2016. Retrieved February 21, 2016 – via YouTube.*

90. Jump up^ Davenport, Christian (June 13, 2016). "Elon Musk provides new details on his 'mind blowing' mission to Mars". Washington Post. Retrieved June 14, 2016.

91. Jump up^ Chang, Kenneth (September 27, 2016). "Elon Musk's Plan: Get Humans to Mars, and Beyond". New York Times. Retrieved September 27, 2016.

92. Jump up^ Lambert, Fred (November 16, 2016). "Elon Musk's stake in SpaceX is actually worth more than his Tesla shares". Electrek. Retrieved November 17, 2016.

93. Jump up^ Elon Musk (29 September 2017). Becoming a Multiplanet Species (video). 68th annual meeting of the International Astronautical Congress in Adelaide, Australia: SpaceX. Retrieved 2017-12-31 – via YouTube.

94. Jump up^ Dent, Steve (29 September 2017). "Elon Musk's Mars dream hinges on a giant new rocket". Engadget. Retrieved 2018-01-01.

95. Jump up^ Burns, Matt (October 8, 2014). "A Brief History of Tesla". TechCrunch. TechCrunch.com. Retrieved June 11, 2015.

96. Jump up^ Nordqvist, Joseph (February 12, 2014). "Tesla Motors Inc.–Company Information". Market Business News. Archived from the original on February 12, 2014. Retrieved April 16, 2014.

97. Jump up^ Musk, Elon (August 2, 2006). "The Secret Tesla Motors Master Plan (just between you and me) No. 124". Tesla Motors. Archived from the original on August 2, 2010. Retrieved October 3, 2010. [self-published source]

98. Jump up^ Musk, Elon. "CEO Elon Musk". Tesla Motors. Retrieved October 20, 2010.

99. Jump up^ Morrison, Chris (October 15, 2008). "Musk steps in as CEO". The New York Times.

100.   Jump up^ *Graham Ruddick. "Tesla's Model X electric car spreads falcon wings at US launch". the Guardian. Retrieved November 4, 2015.*

101.   Jump up^ *"Tesla Model X: Not a model launch".* Fortune. *Retrieved November 4, 2015.*

102.   Jump up^ *"Model X".* Tesla *Motors. October 29, 2012.*

103.   Jump up^ *Joann Muller (June 1, 2013). "What Do Toyota And Mercedes See in Tesla? A Bit of Themselves". Forbes.com.*

104.   Jump up^ *Musk, Elon (August 2, 2006). "The Secret Tesla Motors Master Plan (just between you and me)". Tesla Motors.*

105.   Jump up^ *Hamilton, Tyler (October 12, 2009). "Tesla CEO following in Henry Ford's tracks". Toronto Star. Archived from the original on October 17, 2009.*

106.   Jump up^ *Del Ray, Jason (May 29, 2013), Musk: You'll Be Able to Drive Your Tesla Cross-Country by Year's End With Supercharger Expansion, All Things D*

107.   Jump up^ *Claudia Assis; Jeremy C. Owens. "Elon Musk exercises Tesla options, pays million tax bill with own*
cash". MarketWatch. Retrieved February 21, 2016.

108.   Jump up^ *Chris Ziegler (January 29, 2016). "Elon Musk bought million more worth of Tesla this week". The Verge. Vox Media. Retrieved February 21, 2016.*

109.   Jump up^ *"Tesla's Elon Musk worked for free last year". Fortune. Retrieved November 4, 2015.*

110.   Jump up^ *Durisin, Megan (August 10, 2013). "Musk*

get US$4.3 million of stock options for Model X work".
Bloomberg L.P. Retrieved January 15, 2014.

111.　　　Jump up^ *"All Our Patent Are Belong To You".* Tesla *Motors. Retrieved November 4,2015.*

112.　　　Jump up^ *Dana Hull (February 19, 2016). "Musk Gets Tesla.com Domain Name After Waiting a Decade". Bloomberg L.P. Retrieved March 22, 2016.*

113.　　　Jump up^ *"Management Team".* SolarCity.

114.　　　Jump up^ *Kanellos, Michael (February 15, 2008). "Newsmaker: Elon Musk on rockets, sports cars, and solar power". CNET.*

115.　　　Jump up^ *"2013 Top 250 Solar Contractors".* Solar *Power World. September 13, 2013.*

116.　　　Jump up^ *"Tesla's Acquisition of SolarCity Receives Shareholder Approval". Retrieved 2016-11-17.*

117.　　　Jump up^ *"Early Christmas Present For Elon Musk As Shareholders Bless Tesla-SolarCity Merger". Forbes. 17 November 2016. Retrieved 22 November 2016.*

118.　　　Jump up^ Tesla - Current Report

119.　　　Jump up^ *The unveiling of the Tesla Motors Electric Car. Autoblog. Retrieved July 26,2006.*

120.　　　^ Jump up to:[a] [b] *Diggelen, Alison van. "Tesla and SolarCity Collaborate on Clean Energy Storage". KQED. Retrieved June 25, 2012.*

121.　　　Jump up^ *Aaron Smith (June 17, 2014). "Elon Musk's sunny plans for Buffalo". CNNMoney.*

122.　　　Jump up^ *"Beyond the hype of Hyperloop: An analysis of Elon Musk's proposed transit system". Gizmag.com. August 22, 2013. Retrieved August 23, 2013.*

123. Jump up^ Ashlee Vance. "Revealed: *Elon Musk Explains the Hyperloop, the Solar-Powered High-Speed Future of Inter-City Transportation*". Bloomberg BusinessWeek. Retrieved April 27, 2016.

124. Jump up^ *"Hyperloop Update: Elon Musk Will Start Developing It Himself"*. Forbes.com. Retrieved March 22, 2016.

125. Jump up^ *"Musk announces plans to build Hyperloop demonstrator"*. gizmag.com. Retrieved November 4, 2015.

126. Jump up^ *Musk, Elon (August 12, 2013). "Hyperloop Alpha" (PDF).* SpaceX. *Retrieved August 13, 2013.*

127. Jump up^ *Musk, Elon (August 12, 2013). "Hyperloop".* Tesla. *Retrieved August 13, 2013.*

128. Jump up^ *"Hyperloop Designed for Quick, Convenient Commute".* ABC News. March 9, 2013. Retrieved August 15, 2013.

129. Jump up^ *"Hyperloop".* SpaceX. *Retrieved August 13, 2013.*

130. Jump up^ *Mazza, Sandy (January 29, 2017). "Hyperloop competition brings new mass-transit technology to life in Hawthorne". Daily Bulletin.*

131. Jump up^ *Hawkins, Andrew J. (July 14, 2017). "Talking to Hyperloop One about its big 'Kitty Hawk' moment – and what comes next". The Verge. Retrieved July 14, 2017.*

132. Jump up^ *"Elon Musk Says He Has 'Verbal' OK To Build N.Y.-D.C. Hyperloop". NPR.org. Retrieved July 25, 2017.*

133. Jump up^ *Felton, Ryan (July 20, 2017). "Here's A Running List of Comments From Public Agencies on Elon*

Musk's 'Verbal Govt Approval' To Build A Hyperloop From NYC To
D.C". Jalopnik. Retrieved July 27, 2017.

134.   Jump up^ Markoff, John (December 11, 2015). "Artificial-Intelligence Research Center Is Founded by Silicon Valley Investors". The New York Times. Retrieved December 15, 2015.

135.   Jump up^ Levy, Steven (December 11, 2015). "How Elon Musk and Y Combinator Plan to Stop Computers From Taking Over". Medium/Backchannel. Retrieved December 15, 2015.

136.   Jump up^ "Elon Musk launches Neuralink, a venture to merge the human brain with AI". The Verge. March 27, 2017. Retrieved April 10, 2017.

137.   Jump up^ Golson, Jordan (January 25, 2017). "Elon Musk: "Without tunnels, we will all be in traffic hell forever"". The Verge. Retrieved January 29, 2017.

138.   Jump up^ "Elon Musk Will Begin Digging His "Boring Company" Tunnel in About A Month". Fortune. Retrieved January 29, 2017.

139.   Jump up^ Parnell, Brid-Aine. "Elon Musk Teases Traffic-Busting Tunneling Firm 'The Boring Co.'". Forbes. Retrieved January 29, 2017.

140.   Jump up^ Solon, Olivia (January 26, 2017). "Elon Musk to dig tunnel to ease traffic in LA, but he doesn't yet have permission" – via The Guardian.

141.   Jump up^ Mazza, Sandy. "Elon Musk wants to start digging a traffic-relieving tunnel in Hawthorne 'in a month or so'". Los Angeles Daily Times. Retrieved January 28, 2017.

142.		Jump up^ *Chafkin, Max (February 16, 2017). "Elon Musk Is Really Boring". Bloomberg. Retrieved February 17, 2017.*

143.		Jump up^ *Heathman, Amelia. "Elon Musk's boring machine has already built a 'test trench' in LA". Wired UK. Retrieved February 19, 2017.*

144.		Jump up^ *Hanley, Steve. "Elon Musk Talks About His Vision Of The Future At TED2017". Gas2. Retrieved October 16, 2017.*

145.		Jump up^ *"Elon Musk: The Way Of The Future".* YouTube. *Retrieved November 4,2015.*

146.		Jump up^ *Team, The Transition (December 14, 2016). "President-Elect Trump Announces Additional Members of President's Strategic and Policy Forum". Retrieved December 20, 2016.*

147.		Jump up^ *"Elon Musk and the chief executive of Uber are now advising Donald Trump". Retrieved December 20, 2016.*

148.		Jump up^ *"Donald Trump Adds Elon Musk, Travis Kalanick, and Indra Nooyi to His Team of Advisers". December 14, 2016. Retrieved December 20, 2016.*

149.		Jump up^ *OConnell, Justin (December 23, 2016). "Elon Musk, Appointed to Trump's Team of Advisories, Thinks Bitcoin Is a "Good Thing" - CryptoCoinsNews". CryptoCoinsNews.*
Retrieved April 16, 2017.

150.		Jump up^ *"Elon Musk just got more involved with Trump's administration". businessinsider.com. Retrieved January 29, 2017.*

151.   Jump up^ *"US quits Paris climate pact: Reaction from around the world following the US president's decision on the Paris accord". Retrieved June 1, 2017.*

152.   Jump up^ *"Elon Musk anouncing departing presidential councils on Twitter". Retrieved June 1, 2017.*

153.   Jump up^ *Wattenberg, Ben. "Elon Musk and the frontier of Technology". Think Tank. PBS.org. Retrieved June 12, 2015.*

154.   Jump up^ *Strange, Adario (November 5, 2016). "Elon Musk thinks universal income is answer to automation taking human jobs". mashable.com. Retrieved February 6, 2017.*

155.   Jump up^ *"Elon Musk on Trump presidency: 'I don't think he's the right guy'". businessinsider.in. Retrieved March 21, 2017.*

156.   Jump up^ *Lee, Dave (January 26, 2017). "Elon Musk: I'm Trump's voice of reason". BBC News. Retrieved January 29, 2017.*

157.   ^ Jump up to: [a] [b] *"Elon Musk, SpaceX Founder, Battles Entrenched Rivals Over NASA Contracts". The Huffington Post. February 20, 2013. Retrieved May 30, 2015.*

158.   Jump up^ *"Obama and Congress at odds over Elon Musk". fightforvotes.com. Archived from the original on May 30, 2015. Retrieved May 30, 2015.*

159.   Jump up^ Timothy P. Carney, "Carney: Green stimulus profiteer comes under IRS scrutiny", WashingtonExaminer.com, October 14, 2012.

160.   ^ Jump up to: [a] [b] *"SpaceX blasts off literally and politically". Sunlight Foundation. Retrieved May 30, 2015.*

161.   Jump up^ *Salant, Jonathan D. (September 27,*

2013). "Billionaires Battle as Bezos-Musk Companies Vie for Launch Pad". Bloomberg.com. Bloomberg Business. Retrieved July 1, 2015.

162.   Jump up^ Steven Kovach, "Elon Musk Says He Quit Mark Zuckerberg's PAC Because It Was Too Cynical", BusinessInsider.com, May 31, 2013.

163.   ^ Jump up to: [a][b] Becker, Sean (December 11, 2013). "Elon Musk Donated to Anti-Science Republicans". Mic. Policy.Mic. Retrieved June 10, 2015.

164.   Jump up^ Werber, Cassie. "Elon Musk says tax-free carbon is "the dumbest experiment in history"". Quartz. Retrieved August 30, 2016.

165.   Jump up^ "Taxpayer Subsidies Helped Tesla Motors, So Why Does Elon Musk Slam Them?". Mother Jones. Retrieved April 19, 2015.

166.   Jump up^ Harkinson, Josh (September 2013). "Taxpayer Subsidies Helped Tesla Motors, So Why Does Elon Musk Slam Them?". Mother Jones. Retrieved June 10,2015.

167.   Jump up^ Hirsch, Jerry (May 30, 2015). "Elon Musk's growing empire is fuelled by billion in government subsidies". Los Angeles Times. Retrieved June 2, 2015.

168.   Jump up^ "Going to Mars with Elon Musk". OnInnovation.com. June 2008. Retrieved June 10, 2015.

169.   ^ Jump up to: [a][b] "Elon Musk and Rainn Wilson discuss colonizing Mars, global warming, and the fear of failure". The Verge. March 19, 2013. Retrieved June 12, 2015.

170.   Jump up^ "Elon Musk, CEO and CTO, Space Exploration Technologies Corp (SpaceX), Peter Diamandis, CEO, X Prize Foundation and John Doerr, Venture Capital,

Kleiner Perkins Caufield & Byers". YouTube. Retrieved November 4, 2015.

171.　　　Jump up^ *Anderson, Ross (September 30, 2014). "The Elon Musk Interview on Mars Colonization". Aeon. Retrieved June*
10, 2015.

172.　　　Jump up^ *Gibbs, Samuel (October 27, 2014). "Elon Musk: artificial intelligence is our biggest existential threat". The Guardian. Retrieved December 15, 2015.*

173.　　　Jump up^ *"Elon Musk and Stephen Hawking think we should ban killer robots". Washington Post. July 28,*
2015. Archived from the original on March 8, 2016. Retrieved January 5, 2017.

174.　　　^ Jump up to:[a][b] *Kosoff, Maya (January 15, 2015). "Elon Musk Is Donating Million To Keep Killer Robots From Taking Over The World". Business Insider. Retrieved December 15, 2015.*

175.　　　Jump up^ *Muoio, Danielle (December 11, 2015). "Elon Musk just announced a new artificial intelligence research company". Tech Insider. Retrieved December 11,2015.*

176.　　　Jump up^ *Hern, Alex (June 18, 2014). "Elon Musk says he invested in DeepMind over 'Terminator' fears". Retrieved June 10, 2015 – via The Guardian.*

177.　　　Jump up^ *"We are living in a computer simulation, Elon Musk says". The Independent. June 2, 2016. Retrieved June 30, 2016.*

178.　　　Jump up^ *Kelly, Éanna (23 Nov 2017). "Artificial Intelligence: World is astonishingly pessimistic,' says EU research commissioner". sciencebusiness.net. Retrieved 2017-12-23.*

179.   Jump up^ *Loizos, Connie (19 Jul 2017). "This famous roboticist doesn't think Elon Musk understands AI". TechCrunch. Retrieved 2017-12-23.*

180.   Jump up^ *Chollet, François (16 Jul 2017). "AI/ML makes a few existing threats worse. Unclear that it creates any new*

ones". @fchollet. Retrieved 2017-12-23.

181.   Jump up^ *Domingos, Pedro (16 Jul 2017). "One word:*

sigh". @pmddomingos. Retrieved 2017-12-23.

182.   ^ Jump up to:[a] [b] *Brown, Mike (15 Dec 2017). "Elon Musk Sparks Heated Twitter Debate Over Boring Company's Vision". Inverse. Retrieved 2017-12-23.*

183.   ^ Jump up to:[a] [b] *Hunt, Elle (21 Dec 2017). "'I met my wife on a train platform': Twitter responds to Elon Musk with positive public transport stories". The Guardian. ISSN 0261-3077. Retrieved 2017-12-23.*

184.   Jump up^ *Marshall, Aarian (14 Dec 2017). "Elon Musk Really Doesn't Like Mass Transit Systems He's Trying to Build". WIRED. Retrieved 2017-12-23.*

185.   Jump up^ *Toderian, Brent (18 Dec 2017). "Elon Musk may say bad things about public transit, but I asked Twitter to share their #GreatThingsThatHappenedOnTransit! As usual, Twitter responded in spades. Here are some of my favourites for posterity - please enjoy & share!". @BrentToderian. Retrieved 2017-12-23.*

186.   Jump up^ *Hamilton-Smith, Lexy (23 Mar 2017). "Brisbane's urban planning 'average' and making residents sick, expert says". ABC News. Retrieved 2017-12-26.*

187.   ∧ Jump up to:[a][b] *Morris, David Z. (16 Dec 2017). "Elon Musk Calls Transit Expert 'An Idiot,' Says Public Transport 'Sucks'". Fortune. Retrieved 2017-12-23.*

188.   Jump up∧ *Walker, Jarrett (14 Dec 2017). "In cities, @elonmusk's hatred of sharing space with strangers is a luxury (or pathology) that only the rich can afford. Letting him design cities is the essence of elite projection". @humantransit. Retrieved 2017-12-23.*

189.   Jump up∧ *Walker, Jarrett (31 Jul 2017). "The Dangers of Elite Projection — Human Transit". Human Transit. Retrieved 2017-12-23.*

190.   Jump up∧ *Musk, Elon (14 Dec 2017). "You're an idiot". @elonmusk. Retrieved 2017-12-23.*

191.   Jump up∧ *Musk, Elon (14 Dec 2017). "Sorry". @elonmusk. Retrieved 2017-12-23.*

192.   Jump up∧ *Musk, Elon (14 Dec 2017). "Meant to say "sanctimonious idiot"". @elonmusk. Retrieved 2017-12-23.*

193.   Jump up∧ *Krugman, Paul (19 Dec 2017). "Elon Musk's idea of a cogent argument: "You're an idiot"http://fortune.com/2017/12/16/elon-musk-public-transport/...". @paulkrugman. Retrieved 2017-12-23.*

194.   Jump up∧ *Matt Hardigree. "Elon Musk Explains How He Wrecked An Uninsured Million McLaren F1". Jalopnik.*

195.   Jump up∧ *Wayne, Leslie (February 5, 2006). "A Bold Plan to Go Where Men Have Gone Before". The New York Times.*

196.   Jump up∧ *FlightAware. "Aircraft Registration N900SK". Retrieved June 25, 2012.*

197.   Jump up^ Chris Woodyard,"Tesla's Elon Musk buys 007's sub to make it real", USAToday.com, October 18, 2013; accessed November 13, 2013.

198.   Jump up^ *"Tosca Musk profile at"*. Musk *entertainment.*

199.   Jump up^ Achenbach, Joel. "Elon Musk Wants to Go to Mars" *National Geographic*November 2016. p. 41.

200.   Jump up^ *"Elon Musk and SolarCity Donate Solar Power Project to Coastal Response Center in Alabama". Enhanced Online News. Business Wire.*

201.   Jump up^ *"Elon Musk Donates Solar Power Project to Soma City in Fukushima Prefecture, Japan". BusinessWire.com. Retrieved April 27, 2014.*

202.   Jump up^ *"What it's like to own a Tesla Model S – Part 2 – The Oatmeal". theoatmeal.com.*

203.   Jump up^ *Greg Kumparak. "Elon Musk Donates Million to the Oatmeal's Nikola Tesla Museum". TechCrunch. AOL. Retrieved November 4, 2015.*

204.   Jump up^ *Elon Musk donates M to keep AI beneficial, Future of Life Institute, 2015, retrieved January 20, 2015*

205.   Jump up^ *"Elon Musk Donates M To Make Sure AI Doesn't Go The Way of Skynet". Mashable. 2015. Retrieved June 21, 2015.*

206.   Jump up^ *"Elon Musk". XPRIZE. Retrieved April 19, 2015.*

207.   Jump up^ *Kroll, Luisa (April 19, 2012). "The Giving Pledge Signs on 12 More Wealthy Americans Including Tesla's Elon Musk And Home Depot's Arthur Blank". Forbes.*

208.   Jump up^ Durand Streisand, Elizabeth. "A Look at Elon Musk's Rocky Romantic History". Yahoo. Retrieved May 29, 2017.

209.   Jump up^ Junod, Justine (November 14, 2012). "Elon Musk: Triumph of His Will". Esquire. Retrieved November 28, 2012.

210.   Jump up^ Elliott, Hannah. "Elon Musk – In Photos: Forbes Life Elon Musk". Forbes. Retrieved November 4, 2015.

211.   Jump up^ Lai, Jennifer (January 19, 2012). "Elon Musk Divorce: Announces Split From Talulah Riley On Twitter". The Huffington Post. Retrieved July 23, 2013.

212.   Jump up^ "Elon Musk Divorce: Announces Split From Talulah Riley On Twitter", The Huffington Post, January 19, 2012.

213.   Jump up^ "Billionaire Elon Musk's wife files for divorce", Mashable.com, March 21, 2016.

214.   Jump up^ Kimble, Lindsay (November 18, 2016). "Ion Musk and Talulah Riley Are Divorced for a Second Time". People. Retrieved April 24, 2017.

215.   Jump up^ Ross, Martha (August 6, 2017). "Tesla CEO Elon Musk breaks up with Amber Heard, report says". The Mercury News. Retrieved August 24, 2017.

216.   Jump up^ Elon Musk [@elonmusk] (7 June 2017). "A little red wine, vintage record, some Ambien ... and magic!" (Tweet). Archived from the original on 11 January 2018 – via Twitter.

217.   Jump up^ Matyszczyk, Chris (June 7, 2017). "Elon Musk's strange, strange Ambien tweet". CNET. Retrieved July 9, 2017.

218.   Jump up^ Tan, Yvette (June 7, 2017). "Elon Musk's weird Ambien tweets are back". Mashable. Retrieved July 9, 2017.

219.   Jump up^ Musk, Elon Reeve; Ferguson, Joshua Willard; Zalan, Daryl; Van Dyke, Christopher Hugo (November 12, 2013), United States Patent: 8579635 - Funnel shaped charge inlet, archived from the original on June 2, 2017, retrieved September 23, 2016

220.   Jump up^ Musk, Elon Reeve; Ferguson, Joshua Willard; Zalan, Daryl; Van Dyke, Christopher Hugo (March 10, 2015), United States Patent: D724031 - Vehicle charge inlet, archived from the original on June 2, 2017, retrieved September 23, 2016

221.   Jump up^ Musk, Elon Reeve; von Holzhausen, Franz; Lee, Bernard; Imai, David Tadashi (May 28, 2013), United States Patent: D683268 - Vehicle, archived from the original on June 2, 2017, retrieved September 23, 2016

222.   Jump up^ Musk, Elon Reeve; von Holzhausen, Franz; Lee, Bernard (March 19, 2013), United States Patent: D678154 - Vehicle door, archived from the original on June 2, 2017, retrieved September 23, 2016

223.   Jump up^ Priorities in Space Science Enabled by Nuclear Power And Propulsion. The National Academies Press. 2006. ISBN 9780309180108. Retrieved November 4, 2015.

224.   Jump up^ *"Rocket Man"*. R&D. *September 4, 2007. Retrieved April 20, 2016.*

225.   Jump up^ *Chafkin, Max (December 1, 2007). "Entrepreneur of the Year, 2007: Elon Musk". inc.com.*

226.   Jump up^ *"Tesla Roadster"*. Index. *2007. Archived from the original on January 18, 2012.*

227.   Jump up^ *"Tesla Motors team"*. Tesla *Motors.*

228.   Jump up^ *"SpaceX successfully launches Falcon 1 to orbit"*. Space Exploration Technologies Corp. 2008.

229.   Jump up^ *"Connie Awards"*. National *Wildlife Federation. 2008. Archived from the original on June 29, 2009.*

230.   Jump up^ *Michels, Jennifer (March 4, 2009). "Aviation Week Reveals Laureate Award Winners". Aviation Week.*

231.   Jump up^ *"Space Community Gathers at National Space Society's ISDC 2009" (Press release). National Space Society. June 17, 2009.*

232.   Jump up^ *"Automotive Executive of the Year"*. DNV *Certification. 2010. Retrieved November 4, 2015.*

233.   Jump up^ *Favreau, Jon (April 29, 2010). "The 2010 Time 100". Time.*

234.   Jump up^ *"Barron Hilton and Elon Musk honoured with the highest FAI awards". Fédération Aéronautique Internationale. December 16, 2010. Retrieved March 25, 2015.*

235.   Jump up^ *"Living Legend of Aviation Awards"*. Kittie *Hawk Air Academy. 2010. Retrieved November 4, 2015.*

236.   Jump up^ *"Caltech Elects Two Innovators to Board of Trustees"*.

237.   Jump up^ *"Trustee List"*. The *California Institute of Technology. Retrieved April 19,2015.*

238.   Jump up^ *"Space Foundation Survey Reveals Broad Range of Space Heroes"*.

239.   Jump up^ *Smith, Jacquelyn (February 14, 2011). "America's 20 Most Powerful CEOs 40 And Under". Forbes. Retrieved February 18, 2011. To make this list, you had to be the chief executive of one of the 20 biggest publicly traded companies in the U.S. (as of Feb. 11, by market capitalization) with a CEO aged 40 or under.*

240.   Jump up^ *Dula, Art (June 16, 2011). "Heinlein Prize Honors Elon Musk of SpaceX". The Heinlein Prize. Archived from the original on April 2, 2015.*

241.   Jump up^ *"2011 Churchill Club Awards"*.

242.   Jump up^ *"2012 RAeS Gold Medal"*. Archived *from the original on November 28, 2012.*

243.   Jump up^ *Jonathan Welsh (November 21, 2013). "Tesla's Elon Musk is Fortune Businessperson of the Year". The Wall Street Journal.*

244.   Jump up^ *"IEEE Honorary Membership Recipients"* (PDF). *IEEE. Retrieved March 25,2015.*

245.   Jump up^ *"Social Concepts, Inc: We connect people ™"*. *socialconcepts.com. Retrieved November 4, 2015.*

246.   Jump up^ Elon Musk Named Most Influential Person In The Car Business Teslarati, Retrieved May 11, 2016.

247.   Jump up^ *"The top 10 business visionaries creating value for the world". Business Insider. Business Insider Inc.*

248.   Jump up^ *"Philanthropists & Social Entrepreneurs Top 200: From Elon Musk to Melinda Gates, These Are the Most Influential Do-Gooders in the World". Richtopia. Retrieved March 29, 2017.*

249.   Jump up^ *"200 most influential philanthropists in the world". Naij. Retrieved March 31,2017.*

250.   Jump up^ *"Graduation show, Art Center College of Design". Cumulusassociation.org. November 23, 2010. Retrieved August*
15, 2013.

251.   Jump up^ Surrey celebrates its honorary graduates[*permanent dead link*], Surrey celebrates graduation 2015, Surrey Graduate, Surrey Alumni Society (Autumn/Winter 2009)[*dead link*]

252.   Jump up^ SEAS Celebrates Class of 2015, Honors Innovators Elon Musk and Dean Kamen, 314th commencement (Spring 2015)

253.   Jump up^ *Tate, Ryan. "10 Awkward Hollywood Cameos by Tech Founders". Wired.com. Wired.com. Archived from the original on 1 December 2017. Retrieved 1 December 2017.*

254.   Jump up^ *"Elon Musk SpaceX Tesla on the Simpsons – Business Insider". Business Insider. January 27, 2015. Retrieved April 19, 2015.*

255.   Jump up^ *"Tesla CEO Elon Musk To Appear on Upcoming Episode of the Big Bang Theory - CBS.com". CBS.*
Retrieved December 4, 2015.

256.   Jump up^ Field, Kyle. "Tesla Stars In "Racing Extinction" Documentary". CleanTechnica. Retrieved July 11, 2016.

257.   Jump up^ Bova, Dan. "'Why Him?' Director on Elon Musk's Amazing 'I Can't Come to Work Today' Excuse". entrepreneur.com. Retrieved January 29, 2017.

258.   Jump up^ "'DC's Legends of Tomorrow' Power Rankings, Week 2: Burn, Baby, Burn – Observer". Observer. January 29, 2016. Retrieved February 7, 2016.

259.   Jump up^ Boyle, Alan. "'Star Trek: Discovery' ranks Elon Musk alongside Wright Brothers and warp drive". Geekwire.com. Geek Wire. Archived from the original on October 13, 2017. Retrieved October 13, 2017.

260.   Jump up^ Mack, Eric. "How Elon Musk goes down in history with the Wright Brothers". CNET.com. CNET. Archived from the original on October 13, 2017. Retrieved October 13, 2017.

261.   Jump up^ Etherington, Darrell. "Elon Musk gets a nod as a space pioneer from 'Star Trek: Discovery'". Techcrunch.com. Tech Crunch. Archived from the original on October 13, 2017. Retrieved October 13, 2017.

262.   Jump up^ McCarthy, Tyler. "Young Sheldon Episode 6 recap: Sheldon discovers physics". Foxnews.com. Fox News. Archived from the original on 1 December 2017. Retrieved 1 December 2017.

a.xternal links Marketing information system, Business Dictionary

263.   ∧ Jump up to:^a b *Reid, Robert D.; Bojanic, David C.*
(2010). Hospitality Marketing Management (5th ed.). New
Jersey: John Wiley & Sons,Inc. p. 209. ISBN 9780470088586.

264.   Jump up∧ *Kotler, Philip;* Keller, *Kevin*
Lane (2006). Marketing Management (12 ed.). Pearson Education.

266.   Jump up∧ Robert R. Harmon. (2003). Marketing
Information Systems. Encyclopedia of Information Systems,
Vol. 3. Elsevier Science (USA), 137-151.

267.   ∧ Jump up to:^a b *Shajahan, S.; Priyadharshini, R.*
(2004). Management Information Systems. India:
New Page International(P) Ltd. p. 99. ISBN
8122415490.

268.   Jump up∧ *Pride, William M.; Ferrell, O.C. (2010).*
Marketing. Canada: Cengage Learning,Inc. p. 148. ISBN
9780547167473.

269.   Jump up∧ *Birn, Robin (2004). The Effective Use of*
Market Research: How to Drive and Focus Better Business
Decisions (4th ed.). Great Britain: Kogan Page Limited. p. 22. ISBN
074944200X.

270.   Jump up∧ *Sandhusen, Richard L. (2000). Marketing*
(3rd
ed.). Canada: Barron's Educational Series.
p. 165. ISBN 9780764112775.

271.   Jump up^ Jaideep, S. (2015). "MIS: Marketing Information System (With Diagram)". YourArticleLibrary. Retrieved 1 Nov 2015.

272.   ^ Jump up to:$^{a\,b}$ Bhasin, Hitesh (23 Oct 2015). "8 Advantages of Marketing Information Systems". Marketing 91. Retrieved 23 Oct 2015.

273.   Jump up^ Bhasin, Hitesh (23 Oct 2015).
"MIS – Marketing information system". Marketing
91. Retrieved 23 Oct 2015.

274.   Jump up^ Kotler, Philip; Armstrong, Gary (2010).
Principles of Marketing (13th ed.). United States of
America: Pearson Education,Inc. p. 153. ISBN
9780137006694.

275.   Jump up^ Singh, Awadhesh Kumar; Pandey,
Satyaprakash (2005). Rural Marketing: Indian Perspective.
India: New Age International (P) Ltd. p. 114. ISBN
8122416837

OTHER BOOKS BY STEPHEN AKINTAYO

1. MOBILE MILLIONAIRE:

Making the Most from Digital Marketing Using Mobile Tools

2. HOW TO EARN 7 FIGURES FROM BULK SMS

BUSINESS: Secrets of Building a Successful Mobile Marketing

Empire

3. HOW TO MAKE MONEY FAST FROM
SOCIAL MEDIA MARKETING:

The Ultimate Guide to Social Media Marketing

4. QUICKEST WAYS TO EARN MONEY

BLOGGING: How to Make Money Fast As a

Blogger

5. MILLIONAIRE FREELANCER:

Best Ways to Make Money from Freelance Jobs

6. SCHOLARSHIP MADE EASY:

Fastest Ways to Get Scholarships & Study Abroad

7. SURVIVAL INSTINCTS:

Becoming a Success in a Third World Country

8. TURNING YOUR MESS INTO YOUR MESSE

9. HOW TO EARN 6 FIGURES FROM DIGITAL MARKETING:

Understanding, Monetizing and Consultancy in Digital Marketing

10. SOUL MATE:

Becoming and Finding the Perfect Mate

Made in the USA
Middletown, DE
07 January 2026

24681621R00258